UNDERSTANDING
NELSON ALGREN

Understanding Contemporary American Literature
Matthew J. Bruccoli, Series Editor

Volumes on

Edward Albee • Sherman Alexie • Nelson Algren
Nicholson Baker • John Barth • Donald Barthelme
The Beats • The Black Mountain Poets Robert Bly
Raymond Carver • Fred Chappell • Chicano Literature
Contemporary American Drama
Contemporary American Horror Fiction
Contemporary American Literary Theory
Contemporary American Science Fiction
Contemporary Chicana Literature • Robert Coover
James Dickey • E. L. Doctorow • John Gardner • George Garrett
John Hawkes • Joseph Heller • Lillian Hellman • John Irving
Randall Jarrell • Charles Johnson • William Kennedy • Jack Kerouac
Ursula K. Le Guin • Denise Levertov • Bernard Malamud
Bobbie Ann Mason • Jill McCorkle • Carson McCullers
W. S. Merwin • Arthur Miller • Toni Morrison's Fiction
Vladimir Nabokov • Gloria Naylor • Joyce Carol Oates
Tim O'Brien • Flannery O'Connor • Cynthia Ozick • Walker Percy
Katherine Anne Porter • Richard Powers • Reynolds Price
Annie Proulx • Thomas Pynchon • Theodore Roethke • Philip Roth
May Sarton • Hubert Selby, Jr. • Mary Lee Settle • Neil Simon
Isaac Bashevis Singer • Jane Smiley • Gary Snyder • William Stafford
Anne Tyler • Kurt Vonnegut • David Foster Wallace
Robert Penn Warren • James Welch • Eudora Welty
Tennessee Williams • August Wilson

UNDERSTANDING
NELSON
ALGREN

Brooke Horvath

University of South Carolina Press

© 2005 University of South Carolina

Published in Columbia, South Carolina, by the
University of South Carolina Press

Manufactured in the United States of America

09 08 07 06 05   5 4 3 2 1

Library of Congress Cataloging-in-Publication Data

Horvath, Brooke.
　Understanding Nelson Algren / Brooke Horvath.
　　p. cm. — (Understanding contemporary American literature)
　Includes bibliographical references and index.
　ISBN 1-57003-574-1 (cloth : alk. paper)
　1. Algren, Nelson, 1909– —Criticism and interpretation.   I. Title. II. Series.
PS3501.L4625Z69 2005
813'.52—dc22

　　　　　　　　　　　　　　　　　　　　2004027126

Material from Nelson Algren, "The Chevalier of Vain Regrets," Mi, Midwest
Manuscript Collection, appears courtesy of The Newberry Library, Chicago,
Illinois.

I'm sentimental, if you know what I mean:
I love the country, but I can't stand the scene.
              Leonard Cohen, "Democracy"

For Irving Malin, *hot keinmol nich gegessen in a restaurant vos heist mames*

Contents

Series Editor's Preface / ix

Acknowledgments / xi

Chapter One
  Understanding Nelson Algren / 1

Chapter Two
  Early Work and *Somebody in Boots* / 15

Chapter Three
  The WPA, Early Poems, and *Never Come Morning* / 33

Chapter Four
  The Neon Wilderness / 51

Chapter Five
  The Man with the Golden Arm / 66

Chapter Six
  Chicago: City on the Make and *Nonconformity: Writing on Writing* / 84

Chapter Seven
  A Walk on the Wild Side / 98

Chapter Eight
  Who Lost an American? and *Notes from a Sea Diary* / 114

Chapter Nine
  The Last Carousel and *The Devil's Stocking* / 132

Chapter Ten
  Conclusion / 150

Notes / 157
Bibliography / 187
Index / 207

Series Editor's Preface

The volumes of *Understanding Contemporary American Literature* have been planned as guides or companions for students as well as good nonacademic readers. The editor and publisher perceive a need for these volumes because much of the influential contemporary literature makes special demands. Uninitiated readers encounter difficulty in approaching works that depart from the traditional forms and techniques of prose and poetry. Literature relies on conventions, but the conventions keep evolving; new writers form their own conventions—which in time may become familiar. Put simply, *UCAL* provides instruction in how to read certain contemporary writers—identifying and explicating their material, themes, use of language, point of view, structures, symbolism, and responses to experience.

The word *understanding* in the titles was deliberately chosen. Many willing readers lack an adequate understanding of how contemporary literature works; that is, what the author is attempting to express and the means by which it is conveyed. Although the criticism and analysis in the series have been aimed at a level of general accessibility, these introductory volumes are meant to be applied in conjunction with the works they cover. They do not provide a substitute for the works and authors they introduce, but rather prepare the reader for more profitable literary experiences.

M. J. B.

Acknowledgments

I wish first to thank Kent State University for the sabbatical that allowed me to write this book. More specific thanks go to my sometime coauthor and full-time friend Joseph Dewey, who provided some helpful advice as I was getting my thoughts up and running, and to Roger Davis of the Kent State University libraries. Roger processed a shameless number of interlibrary loan requests, all the while projecting a plausible imitation of someone who enjoyed helping me. Also deserving my thanks are Kent State librarians Mary Birtalan, who fetched books for me, and Maureen Kilcullen, who explained in the nicest terms possible why I keep falling off my board when surfing the Web. I am likewise grateful to Elva Griffith of the Ohio State University libraries for helping me find what I needed in the Nelson Algren archive, and to Alison Hinderliter for finding and copying Algren materials held by the Newberry Library (Chicago). I also appreciated the interest, encouragement, and generosity of Bill Savage of Northwestern University and Warren Leming, cofounder of the Nelson Algren Committee.

To my daughters, Susan and Jordan: thanks for tolerating six months' worth of weekends less filled with adventures than they usually are. And my profound apologies to my wife, Virginia, for making her endure too many evenings when I tried out ideas on her and ranted obsessively against word counts. Ginny also deserves the reader's thanks for her courageous persistence in facing me down over matters of style. I do not, however, always accept criticism graciously, and whatever problems the reader finds in the pages that follow are entirely of my making. Readers of this book should know that she did her best.

CHAPTER ONE

Understanding Nelson Algren

Nelson Algren's friend Art Shay tells a story. It is 1952, and Shay, his wife, and their two small children are having breakfast with Algren:

> As we sat at the table reading the morning paper, a front-page story illustrated by two pictures caught Algren's eye. Two large white coffins and three small ones were arrayed in a church. A hitchhiker had murdered a father, mother, and three children. Next to this picture was a close-up of the killer, who was holding his knuckles up to the camera. On each of eight knuckles was tattooed a letter, H-A-R-D-L-U-C-K.
>
> Algren looked at the picture and said, "That poor S.O.B."
> My wife didn't understand him at first.
> "You mean the father?" she said.
> "No, the hitchhiker."
> As my wife swatted him with the paper, Algren, surprised, said, "Can you imagine what it took to make a guy do a thing like that?"[1]

To understand this story is to go a long way toward understanding Nelson Algren.

Unlike many modern American writers, Algren does not present the usual obstacles to comprehension. His plots are straightforward, and his prose, although often laced with now-dated street slang, is accessible. Nor does he traffic (in the manner, say, of

Thomas Pynchon and Richard Powers) in esoteric lore and difficult scientific concepts—although some readers may find his detailed stories of life among America's poor as mysterious as fiction set long ago and far away. Rather, what may impede an appreciative understanding of Nelson Algren is difficulty understanding his attachment to America's permanently down-and-out: his passionate fascination with how they live from day to day, why they make the choices they do, what the rest of America has done or failed to do to create and perpetuate this underclass, and what one's response to such truths should be.

To understand Nelson Algren, one needs to understand the trajectory of his work—from his Marxist-oriented early fiction and the sometimes comic, often grimly poetic realism of *Never Come Morning* and *The Man with the Golden Arm,* through his twenty-year abandonment of the novel, to the posthumously published *The Devil's Stocking.* To understand Nelson Algren is to understand his fifty-year career as a continuous search for a way to remain true to his convictions and for the means of convincingly articulating those convictions as America moved through the Depression, a world war, and cold war, from the conformist 1950s through the radical 1960s and into the narcissistic 1970s.[2] To understand Algren is to see him, start to finish, as someone who, to paraphrase the poet Leonard Cohen, loved the country but couldn't stand the scene—and to appreciate why an author once praised by Ernest Hemingway and Carl Sandburg came to see himself as "the tin whistle of American letters."[3]

What Algren wished his work to communicate is clear, for he explained his intentions on numerous occasions: in interviews and introductions to his books, in reviews and essays. As he told interviewer H. E. F. Donohue in 1964, he wrote "to catch the emotional ebb and flow and something of the fear and the terror and the dangers and the kind of life that multitudes of people had been forced into with no recognition that such a world existed." American literature, he explained, "is the woman in the courtroom who, finding herself undefended on a charge, asked, 'Isn't anybody on my side?'" In his afterword to *Chicago: City on the Make,* Algren elaborated on this point, insisting that "literature is made upon any occasion that a challenge is put to the legal apparatus by conscience in touch with humanity," that "the hard necessity of bringing the judge on the bench down into the dock has been the peculiar responsibility of the writer in all ages of man."[4]

In stories littered with what polite society may deem human refuse, Algren explores the causes and consequences of crime and addiction, poverty and racism, exploitation and alienation. Yet he does not propose solutions to the perennial social problems he addresses. Even his most ideologically driven novel, *Somebody in Boots,* is ultimately less a call for revolution than a testament to revolution's unlikelihood. Rather, Algren, whose fiction portrays a godforsaken world, assumes a prophetic stance toward his culture, offering jeremiads and lamentations to speak against society's betrayal of its professed ideals, its numbness to suffering and blindness to its sundry moral failures, its willingness to cast the first stone of blame over the economic fences behind which society's bottom dogs suffer abuse and neglect. Thus, Algren would redeem his chosen people's endangered humanity; give them a sometimes tragic, sometimes humorous, but always poetically revelatory voice; and, by exposing societal failures, make possible repentance and a new beginning.[5]

Algren's countercultural perspective, however, originates not in any desire to emulate biblical prophecy but in an early allegiance to the political left and in firsthand experiences of life lived hand-to-mouth. Born Nelson Ahlgren Abraham in Detroit, Michigan, on March 28, 1909, Algren grew up in Chicago, the city with which he will always be most closely identified.[6] The youngest of three children (his siblings were sisters Irene and Bernice), Nelson was descended on his father Gerson's side from a Swedish grandfather, who converted to Judaism before emigrating to America. Nelson's mother, Goldie, came from German-Jewish stock. The family, however, did not practice their inherited faith; indeed, Nelson attended Sunday school at a nearby Congregationalist church.

An indifferent student, Algren enjoyed a typical childhood —playing with the neighborhood kids, selling newspapers, cheering for the White Sox—although a certain amount of tension existed in the home because Goldie was dissatisfied with Gerson's lack of ambition (he ran a tire and battery shop and worked as a machinist). In later years, Algren recalled that he was fond but also contemptuous of his father and never particularly comfortable around his mother.

Graduating from high school in 1928, Algren (with Bernice's help and encouragement) entered the University of Illinois, where he majored in journalism. Graduating in 1931, Algren expected to find work as a journalist. As he later remarked, "I'd been assured it was a strive and succeed world. You got yourself an education and a degree and then you went to work for a family newspaper and then married a nice girl and raised children and this was what America was."[7] The Great Depression, however, spoiled Algren's plans, and his on-the-road search for newspaper work turned into the tramping and odd-jobbing undertaken by so many others during those hardscrabble years: he hopped freights, shilled at a carnival wheel-of-fortune, sold coffee and bogus beauty parlor certificates door-to-door; he experienced discrimination and was jailed for vagrancy, stood in line at soup kitchens, slept in hobo jungles. What he experienced radicalized his thinking, and he became convinced that the American Dream was a nightmare for too many Americans.[8]

Returning to Chicago, he began attending meetings of the John Reed Club (the literary arm of the American Communist Party) and of other writers' groups. His first published story, "So Help Me" (1933)—begun as letters from Texas to friends back home—sufficiently impressed the president of Vanguard Press that Algren was offered a contract (and the princely sum of thirty dollars a month for three months) to produce a novel.[9] Back in Texas to do research, Algren stole a typewriter from a college and was caught and jailed for a month before being handed a suspended sentence and told to leave the state. These and other personal experiences found their way into *Somebody in Boots* (1935), the story of a poor Texas boy who flees his dysfunctional family for a humiliating life on the road before turning to a life of crime on the streets of Chicago.

Although Walter B. Rideout has included *Somebody in Boots* among the handful of titles he believes constitutes "the most durable achievements of the radical novel of the thirties," the book sold poorly and received at the time few and mostly mixed notices.[10] Reviewers faulted Algren's prose and characterization while finding the subject matter compelling. In 1936, Algren married Amanda Kontowicz, whom he had met at a party organized by novelist Richard Wright to celebrate the publication of *Somebody in Boots,* and Algren soon joined the Federal Writers' Project (part of President Franklin Delano Roosevelt's Works Progress Administration) to earn a living, working as researcher, writer, and editor on several projects, including an unpublished collection of industrial folklore and a guidebook to Galena, Illinois. A book-length account of midwestern cuisine he authored in the late 1930s was published in 1992 as *America Eats*.

As the country moved toward World War II, Algren worked for the Chicago Board of Health and its Venereal Disease Control project. He wrote poems and reviews until his friend Richard Wright's celebrated novel *Native Son* (the title a gift from Algren, who had used it as the working title of his first novel) revived his sense of vocation by convincing him that perhaps Americans did want to know the truth about the country's underclass. *Never Come Morning*, the novel he saw taking shape in the stories he had been writing, was the result: a gritty foray into the constricted life of Bruno Bicek, a boy with dreams of boxing fame who is eventually fingered for a murder committed during the gang rape of his girlfriend, Steffi Rostenkowski, who is as a result forced into a life of prostitution. The novel horrified Polish Americans, some of whom claimed it was Nazi propaganda, yet it earned its author praise from such influential critics as Clifton Fadiman, Malcolm Cowley, and Philip Rahv. Cowley dubbed Algren "a poet of the Chicago slums," and Ernest Hemingway announced that *Never Come Morning* was "about the best book to come out of Chicago."[11]

Drafted into military service in 1943, Algren served as a private in an army field artillery unit and in the medical corps but saw little combat.[12] Discharged in 1945 (the year he legally changed his name to Nelson Algren, which had been his pen name since 1933), Algren returned to Chicago, completing before decade's end both the story collection *The Neon Wilderness* (1947) and the novel *The Man with the Golden Arm* (1949). The stories offer glimpses down America's mean streets, behind its tenement and tavern doors, inside its jails and prisons. Among the stories collected were three prizewinners, and although reviews were again sparse and sometimes lackluster, the book gained a reputation as, according to Maxwell Geismar, perhaps the best collection of short fiction to appear in the 1940s.[13] For Tom Carson, the stories "inaugurated the idiosyncratic, bedevilled, cantankerously poetic sensibility that would see [Algren] ranked among the few literary originals of his time."[14]

The Man with the Golden Arm marked the high point of Algren's reputation. Telling in lush, poetic prose the squalid life and eventual downfall of Frankie Machine, a war veteran and morphine addict who one night accidentally kills his drug connection, the novel won over even those reviewers put off by the dismaying subject matter (poverty, vice in thirty-nine flavors, murder, familial dysfunction, drug addiction), and American icons Carl Sandburg and Ernest Hemingway praised the book lavishly. Algren's biographer writes that at one book signing, "for three hours the book sold a copy a minute"—and more than a thousand sales in one night, according to the bookstore owner.[15]

In 1949, Algren was acknowledged to be among the first rank of modern American writers. Hemingway told his editor, Maxwell Perkins, in a letter dated October 11, 1949, that Algren was "probably the best writer under 50 . . . writing today."[16] During this period, Algren, whose 1936 marriage had faltered, was also energized by his affair with the French writer, feminist, and existentialist Simone de Beauvoir, whom he had first met when she visited America in 1947. As he would remark later of the years devoted to writing *The Man with the Golden Arm,* "I can say that at the time I was the only person I [knew] of in Chicago who was doing something that was actually worth while."[17]

The cold war, however, was taking a toll on Algren's peace of mind. In his opinion, the country was failing to live up to its ideals, was being turned into a paranoid, conformist fortress. Meanwhile, de Beauvoir was most of the time an ocean away and unwilling to end her longstanding relationship with philosopher Jean-Paul Sartre and make a serious commitment to Algren, who was himself unable to get a passport and was dogged by the FBI because of his leftist ties and activities.[18] Moreover, following Otto Preminger's movie version of *The Man with the Golden Arm*, Algren began to doubt that many readers really cared about his work's integrity. He considered the film a travesty of his work and knew he had been cheated financially by Hollywood, receiving only $15,000 from a movie that made millions. "I wouldn't do [a book like *Arm*] again," he remarked in 1964: "You don't have to do this to get money. And you've lost two or three years. . . . You'd do it for the real satisfaction—you'd assume—that it's wanted. But the real deception, the real disappointment is that actually it's not wanted." He added that there "were people who wanted answers in the thirties and into the 1950's. . . . Now the scene is changed. There is no feeling of this being wanted. Now the whole atmosphere is, 'What's the difference? We won't miss it if it don't [sic] appear. We don't need it.'"[19]

Before Algren reached this stifling malaise, he had produced two pamphlet-length essays: *Chicago: City on the Make* (1951) —a bittersweet prose poem to the city seen as a microcosm of what ails America—and *Nonconformity: Writing on Writing* (1996). *Nonconformity* (written 1950–53) went unpublished at the time because of its harsh attack on America's postwar failures and Algren's chastisement of writers unwilling to take a stand in a time of air-conditioned national crisis. Otherwise preoccupied with a novel he would never finish (and which he was calling

"Entrapment"), Algren produced his next novel, *A Walk on the Wild Side* (1956), accidentally. Asked by his publisher for permission to reissue *Somebody in Boots* to capitalize on the success of *Arm,* Algren had agreed on the condition that he be permitted to make changes. That revision eventually proved so extensive that the result was an entirely different book, a tragicomic burlesque of the American Dream as enacted by Dove Linkhorn, good-natured naïf and maker of condoms, hayseed confidence man and performer in sexual peep shows, whose story ends with him beaten and blinded but unbroken.

A Walk on the Wild Side was the book that Algren thought his best—in 1969 he described the book as "surely the best I've written or will write"—and it has enjoyed critical acclaim as the equal of *The Man with the Golden Arm*.[20] *A Walk on the Wild Side* was also filmed (1962), although Algren claimed never to have seen the result, and both novels have been staged (*Walk* as a musical). Yet Algren's fourth novel also provided an occasion to chart how far Algren's fiction had fallen from favor among those professional critics and academics whose business was guarding the gates of American literature. Seen as an anachronistic leftist, an ideological relic of the 1930s with an embarrassingly sentimental attachment to America's losers, Algren was dubbed "the man with the golden beef" by the *New Yorker* and "a museum piece" by Leslie Fiedler. Although Ralph Gleason would later assert that *A Walk on the Wild Side* had made possible the work of Bob Dylan as well as of novelists Joseph Heller and Ken Kesey, opinion at the time did nothing but sour Algren on the state of contemporary American literature and strengthen his conviction that his work was not wanted.[21]

Despite his war with the critics and the gradual disappearance of his work from anthologies and textbooks, despite personal problems and disenchantment with the American scene, Algren continued to write. In a 1955 interview, Algren claimed that "a writer doesn't really *live,* he observes," and from the second half of the 1950s into the 1970s, Algren's life dramatized this conviction.[22] He allowed his name to be used in the title of a collection of stories by contemporary writers—*Nelson Algren's Own Book of Lonesome Monsters* (1962)—which he selected and to which he contributed an introduction and a story, and in 1964 H. E. F. Donohue's *Conversations with Nelson Algren,* a book-length series of interviews, appeared. While never entirely abandoning his novel-in-progress, he earned a living writing for magazines, keeping his earlier work in circulation, and trying his hand at teaching—with a spectacular lack of success. He tried marriage again in 1965 with an equal lack of success. He continued to follow the horses and professional boxing, to play poker, and to travel, turning his experiences into *Who Lost an American?* (1963) and *Notes from a Sea Diary: Hemingway All the Way* (1965)—curious amalgams of travel writing, literary criticism, tall tales, social criticism, and often sardonic meditations on the writing life.

Both *Who Lost an American?* and *Notes from a Sea Diary* met with indifferent reviews, and by 1969 Sheldon Norman Grebstein could casually explain that Algren's "journalistic writing" was work that "hardly warrants our concern."[23] Included in Grebstein's dismissal were Algren's dispatches from Vietnam and other essays eventually included in the miscellany *The Last Carousel* (1973). Although Hilton Kramer might complain of *Who Lost an American?* that "Algren seems to have lost all sense of what useful literary tasks might remain open to him," Conrad Knickerbocker, reviewing *Sea Diary,* felt Algren possessed "the poker player's sense of when to fold his hand," when to stop bearing witness for the downtrodden in a manner to which few are still willing to listen.[24] However, it is possible to read both books, as well as *The Last Carousel,* as experiments, as forays in search of new ways of bearing witness.

In 1974, Algren was asked by *Esquire* magazine to do an article on Rubin "Hurricane" Carter, once the number-one contender for the middleweight boxing crown until arrested in 1966 as the alleged killer of three people in a New Jersey bar. Although the article was rejected, Algren's interest in Carter remained. He had moved to New Jersey (first to Paterson, then to Hackensack) to be close to the story, eventually producing a book-length journalistic account for which he could not find a publisher (in part because a 1976 retrial failed to exonerate Carter). Relocating to Sag Harbor, Long Island, Algren reworked the material until, again almost despite himself, he had a new novel, *The Devil's Stocking.* When Algren died on May 9, 1981, just days before his belated induction into the American Academy and Institute for Arts and Letters, his last novel had yet to find a publisher.[25]

Thus, the man who came to see himself as "the tin whistle of American letters" died the disenchanted American Dreamer he had been for so long. A leftist understood first as a writer of proletarian protest fiction, Algren has been more habitually described as a literary naturalist, although he is also readable as an existential absurdist, a "documentary" novelist, idiosyncratic prose stylist, black humorist, Christian allegorist, sentimentalist, streetwise tough guy, or postmodern practitioner of parodic, genre-conflating bricolage.[26] Novelist and reporter, poet and social conscience through fifty years of drastic change in America, including changes of literary fashion, Algren repeatedly located himself among those who have stood up for the accused and the down-and-out: a tradition in American literature that he saw extending from Walt Whitman and Herman Melville through Stephen Crane, Sherwood Anderson, Theodore Dreiser, and Eugene O'Neill to Richard Wright, Jack Conroy, and himself. Insofar as he was a Chicago writer, Algren took his place among a group of socially concerned writers that included Frank Norris, Upton Sinclair, James T. Farrell, Vachel Lindsay, Carl Sandburg, Edgar Lee Masters, and Edna St. Vincent Millay.[27]

Stylistically, Algren commanded a range of voices, each recognizably his own. He could write straightforward expository prose, and he could be charmingly breezy. In the space of a single sentence, he could drop from mellifluous lyricism to brutal facticity, from profundity into slapstick. He was as comfortable psychologizing as he was speaking street slang. A dangerous satirist armed with several lethal varieties of scorn, he could succinctly disembowel a bad novel or worse critic. Best known for his evocative poetic prose, Algren could capture with photographic accuracy the details of an El Paso jail or the blow-by-blow progress of a ten-round fight. He could be wildly humorous and heartbreakingly bleak.

Although no feminist, Algren created female characters that often transcended stereotypes to step forth as complex, sympathetically imagined women. Grounded in the tenets of literary naturalism with its realistic if melodramatic depiction of downtrodden lives controlled by larger forces within an indifferent universe, Algren's fictional world was sufficiently riddled by dread, anxiety, alienation, and the troubled sleep of profound introspection to explain his appeal to existentialists de Beauvoir and Sartre. Although sometimes viewed as a writer stuck in the 1930s, Algren in his fifties could respond enthusiastically to the work of such unconventional new voices as Joseph Heller, Terry Southern, Thomas Pynchon, and, later, Gabriel García Márquez, Don DeLillo, and Salman Rushdie. To judge from his more than 230 book reviews, his tastes were catholic, and he seemed predisposed to dislike only the work of academics and professional critics, too many of whom, he felt, worked "a sealed-off field" in which finding fault with their betters "can be turned into a comfortable livelihood."[28]

In addition to reviews, Algren published dozens of articles, stories, and poems over the course of his career, much of which never found its way into any of his books; he granted many interviews, frequently made statements to the press when asked, and fired off letters to periodicals as diverse as the *Nation* and the men's magazine *Rogue*. Yet wherever one looks in Algren's body of work, one invariably finds a witness committed to advocating on behalf of society's victims, including those more routinely judged its felons and misdemeanor outlaws. The depth of Algren's sympathetic commitment to understanding such people can be seen in his 1965 comment on Lee Harvey Oswald, the presumed assassin of John F. Kennedy: "Belonging neither to the bourgeoisie nor to a working class, seeking roots in revolution one week and in reaction the next, not knowing what to cling to nor what to abandon," Algren's Oswald "murders a man he does not even hate, simply, by that act, to join the company of men at last."[29] Thus, while neither excusing nor forgiving Oswald's actions, Algren refuses simply to demonize and dismiss the man who did the deed. Such empathetic allegiance to those he felt were as much sinned against as sinning perhaps explains why Algren's readers are likeliest found not among scholars and their students but, as Studs Terkel has repeatedly observed, among welfare mothers, coal miners, and other working men and women.[30]

One evening in the late 1940s, Algren took bookstore owner Stuart Brent for a walk on Chicago's wild side. Brent later recalled a Clark Street tavern, seedy and unsavory, where after "several beers" he suffered an epiphany. Those drinking around him were suddenly no longer "dregs" and "strays"; instead, he saw "something terrible, humiliating, too outrageous for words." His earlier smugness and distaste now disgusted him as he realized the extent to which he had been "the epitome of what I had long viewed with scorn in others." Brent concludes, "I lived for days with this nightmare, asking myself why I should feel guilt for those who no longer feel responsible for themselves. Then it occurred to me that the question was never one of guilt, but only of love."[31]

If Art Shay, with whom this introduction began, locates the heart of Nelson Algren's obsession, Brent surely suggests the response to Algren's work that its author would welcome most.

CHAPTER TWO

Early Work and *Somebody in Boots*

When Algren graduated from college, he hit the road looking for a job. Eighteen months later and still jobless, he returned to Chicago, began trying his hand at fiction, and found a career. As he said years later, in America "you get to be a writer when there's absolutely nothing else you can do."[1] He began to publish stories and excerpts from *Somebody in Boots,* his novel-in-progress, in left-leaning magazines such as *Masses,* the *Anvil, Partisan Review,* and the *New Masses.* Active in the Chicago chapter of the John Reed Club, Algren also contributed an article to the *New Republic* on efforts to break mine unions in southern Illinois where, according to Algren, local strong-arm tactics were a transparent reaction to the "growth of political control by radicals in the mining centers."[2] In January 1935, he signed an open letter calling for a congress of writers committed to "proletarian revolution" and willing to help "accelerate the destruction of capitalism and the establishment of a workers' government."[3]

It is against this radical commitment that Algren's early writing (including *Somebody in Boots*) must be read. In many respects apprentice work, his early efforts reveal that several of the author's signature concerns were firmly in place from the start of his career: a disenchanted leftist perspective on whatever caught his attention; a preference for social outcasts and admiration for their resilience and vitality; a suspicion of things middle class; doubt that the chains of ingrained prejudice and environment could be broken; pity for the essential aloneness of those without love.

With his perhaps sentimental belief in humanity's innate if much-abused goodness and his desire to see society reformed and its downtrodden uplifted, Algren in the 1930s saw himself as a spokesman for those society considered human refuse, and his message—albeit never untroubled or without qualification in the fiction—was that, come the revolution, the last would be first. In "For the Homeless Youth of America" (material deleted from *Somebody in Boots*), Algren speaks directly to "you ones that live in houses, that eat at tables, that sleep in beds" to prophesy a time when "oppressed man will rise up!"[4] "Within the City" and "American Obituary"—two brief sketches—make the same point. The former offers a vignette of Chicago, where "every man seems to go alone" and the army is the only use society has for its unemployed. "This is Chicago," Algren writes, a city that "will one day flame into revolt." Similarly, "American Obituary" limns one of the decade's homeless, a young man who has come to Chicago from the country only to get drunk, "slugged for ninety cents," and dumped into the river for the simple reason that he hadn't "a day's work to do."[5]

If the Depression was responsible for such unfortunates, the Depression was itself proof (the argument from the left ran) of the failure of capitalism, of the mishandled power of owners over workers who, once unemployed, could soon join the ranks of the lumpen proletariat: those at the very bottom of the social barrel, degraded and lacking any social consciousness. "A Holiday in Texas" offers an allegory of such workers and the coming revolution—an allegory that challenges the very hopes Algren would seem intent on propagating.[6] As the story opens, cattle first exploit and eventually murder David, a "Jew high-school kid" (272) who has gone on the road in the hope of finding a job that will allow him to marry the girl he has got pregnant. Told in first-person by Homer, who is speaking to a lawyer in an attempt to shift blame onto Luther, the story is unclear on the role anti-Semitism plays in sealing the boy's fate although it certainly adds to the men's sense that David is not of their ilk. It is perhaps sufficient to say that Homer and Luther take advantage of the kid, then kill him, because they can, because he is a pigeon, and because they have no feeling for a much younger person as down on his luck as are they. This lack of human connection would seem to be what the boy intuits with terror, awakening from sleep more than once to cry out, "We're cut apart!—cut apart!—cut apart!" (275).

A lack of solicitude, of any sense of brotherhood, leads Algren's characters in these early stories into depravity and a denial of love and away from the prerequisites of collective political action. Prejudice again drives in its wedge in "Forgive Them, Lord."[11] Here, World War I veteran Christopher Morgan, a black man in Alabama, witnesses three white men—a father and his two sons—gun down an old black man and his daughter because the younger son, Lloyd, has impregnated the girl, making murder seem to the three the most efficient and foolproof means of avoiding scandal. Christopher, too afraid at the time of the murder to do more than cower, wrestles with his conscience before finding comfort in the "ancient flummery" of religion and some tortured sophistry, both of which leave him convinced that the whites in town can know nothing of what really happened (the deaths were written off as suicides) and even that the father and his sons probably had good reasons for doing what they did: "Maybe the girl had wronged Lloyd first.

Maybe it was for her own good that they had killed her" (148). But no rationalization will save Christopher, whose story ends with four "hard" white faces confronting him menacingly as he sits one night on the courthouse steps.

Thus, for Christopher, neither religion nor American justice (symbolized by the courthouse), neither patriotic gratitude nor racial fellow feeling, can bind him meaningfully to others—just as Lloyd feels no connection to the woman he has slept with and who is carrying his child. And if family seems a locus of solidarity—father and older brother helping Lloyd clean up the mess he has made—a final early Algren story, "The Brothers' House," suggests that familial bonds are likewise fragile.[12] Here David, a young man who has been on the bum and in and out of jail since his mother died, returns after his most recent pardon to his boyhood home and his four brothers. Yet David "hated his brothers" (143) and comes home because, quite simply, he has nowhere else to go. If the sight of his former home allows David to imagine for a moment a nonexistent comfort, he is quickly disabused when he confronts his brother Jesse, who can only ask as the story ends, "Well, what do you want?" (146).

By depicting what life is like for society's bottom dogs, Algren's earliest work calls for brotherhood and radical change predicated on collective action while simultaneously questioning the likelihood that human beings can effect positive social (or personal) change, victimized as they have been by the way things are and by the compensatory mechanisms—racism, mistrust, crime, violence, servility—on which they have come to rely. This same critique and troubled call for radical action can be heard as well in Algren's first novel, *Somebody in Boots* (1935).

Dedicated to "The Homeless Boys of America," *Somebody in Boots* is perhaps best remembered for its Marxist-oriented depiction of vagrant life.[13] Walter B. Rideout, for instance, has judged the novel to be among the best radical fiction of the 1930s, and Maxwell Geismar has characterized the book as "a thesis novel of social protest" in which Marxist revolution is the solution to the poverty and depravity spawned by capitalism.[14] In his preface to the 1965 paperback reprint of the novel, Algren articulated part of his thematic intentions: "to show what had happened to a single descendent of that wild and hardy tribe that had given [Andrew] Jackson and Lincoln birth." His protagonist was "a man representing the desolation of the hinterland as well as the disorder of the great city, exiled from himself and expatriated within his own frontiers. A man who felt no responsibility even toward himself."[15]

Opening in west Texas in 1926 when protagonist Cass McKay is fifteen years old and concluding in the fall of 1934, *Somebody in Boots* tells the story of one soon-to-be-homeless boy and of the impossibility of the life from which he fled. Under different circumstances, Cass might have enjoyed an absolutely normal childhood. He possesses a capacity for wonder and dreams, enjoys flying kites, hopes to make money in town shining shoes, and kicks around with his friend Johnny. He seems to care sincerely about his siblings and responds passionately to the world around him: "A common bush would become a glory, a careless sparrow on a swinging bough a wonder to behold" (14). Yet Cass, who "looked as though he had not laughed four times in all his life" (14), is forced to grow up amid squalor, communal scorn, and familial dysfunction. His father, Stubby, is a violent and embittered man whose insolence and scattershot anger cost him every menial job he finds. His broken older brother, Bryan, has been lost and alcoholic since returning from World War I, and his once-happy sister, Nancy, has lost her laughter and now "cried for the utter joylessness of her life" (78).

Revealing the poverty and deracination that predated the onset of the Depression, the novel's first section, "The Native Son," details Cass's adolescent life of hunger, shame, petty crime, and brutality—a life from which Cass first runs after witnessing his father viciously beat ne'er-do-well Bryan for coming home drunk once too often. Returning "sick and lonely" (59) after a week on the road (during which time he is himself severely beaten after sleeping with a prostitute without a penny in his pocket), Cass finds himself forced to flee once more after Stubby inflames the town by killing the man who has been working the job Stubby had most recently lost. Having irreparably insulted his sister by suggesting that she should now look for work "in a spik whorehouse"—"a thing that all his life he regretted" (89)—Cass knows this second departure will be permanent, that "this time there would be no one to turn back to" (90).

Part 1, then, establishes the connection between the personal and the social, proceeding in the manner of literary naturalism to present a realistic—if pessimistically melodramatic—picture of life at its lower depths wherein free choice is checked and deterministically conditioned by economic and environmental forces beyond one's control and blinded at every turn by the harsh light of chance. The novel notices what seem to be personal bad choices: Cass can barely read and write, not because no schooling was available but because his racist father pulled him out "in protest" when the school board hired a "half-Mexican" teacher (14). Yet the novel posits larger forces at work on the McKays and implies that their choices are the sort likely to be made by people whom the world has left psychologically scarred and emotionally calloused. Hunger and shame; crime and cruelty and casual death; racial and ethnic hatred; stunted, frustrated lives: all are endemic in west Texas. Even before Cass has hit the road for good, he has learned the fundamental lesson of his life: "that for him, Cass McKay, there was no escape from brutality. He had learned that, for him, there was no asylum from evil or pain or long loneliness. . . . The world was a cruel place, all men went alone in it" (61).

It is the town, for instance, that has labeled all of the McKays "bad hats," that visits the sins of the father on his children, and responds with indifference to the misfortune of others —as when the death of a young Mexican girl beneath the wheels of a freight train elicits only the wan observation that "she must of just slipped a little" (26). Moreover, the novel makes clear that the McKays are not alone in their poverty: much of west Texas is suffering, hobo jungles are strung along the tracks of the Santa Fe, and a crowd gathers every time a coal train passes through to raid it for fuel. Moreover, Algren does not ask his readers to challenge Stubby's conviction that he is somehow tricked and cheated daily by "someone behind him or someone above" (3), and Bryan's dissolute floundering is explained as the effects of war on his psyche. "Nothin' but lies," he tells Cass drunkenly one morning, "Nobody told nothin' but Jesus-killin' lies. Told us it was *dooty* to fight fo' this pesthole—told me. . . . Now, look at me" (21). Again, the reader is encouraged to understand this as more than Bryan brazenly making excuses.

To the unconcern of the secular world must be added the failure of the church. The violent Stubby, unmoved by his children's suffering, has nonetheless "never missed a Sunday morning at the Church of Christ of the Campbellites" (4), and Cass, when asked by Nancy to consider attending church again, can merely observe that "God ain't never fed us, Nance—not wunst he ain't" (80). The church provides assistance as meager as the allotment of oatmeal and rice doled out by the local relief station or the inedible slop spooned up in mission soup kitchens while army recruiters work the line outside the door, preying on the down-and-out in a search for cannon fodder.

As a boy, Cass had visited the hobo encampment outside of town, where he had been impressed by the romantic lies he heard—how such "underdogs" drew no lines between "black, white, or brown" but cared only about whether a man was down on his luck; how any one of them was happy to "[assist] those of his own class, and when he himself was down his class would help him" (12). Yet Cass's four years on the road teach him otherwise: life among the disinherited is rotten with racism and the often violent exploitation of one another—as Algren's short stories of the period also made clear. The hundred pages constituting part 2 of the novel ("The Big Trouble") are, for Cass as for the reader, a blur of painful humiliation and criminal depravity. Jailed in El Paso for vagrancy, he is victimized by the "kangaroo court" (where inmate "justice" takes sadistic advantage of any newcomer) and witnesses the sexual abuse prisoners inflict on one another. He is harassed by the police and by railroad detectives, propositioned by a pervert while attempting to sleep on a park bench, twice locked accidentally in a refrigerated boxcar (a reefer), escaping death both times by blind luck alone. He fishes scraps from garbage cans, begs spare change on the street, learns to steal, and participates in a gang rape; aroused by a prostitute he cannot afford, he assaults a young girl on a darkened street. He learns that "spiks," "kikes," and "shokes" (Mexicans, Jews, and blacks) are always fair game and is quick to blame any recent immigrant for the country's problems.

Brotherhood among the lumpen proletariat, Algren insists, turns on self-interest and the whims of chance—stowaways needing to work together to escape from a locked boxcar, or one grifter needing another to work a con. Yet even such fortuitous friendships are often poisoned and doomed. Befriended by Matches, for instance, whom Cass had ineptly assisted when a woman in the reefer the three are riding goes into labor (what might be imagined to be a bonding experience), Cass does not even bother to ask the man his proper name and can only think that he had "better shake this shine" (145) before consorting with a black man gets him into trouble. Both men leave the exhausted woman asleep in a train depot, her dead baby at her feet and her cigarettes in their possession. And in the El Paso jail, where men are thrown together for months at a time and camaraderie would be to everyone's advantage, Nubby O'Neill will subject the weakest sheep to physical and verbal abuse in the interests of taking their money, enlivening a dull hour, enhancing his self-esteem, or affirming white supremacy—and the men will readily join in against whoever is the scapegoat of the moment. Indeed, most of the laughter in the book comes at the expense of one downtrodden person or another: "men bark laughter" while committing rape (109), and the cell block "roar[s] with laughter" when Nubby makes the Jew "Creepy" Edelbaum scour the communal toilet.

Somebody in Boots makes clear that all of the souls drifting through its pages have been conned and brutalized, shamed and dehumanized, in one way or another because of their poverty and lack of home, friends, and family; because of their sex, their race, their ignorance, and/or their lack of physical strength; because they are defenseless transients in tatters. Thus, the ill and exhausted Matches is clubbed and manhandled by a boorish cop beyond what even the gathering white crowd is willing to tolerate simply because it is possible to abuse a black man in

Texas with such impunity. Or again, the immigrant Carl Jusitska, tricked into leaving Latvia for America with promises of "fine wages" in the factories of Detroit, not knowing he will be used as scab labor against striking workers, is left jobless, friendless, and bereft after choosing to join the union himself (129–30).

In the novel's final sections, "Chicago" and "One Spring in This City," Cass temporarily finds respite from his hard traveling. Accompanied by former cell mate Nubby O'Neill, he alights in Chicago to commence a life of armed robbery and to enjoy a brief few months of genuine love with Norah Egan, a prostitute he meets one drunken night when she attempts to roll him. Fresh out of high school, Norah had attempted honest work only to be underpaid, mistreated, and eventually fired from the few such jobs she found (dress-shop seamstress, window washer). Despite having "spirit" (198) and a diploma, Norah cannot find "honest" work, and she is forced to become a stripper in the Little Rialto burlesque house. By the time she meets Cass, however, she has lost even that job and, indeed, has fallen to the lowest rank of prostitute: one who picks up drunks. If Norah's story emphasizes her persistence, her desire to support herself, and her unwillingness to let anyone take advantage of her, it likewise reveals how much she, too, is a victim of circumstances beyond her control, someone whose choices are few and unsavory.

Algren opens part 3 with an epigraph taken from *The Communist Manifesto* that brands the likes of Cass and Norah "social scum" (189), but Norah's story, like Cass's life of crime, is meant to picture illicit activities as the recourses of those with no other options for survival. Disease, jail, or death (among many other evils) may await the prostitute, just as prison or death may await the armed robber, but the novel makes clear that such fates are less the proof that crime does not pay than that the wages of poverty are social damnation.

When Cass meets Norah, he is the same weak, scared, and confused young man he has always been, "exiled from himself" as Algren later put it, and as irresponsible as the soup lines are long. He is still riddled with guilt over the harsh words spoken years ago to his sister, a memory he revisits obsessively as though one personal mistake might explain all that has since happened to him. His ambitions before meeting Norah had extended no farther than the desire for a tattoo and the wish to hurt somebody as badly as he has been hurt. What pride he was able to muster rested uncertainly on the fact that he was white and a braggart's unconvincing self-inflation. Without question, the high point of his life has been the butcher-shop robbery he and Nubby recently pulled off. Yet what he feels for Norah surpasses even that criminal high.

Screwing up his courage, he begins with Norah a life of crime so that the two can stay together, for in her arms shame, fear, and pain dissolve: "Heretofore he had been ill. He had been ill and he had not known. His head had been clogged with darkness, and now it was clear" (237). Laughter enters his life, and "once from a bus-top he felt like calling out to some strangers walking below him, 'Poor blind ones down there! Look up to where Cass is! This is me, this is Cass—up here with Norah! . . . I'm Cass—you remember?'" (245). What the few months with Norah demonstrate is the ineradicable humanity of people like Cass and Norah, the resilience of redemptive dreams and desires, the power of love to bring meaning to anyone's life and to give even the most brutalized men and women a sense of identity.

It is, of course, not surprising that such a hiatus cannot last, that such attacks on society will not sooner or later be countered.

28 / Understanding Nelson Algren

Consequently, it seems all but inevitable that Cass should be arrested while attempting a heist and sent off to jail, while Norah, left to her own devices, should return to the street, where she soon contracts a venereal disease. Released from jail ten months later, Cass searches for Norah while working his first steady job as a barker and candy and pornography salesman at the Little Rialto, but his dreams of a better life are dimming as he comes to feel as his father once had felt, that he and Norah "had both been robbed, some way, and he did not understand quite how. But whenever he thought of one man robbed by another, he thought of somebody in boots" (289)—the novel's recurrent symbol of repressive, vilifying, generic power.

The novel's brief part 4 ("One Spring in This City") is prefaced with a second epigraph taken from *The Communist Manifesto:* "In place of the old bourgeois society, with its classes and class antagonisms, we shall have an association, in which the free development of each is the condition for the free development of all" (293). The beginnings of that association are present at the Washington Park political rallies that Cass begins attending, thanks to his growing friendship with Dill Doak, the unfortunately named black man with a social conscience who works with Cass at the Little Rialto. A charismatic individual, Dill is ideologically on the left, is often seen backstage "brooding over the foreign-news page of a daily paper" (303), and enjoys preaching the advantages of Communism.

At the rallies, white and black speakers agitate for unemployment insurance, lambaste religion as a tool of the establishment, attack "discrimination against both Negroes and Jews," and call for "the day when the workers of the world take over their earth" (309). It is at these rallies that, had Cass ears to hear, he would learn who it was that has robbed him of Norah.

Finally found, she is immediately lost again because she feels her venereal sickness makes a life together impossible, although what Norah may find impossible at this point is believing in anything but defeat. The rallies, however, leave Cass mostly bored, and he attends only because Dill is his sole friend. When Nubby returns, first pummeling Cass for "walkin' with a nigger so black he looks like a raincloud comin' down the street" (312), Dill, revolution, and any concern about who robbed whom are quickly forgotten.

Set against the 1933–34 Chicago World's Fair—ironically dubbed "The Century of Progress"—the closing sections of *Somebody in Boots* belie the likelihood of "the old bourgeois society" being replaced anytime soon. Despite Algren's characterization of the novel as "a trumpet-call to arms" whose theme was revolution, the novel suggests that the likes of Cass McKay and Nubby O'Neill may be beyond political redemption.[16] In part, as some of Algren's recent critics have observed, Cass and Nubby are unpromising comrades in revolution because, made weak by their oppression, their compensatory racism is stronger than any reason they might discover for wanting to make common cause with anyone they have learned to consider beneath even themselves.[17] Additionally, the novel doubts the chances for revolution to the extent it judges the "old bourgeois society" to be perhaps too formidable to be overturned.

The power of the status quo is symbolized in the closing chapters by the World's Fair, whose flags decorate Chicago's "hunger-ridden streets" of "misery unspeakable" (275) while the fair itself "conceal[s] the decadence of a city sick to death" and "hide[s] the corruption that private ownership had brought it" (276). Business, government, organized religion, the schools, and the media are viewed as united against "any change in an order of society so beautifully calculated to permit the plundering of the millions by the few, so ideally suited to enhance private interest at the cost of the masses: The system which requires of each generation that millions be slain in wars for world-markets" (276). Algren's disgust is expressed in the harshest terms possible:

> Sometimes visitors to the Fair saw puzzling incidents on the way back to their hotels. Late at night, after a day spent on the grounds, they saw old men, like unclaimed curs with tentative claws, pawing in garbage barrels or ash cans; or they heard the voices of children begging from some unlit doorway. The *Tribute* had nothing to say of this, for the *Tribute* was owned by the pure-in-heart, and the pure-in-heart averted their eyes. They were good Christian editors proud of their paper, of the greed-inspired lies and the sweet christfablings and the star-spangled spew that they termed "editorials." They were proud of their souls, for their souls were clean; and proud of their churches, for their churches were large; and proud of their schools, for their schools taught conformity; but proudest by far were they of their Fair, their great Century-of-Progress slut stretched out on a six-mile bed along the lake with Buicks for breasts and a mayor standing up to his neck in her navel making a squib-like noise. (300)

Yet as the novel ends amid the first flakes of a late November snow, Cass and Nubby are preparing for nothing more radical than hitting the road again, Nubby berating Cass on his shortcomings, Cass dreaming once more about getting tattooed at the first opportunity. If, as Jon Christian Suggs contends, "The proletarian novel in America assumed that class struggle made history and that art could be a weapon" in that struggle, *Somebody in Boots* abets the cause by delineating the social problems faced by America's disinherited and the considerable impediments to a brotherhood of workers.[18] Algren may have wished to sound "a trumpet-call to arms," but his readers—like Cass at the Washington Park rallies—had to be willing both to listen and to be changed. The accomplishment of such a task was perhaps hampered by a second characteristic of the proletarian novel, what Suggs describes as the "air of defeatism that hung over the works themselves," which typically end with the powers-that-be intact and the radicals "in flight or disarray"—or, as in *Somebody in Boots,* unheard and abandoned.[19]

If Algren cannot imagine a way out of the impasse of defeatism noticed by Suggs, it is because he is writing realism, the fictional depiction of life as it is. One man does not make a revolution, and to present the successful escape from poverty and exploitation of the single individual (in the manner of Abraham Cahan's *The Rise of David Levinsky* or Horatio Alger's *Ragged Dick*) would have been only to validate the familiar myth of the self-made man. Thus, Cass cannot prosper in the absence of revolution. This being the case, it is also true that *Somebody in Boots* is no more defeatist—or grim, sensational, or crudely written—than, say, Upton Sinclair's *The Jungle* or Michael Gold's *Jews without Money.* Nor does *Somebody in Boots* overstate Algren's case, the roots of which extend beyond proletarian protest, the tenets of literary naturalism, and Communist Party ideology. The burden of Algren's novel can be heard in the speeches of Eugene V. Debs and Emma Goldman; of labor leaders, Progressive Party candidates, and Populist reformers such as Mary Ellen Lease, who at the end of the nineteenth century charged that in America it "is no longer a government of the people, by the people, and for the people, but a government of Wall Street, by Wall Street, and for Wall Street." Indeed, the novel's message can be traced back to the Christian Gospels and to Psalms: "For the needy shall not alway be forgotten: the expectation of the poor shall *not* perish for ever."[20]

In the course of his philippic against the World's Fair, Algren offers a small portrait gallery of those left behind by the Century of Progress, among them Young Finnegan, who will be "eighteen in August, if he lives that long," and who at present, when not turning a buck pimping, "gets six dollars every Saturday night for fighting at White City if he wins in six rounds" (299). With a change of ethnic background, this thumbnail sketch is a fair foreshadowing of Bruno "Lefty" Bicek, protagonist of Algren's next novel, *Never Come Morning*. If Bruno's story is largely free of the explicit radical didacticism of Algren's first novel, *Never Come Morning*, no less than *Somebody in Boots*, insists on being understood sociologically—as more than a story of personal failures and individual bad choices. In both novels, the question remains the same: how are these characters the victims of circumstance, of social injustice, of choices indelibly colored by where and how they live?

CHAPTER THREE

The WPA, Early Poems, and *Never Come Morning*

Nelson Algren remarked of *Somebody in Boots*, "That was the only work I did between graduation [from college] and 1936 when the WPA [Works Progress Administration] opened up. I got married in 1936 and the book wasn't a success at all, so I didn't try writing another novel until 1940."[1] Yet Algren in fact did other work in the early 1930s, and if this inadvertent novelist let more than five years pass before attempting a second novel, he was busy during those years as an editor, researcher, and writer for the Illinois Writers' Project (a branch of the Federal Writers' Project of the WPA), working on the *Galena Guide* —an illustrated, booklet-length historical portrait of Galena, Illinois—an unpublished piece on a Revolutionary War financier, and an unpublished oral-history collection of industrial folklore.[2] Of greatest significance, perhaps, is the book-length ethnographic study Algren authored that was eventually published in 1992 as *America Eats*.

Written in the late 1930s and intended as part of the national America Eats project, the purpose of which was to collect information about regional cuisine as a window onto ethnicity and regionalism, *America Eats* describes the production and preparation of midwestern fare—everyday staples, special-occasion dishes, and ethnic favorites—as well as accompanying social customs. Making use of anecdote, folklore, and song, and including more than sixty recipes, Algren covers his subject from the days when "America's great inland plains were carpeted by a spiraling wild grass called bluestem" to the time of the book's composition with special attention to the fare of homesteaders, farm families, and the many immigrant populations that congregated in midwestern locales.[3] The foods described are both familiar and forgotten: from cracklin' bread and vinegar pie to hoecakes and hasenpfeffer, burgoo and fish pudding. Each dish is considered in the context of when and where it might have been served—at family reunions or quilting bees, threshing dinners or box socials—and collectively serve to symbolize the American melting pot (here, perhaps, a bubbling stew pot): "These are the foods of many nations, brought from many lands to nourish one land . . . passed down an endless boardinghouse table from a brave in buckskin to a blue-turbaned voyageur, from a coonskin Yankee to a drawling steamboatman, from a Negro fish-vendor to an Irish section hand" (78–79).

In *America Eats,* Algren's politics are kept mostly under wraps in favor of the *e pluribus unum* message that, as Algren understood, the project wished to forward. Only occasionally does he let slip a telling aside—as when observing how Europeans "modified the Indian's natural diet" until they had "just about put a stop to it altogether" (9) or imagining present-day farmers "glanc[ing] quickly at the war news" before scouring the paper for what most concerned them: the next public "lutefish supper" (62).

If *America Eats* was of necessity politically circumspect, the poetry Algren was writing at the time gave him a chance to speak freely. Stylistically and topically, the nine poems published between 1939 and 1942 are a mixed bag. A couple are rhymed and loosely formal, but for the most part they are unrhymed free verse, and over them all hangs an air of disenchanted gloom, of

The WPA, Early Poems, and *Never Come Morning* / 35

closing time. "How Long Blues," for instance, sees a nightclub's closing on the eve of America's entrance into World War II as the end of life as Chicagoans had known it, whereas "Local South," which wants to know, "What time will it be when the last El crashes?" imagines the city's menial laborers on the brink of some unspecified apocalypse. "Home and Goodnight" is another closing-time poem about late-night workers at the end of their day—the "boys in the three-piece orchestra," the "ex-pug" sweeping out the sideshow after the last "fake [boxing] match," the prostitute "in the little room smelling of Lifebuoy" —while "Travelog" paints a bleak nightscape of "pale Americans stricken with pale blue sleep" beneath a "rented neon moon." "Makers of Music" offers yet another glum portrait of Chicago, where there "is no hope" and "a million friendless faces" avoid "a million friendless hands." Who, the poem asks, "will play Lenin to Chicago" and redeem the "laughing fairy in a Clark Street car," the "woman weeping on a flyspecked bar"?[4]

Loss and defeat inhabit every poem. "This Table on Time Only" narrates the murder of a mobster "born above a rear-lot garage facing an alley" who is shot three times in the back of the head then tossed into the street. "The Swede Was a Hard Guy" recalls the Chicago Black Sox scandal of 1919, seeing the ballplayers as having taken the fall for throwing the World Series while the team's owner, "Old Comiskey," got an "immunity bath" and was portrayed in the press as a long-suffering victim despite the fact that the players were driven to their actions because so poorly paid. Not surprisingly, the most politically outspoken poems appeared in the leftist magazine the *New Anvil*. The prose poem "Utility Magnate" contrasts the life of a dishonest business tycoon "low enough to sit on a cigarette paper and swing both legs" with the cynical eulogy prepared by a newspaper's "star feature writer"—whose knowing lies will become the truth of the man even for those "he defrauded, one time or another, one way or another." Finally, "Program for Appeasement" imagines the country on the brink of war as a theater on fire wherein, should panic ensue, it will be "every man for himself."[5]

These poems gave Algren a venue for his dismay as the country prepared for war and allowed him to try out Chicago material in small narratives. They also perhaps taught him something about language and style—lessons he articulated in some of the book reviews he was writing in the early 1940s. In one, he asserts that "patient documentation doesn't of itself make authentic history," and in a second observes that "words, unless they bring us a tactile sense either of the outer or of an inner world, remain dead" even when artfully deployed.[6] Here can be seen the emphasis on emotional investment via concrete poetic prose that would characterize Algren's mature fiction.

Of utmost importance to Algren's development as a writer was, however, the work done for the Writers' Project. Carla Cappetti has demonstrated that the training project writers received included the techniques and procedures of sociologists and ethnographers studying "immigrant and urban history," and as the folklorist B. A. Botkin explained, the Federal Writers' Project "trained writers to record what they heard as well as what they saw with an ear for the characteristic phrase and rhythm of the vernacular."[7] Such work must have encouraged Algren's respect for the use of telling factual details when describing the lives of people of a specific walk of life, social class, race, or ethnicity.

Indeed, when the staff of the Chicago urban folklore project met on July 13, 1939, Algren mentioned that researchers in

New York were recording "almost straight dialogue," by which he meant the verbatim transcription of whatever interviewees said. Referring to the technique as documentary realism, as naturalism, and as "the most contemporary form of folk literature," Algren urged the Chicago group to adopt this "new way of writing" that he believed in the future would be looked back on as genuine "proletarian literature."[8] That Algren employed this "new way of writing" when he returned to fiction is evident from a comparison of two texts. The first is a passage from an interview with a Chicago prostitute conducted by Algren on July 17, 1939:

> Say, I know every window, every alley, every bust-out lamp, every car-line, every newsboy, every cigar store, every cop, every Chinaman—say, I even notice where somebody tossed out a cigarette against a wall and the next day the wind has blew the snipe into the middle of the street.

The second presents brothel keeper Mama Tomek speaking in *Never Come Morning*:

> I know every window, every alley, every bust-out lamp, every car-line, every newsie, every Polack cop, every cigar store with a bookie in the back—I even notice where somebody tossed out a cigarette 'n bust a milk bottle against a wall 'n the next day the wind has blew the glass into the street.[9]

It is certainly not the case that all dialogue in *Never Come Morning* should be understood to have come from transcribed interviews. However, this means of acquiring authentic material, along with the other techniques Algren was refining, is important to notice when attempting to understand Algren's growth as a writer, for despite Chester Eisinger's contention that Algren may have written "better books than *Somebody in Boots*, but not very different books," there is in fact a difference.[10] That difference turns, at least in part, on what Algren seems to have learned from writing poetry and from collecting and writing up material for the Writers' Project: that aesthetically effective authenticity hinges on the accurate rendering of idiolect and dialect, the strategic deployment of revelatory factual detail, and the creation of a prose style able to enliven subjects emotionally and sensually, to conjure mood, and to convey ideas without intrusive authorial editorializing. The poetic prose of *Never Come Morning*, with its internal monologues, surreal dreams, expressionistic descriptions of setting and character, and exact replication of the argot and speech rhythms of the street, is the result.[11]

Reviewers recognized what was new about Algren's second novel, which Ernest Hemingway believed to be "as fine and good stuff to come out of Chicago as James [T.] Farrell is flat, repetitious, and worthless" and which France's leading intellectual, Jean-Paul Sartre, admired sufficiently to help translate into French.[12] Malcolm Cowley praised its "poetry of familiar things" and nominated Algren as Carl Sandburg's successor as the poet of Chicago. Similarly, Benjamin Appel pronounced the book "a knockout" and noted "the powerful positive achievements on almost every page of character, of color, of poetry, of understanding."[13] James T. Farrell thought the novel "one of the finest works of American literature . . . of recent years" in large part because of its success as "telling social indictment," and for Philip Rahv the novel succeeded because it avoided both "the tedium of the naturalistic stereotype" and "the manner of the left-wing novelists" of the 1930s to attain "utter sincerity and psychological truth" as well as "complete unity of action, mood, and form."[14]

Certainly, *Never Come Morning* is less thesis novel (in which everything works to forward a solution to some problem) than the vivid rendering of life on Chicago's mean and unforgiving streets. Yet, that the novel had social commentary as its aim is also clear. In a preface supplied for the 1963 edition of the novel, Algren explains precisely what truth he had hoped his book would communicate:

> The novel attempted to say, about the American outcast, what James Baldwin has observed more recently of the American Negro: if you don't know my name you don't know your own. I felt that if we did not understand what was happening to men and women who shared all the horrors but none of the privileges of our civilization, then we did not know what was happening to ourselves.

Observing that nothing will reduce the crime rate as long as those in positions of authority "feel no identification with the outcast man and the outcast woman," Algren insists that "anything less than such identification is contempt," adding that crime originates "not in the criminal but in the righteous man: the man too complacent ever to feel that he—even *he*—belongs to those convicts and prostitutes himself."[15] This is in fact the burden of the epigraph (taken from Walt Whitman's "You Felons on Trial in Courts") that has always prefaced the novel:

> I feel I am one of them—
> I belong to those convicts and prostitutes myself—
> And henceforth I will not deny them—
> For how can I deny myself?

The principal criminal outcasts in *Never Come Morning* are Bruno "Lefty" Bicek (also known as "Biceps") and Steffi

Rostenkowski, both fatherless seventeen-year-olds when the novel opens and both living constricted lives in the west-side Polish neighborhood known as the Triangle—an area defined by "Chicago, Ashland and Milwaukee Avenues" (8)—in the late 1930s and early 1940s.[16] Their story, told in four "books," is in outline as simple as it is discouraging: Steffi, betrayed by Bruno's cowardice, is raped beneath the El by members of Bruno's street gang, then forced into prostitution in Mama Tomek's brothel by Bonifacy "The Barber" Konstantine—procurer, fence, fight promoter, and organizer of local teenagers into criminal gangs. Bruno, having lashed out in his shame at not protecting Steffi by killing a Greek kid waiting in the rape line, takes the rap for a mugging he and two friends attempted and is put away for six months. Upon his release, he eventually tries to set things right with the understandably wary Steffi but crosses the Barber by going around him to get a professional fight—the realization of a dream that ends minutes after the match with his arrest because Bonifacy, seeking revenge, has given the police all that they need to convict Bruno for murder.

"I'm a neighborhood kid is all," Bruno tells the police (119), and book 1, "Below the Belt," offers a detailed picture of what life in that neighborhood is like. Concluding with Steffi's rape, book 1 details Bruno's stumbling romantic relationship with the girl; the monotony of a life enlivened only by baseball; opportunities for petty larceny afforded by membership in the Baldheads; efforts to meet girls who might let one "joop" them; and Bruno's graduation from "vandalism to hoodlumhood" (50) when he and two friends venture beyond their turf to steal a slot machine from a roadhouse.

It is a world in which, as Bruno maintains, the principal rule of life is "to take care of number one" and let tomorrow "take care of itself" (46). He is completely indifferent to his mother, whose health is failing and whose income is not enough to afford food and medicine, and he shows every sign of having been shaped by peer pressure his entire life—acting tougher than he is, scorning honest work, forcing himself sexually on Steffi because he "needed to prove himself" (59), possessing no intellectual interests, and dreaming of success in the only terms available to him: as athlete or criminal.

Steffi is presented in book 1 as a young woman who lives by a code similar to Bruno's. She is described as "one of those women of the very poor who feign helplessness to camouflage indolence," having learned early that the successful completion of any household task will only mean being burdened with other, "less pleasant" ones (26). Living above the pool hall her mother runs, Steffi, like Bruno, is in many ways still a child: ignorant, dreamy, delighted by a stuffed doll Bruno wins for her at the amusement park.

Books 2 and 3 ("A Bottle of Milk for Mother" and "Others") initially treat Bruno and Steffi separately. The former details Bruno's arrest for jackrolling a drunk, the brutal and humiliating treatment he receives at the hands of the police, and his six months in the workhouse. As Bruno stews in the guilt he feels for betraying Steffi's trust, book 3 shows Steffi enduring her own humiliations as she drifts farther and farther into a world of menacing dreams and waking indifference as she prostitutes herself for the profit of the heroin-snorting Mama Tomek and the Barber, who has made her his personal prize during her off hours. Bruno's return and employment by Mama (pimping and rousting customers who get too rowdy) draw Steffi and Bruno charily together again. As book 3 ends, Steffi, ready to give Bruno another chance, betrays the Barber first by helping Bruno cheat him at cards, then by warning Bruno on the night before his fight that Bonifacy is sending some of his boys around to give him a beating. The brief book 4, "Toward Evening Lands," details, punch by punch, Bruno's eight-round pugilistic victory but ultimate life defeat as he is arrested for murder.

Bruno and Steffi cannot be said to lead uneventful lives, which, indeed, are overfilled with emotion and struggle beyond what they seem prepared adequately to handle. Consequently, they deserve credit for surviving their circumstances without being broken or cowed any more than they have been—although by the book's final pages their luck seems to be running out. Yet these are likewise stunted, demon-haunted lives: "I been hungry all my life, all the time," Bruno concludes at one point (32), and Steffi, following her booze-toting boyfriend into the shed where she will soon be raped repeatedly, can think only, "I got nothin,' so I got nothin' to lose" (64). In this respect, they are little different from anyone else in the Triangle—gang members Catfoot Nowogrodski and Finger Idzikowski, Fireball Kodadek and Bibleback Watrobinski; the whores Chickadee, Roxy, and Fat Josie. All of them are still in many ways children: they hope for new baseball uniforms or read movie magazines and gossip about the stars, gamble for nickels in their three-walled clubhouse or drop them into the jukebox, commit acts of petty crime while waiting to be recruited for larger criminal activities, and still believe in the possibility of putting a jinx on someone to win a game. What Steffi understands about Bruno is true of all the boys: each "wished only to be a man" (209).

Never Come Morning, then, is readable as literary naturalism—as a novel that documents the detrimental effects of environment on those trapped in the sort of world that is the Triangle. Girls are objects to be shared communally, then discarded and ridiculed. To speak of love is to admit a weakness, and sex is merely the gratification of lust and the stuff of which boasts are made. In this world, arrest and jail time are inevitabilities unless the cops can be bought off or one knows the ward alderman; vandalism and crime are necessities at times and always a means of "breakin' the old monotony" (119); work is something to be avoided if only because the jobs available are unsteady, poorly paid, and more difficult in their demands than less legal ways of picking up some change—and anyway, as Bruno explains to the Widow Rostenkowski, "Ever'thin's crooked" (26). A truism among the girls at Mama Tomek's is that prostitution is preferable to employment as a salesgirl or housekeeper because "the lower the wage the greater the morality demanded of you off the job"; as a hooker, at least "you had your own racket" and did not have to answer to anyone about "where you were last night" (210).

Riddled with prejudice—against blacks, Jews, indeed anyone not Polish—preyed on by both the Barber and by the police, Bruno and the others cultivate "a ceaseless series of lusts: for tobacco so good [they] could eat it like meat; for meat, for coffee, for bread, for sleep, for whisky, for women, for dice games and ball games and personal triumphs in public places" (31). They rely on brutal cunning and street smarts, as when Bruno explains to his cell mate what it will cost to buy his way out of a charge of statutory rape (100–101), or when he wishes the police had beat him when they first picked him up because "if they did it in the car they got it all out of their system, without being as accurate about it as they were in the cell" (105). Acceptance turns on proving oneself by ruining some girl (59), standing up to the cops, or showing you can take more punishment than the next guy: "the crowd had come out to see [him] kayoed," Bruno thinks proudly of himself during his boxing match with Honeyboy Tucker; "they were all here because he was going to get it. Casey thought so, Finger thought so, Steffi thought so, they all thought so. . . . Well, he wasn't going to get it. The jig was going to get it" (277).

In a world of decidedly limited options where reading material is limited to *Superman* comics and *Kayo: World's Foremost Boxing Magazine*, where WPA relief work or perhaps a few uncertain thirty-cent hours pushing freight around a dock cannot compete with the profitable thrill of a heist, and where everyone has been "crippled by the city streets" (216), depravity and immorality thrive, "burning embarrassment" (151) lurks in every moment, and an internalized sense of one's inferiority threatens constantly to undermine love and trust. Guilt, a remorse-laden loneliness, and the conviction that somehow one has been cheated and betrayed are among the results of such an existence. "Everthin's a fake," Bruno tells Steffi at the amusement park to explain why he has just destroyed the doll he won for her, leaving the girl feeling "alone," "unloved," and "abandoned in the dark" (62–63). And later, trying to work up some pride in having refused to implicate Casey and Finger for the mugging that sent him to jail, Bruno nevertheless feels "the same sense of defeat he had had when he had crept up the steps of the shed away from Steffi and Fireball" on the night that left her a prostitute (132), understanding that "no punishment was too great for such a betrayal" (133). Steffi, lamenting the "lack of humanness" (217) of the men with whom she shares her bed for pay, can only feel (as will Sophie in *The Man with the Golden Arm*) that "God has forgotten us all. . . . He has even forgotten our names" (215). Mama Tomek recites a litany to herself

The WPA, Early Poems, and *Never Come Morning* / 45

nightly: "You got to kid ever'body, mostly yourself. When you live like I done you don't believe *nobody*" (180).

"The world," Steffi thinks one lonely night, "was a curtained brothel," the city "a sealed-up room . . . a madhouse" (208–9). "And whoever wanted it so?" she asks herself, knowing that no one does; it is just that "they were all trying not to be cheated" (209). To avoid being taken advantage of, each resorts to stratagems both damning and illegal, and then is made to feel guilty for having fought back. The motto hung above One-Eye Tenczara's desk in the police query room reads "I HAVE ONLY MYSELF TO BLAME FOR MY FALL" (81), and Steffi can only unwittingly concur when, attending mass one Sunday, she leaves convinced that she must be sinful beyond salvation and "got only myself to blame" (228). Just so, Bruno knows that even when eventually released from jail, "he would never be free again" (95).

The poverty and threadbare sense of self, the moral turpitude and pervasive sense of powerlessness and exploitation, humiliation and ignorance, that characterize the world of *Never Come Morning* can, then, be accounted for circumstantially and environmentally. Yet to focus too exclusively on these ravaged lives alone, whether to condemn or pity them, is to ignore a large part of Algren's message as articulated in his 1963 preface. It is not simply that to attend overmuch to the shortcomings and moral horrors of the novel is to overlook the fact that Bruno and Steffi are perspicacious people, capable of compassion and trust, recognizable hopes and dreams, and in need of love and security. It is not just to ignore the fact that they are often electrically alive and morally aware despite environment and upbringing, little schooling and less encouragement to cultivate an internal life. The point not to be missed is this: readers who do not recognize the important ways in which they are not so different from Bruno and Steffi do not fully know themselves; consequently, whatever such readers think they feel for those inhabiting the Triangle, it amounts in the end to contempt.

But what can such contentions mean? First, they mean that until the middle class (whose representative the reader is) achieves empathic identification with America's outcasts, it cannot understand why its philanthropic efforts and wars against crime are doomed, which they are insofar as the former cannot earn trust and gratitude or the latter respect and compliance when they smack of noblesse oblige or of fear-driven efforts to shore up societal power and control. This would seem to be the adjuration with which Algren leaves us at the close of his 1963 preface:

> Nor all your piety nor all your preaching, nor all your crusades nor all your threats can stop one girl from going on the turf, can stop one mugging, can keep one promising youth from becoming a drug addict, so long as the force that drives the owners of our civilization is *away* from those who own nothing at all.[17]

In *Never Come Morning*, the ineffectuality of corrective interventions is presented on four fronts. First, the novel shows the impotence of parents to guide their children when, struggling to achieve the American Dream, the parents are themselves caught between unpersuasive Old World values and a new world whose ways are pulling their children away from them. Bruno's mother may believe in "work as a cure-all" (15), for example, but for the boy this is just "peasant" nonsense. Eventually, an abdication of parental responsibility is the result. Thus, Bruno's mother fails to visit her son in the workhouse even once, just as Steffi's mother makes no effort to contact Steffi once she has fallen into the clutches of the Barber. No other parents even make an appearance in the novel.

Secondly, the police, while effective in harassing the criminal small fry, are shown to be as brutal, manipulative, and corrupt as the other older adults from the neighborhood—Casey Benkowski, Bonifacy the Barber, Mama Tomek, the indicted ward alderman. Bruno has learned enough on the streets to know that, where the police are concerned, the "right answers never had gotten anyone out of trouble yet" (96) and, refusing to believe a deal Tenczara is pretending to offer him, reflects that "he didn't trust anything in uniform because he had never met up with any uniform that had ever learned how to deal with a man in any other fashion than by beating him" (116).

Thirdly, the church, although it has instilled in Steffi a sense of moral depravity, is otherwise forceless and indifferent to her fate. Mocked throughout, the church offers its sinners little. When Steffi, for instance, leaves Mama Tomek's for anguished hours of soul-searching at mass, her priest, noticing her "little white face beside the first pew" and seeing that she is "unwell," offers her nothing more than the homily that "God has more than He has spent" (227)—shortly after which the collection is taken, and things are as they have always been: "The poor were giving. The priests were taking" (228). It is certainly not coincidental that Bibleback, the only devout boy in Bruno's gang, feels free to join the rape line because he intends to do penance later and is one of the boys who eventually agrees to finger Bruno for murder.

Finally, of equal uselessness is the relief worker, Algren's symbol of social concern, who shows up early in the novel to lecture Bruno self-righteously on his responsibilities, quiz him on why he has not followed up on a job lead she gave him, and explain that assistance hinges on sundry rules and regulations that disqualify his mother from receiving the help she needs. It is unlikely, however, that even a more sympathetic, less condescending caseworker would meet with greater success, for she, too, would come "from the same world as did detectives and truant officers and park policemen" (13): the middle-class world Bruno and the others have learned to distrust.

In short, the middle class has managed to convey to every "promising youth" of the Triangle that everything is crooked—and nothing more so than the middle class, which masks its indifference and hypocrisy in shows of concern and lip service to statutes and holy commandments. Yet the truth keeps breaking through: in the women "seated comfortably, as though for a double-feature" and "titter[ing] their enjoyment" of the men being so comically grilled by Captain Tenczara (137, 141); in Sergeant Adamovitch's admission to Bruno that "we just don't want you turning out a criminal, costing the taxpayers money" (112) and his dislike of Bruno because kids like him "kept spoiling things for the high-class Polacks" (127). In short, not to know Steffi and Bruno—and the countless others similarly situated—is not to know in what ways one is already responsible for how they live and think, implicated in their actions and desires, guilty of selling the "spring-blade knife with a six-inch blade" (84) that may one day be held against one's own throat.

But Algren has yet a further point to make beyond indicting the middle class for the contemptuous self-righteousness that makes unlikely any heartfelt compliance with laws and ideals seen to be ignored by those paid to preach and enforce them. This final point is that nothing of greater moral authority than money and what it can buy separates "us" from "them," that "we" do just as "they" do, only in more pleasant surroundings; as Steffi understands, money alone can "get people like herself and Bruno out of almost any trouble, because it was usually just through lack of a ten-dollar bill that they'd gotten into trouble in the first place" (241). As the novel makes clear, many of the men visiting Mama Tomek's come from the middle class, just as does a good part of the rowdy crowd jeering the "white hope" Bruno as he and the African American Tucker beat each other senseless. Indeed, as Steffi comes to feel after several months of prostitution, "There was no bottom to [men's] depravity. . . . The more respectable they appeared the deeper their depravity":

> To Steffi the terror of them lay in this: that they went to work and joked and lived sensibly with their mothers and saved their money and married and grew conservative and cared for their health by day, while practicing, all their lives by night, the madnesses of the streets as though their madnesses were the reward of being virtuous by day. (216)

Thus, for Algren, not to know Bruno is not to know that all men and women, oneself included, are among the poor in spirit, just as is it not to know that one supports and profits shamelessly from a system that functions most efficiently when able most completely and contemptuously to ignore "those who own nothing at all."

Perhaps, as John Clellon Holmes has suggested, Algren preferred America's outcasts to its respectable citizens because Bruno's and Steffi's "air of forthright larceny, naked appetite, no-shit con" appealed to him as more honest than the smug duplicity, the pious scorn, of Steffi's priest, Bruno's caseworker, or the Triangle's indicted alderman. "The essence of [Algren's] work," writes Holmes, "was to bring the day-to-day, deal-to-deal, fix-to-fix lives of [his chosen] people out of the shadows . . . exposing by comparison the impoverishment of most middle class values," which pretend to prize rectitude while permitting all that they condemn.[18] As Mama Tomek puts it, "We're all responsible" (182). Algren wishes his readers to understand that to know such things is to know oneself; not to know such things is to allow Steffi to die "without having lived" (213) and to confirm Bruno in his belief that he would "never get t' be twenty-one anyhow" (284). For readers not to know such things is to be as irresponsible as those their society condemns and to guarantee that everyone remains trapped "in the same big room" in which "nobody's speakin' to anyone else, 'n nobody got a key" (215), and the morning of a better day never comes.

CHAPTER FOUR

The Neon Wilderness

Between the publication of *Never Come Morning* and the release of *The Neon Wilderness* in January 1947, Algren had spent almost two and a half years in the army before returning to Chicago, where, armed with his veteran's benefits and a sixty dollar a week advance from his new publisher, Doubleday, he found a place in the city's impoverished Polish district to begin writing again in earnest. As he worked on the stories that would comprise *The Neon Wilderness,* he was also writing book reviews for *Poetry,* the *Chicago Sun,* and *Chicago Daily News.*

The thirty-two short reviews Algren produced from 1942 through 1946 were primarily quick ways of making a little money. They do, however, offer brief glimpses into his intact political convictions and maturing aesthetic. He observes, for instance, that *Sun in Their Eyes,* a novel by Monte Barrett, offers "history according to the slick-paper magazines" while nevertheless revealing how "early American imperialism was fought and resisted." Algren criticizes Sinclair Lewis's novel *Gideon Planish* for its inability to speak "in positive democratic terms" and dismisses Salom Rizk's novel *Syrian Yankee* for its "Rotarian" blindness to what America's technological civilization has "cost in terms of human values."[1] On the other hand, he applauds Dorothy Stockbridge's *Angry Dust,* a novel about labor disputes, for its timeliness; praises Jean Giono's *Blue Boy* for its conviction that "there are no truly evil men and women"; and commends Niven Busch's World War II novel *They Dream of Home* for showing readers how a man who has been "violated" by warfare "will violate society in return."[2] On aesthetic matters, Algren found the poems of the African-American poet Margaret Walker an occasion to observe how "music and message" can derive "from sheer weight of social pressure" while elsewhere panning Benedict Thielen's novel *The Lost Men,* which follows a group of World War I veterans through the Depression years, as "too literary for the job." Similarly, he faults Robert Henriques's *The Voice of the Trumpet,* a memoir of life as a commando in World War II, for being too poetic and "overwritten"—risks that, as Algren knew, he was himself repeatedly running.[3]

Of particular interest is a 1943 essay on writing entitled "Do It the Hard Way." Algren advises would-be writers to carry a camera to assist in accurate visual detail and, more important, to "listen to people talk" until "the commonest speech" of "the ball-park and the dance hall, of the drug store at noon, of the pool room and the corner newsstand" begins "to ring like poetry." He urges his readers "to share, as fully as one is able, in the common experiences of common humanity" and, fresh from his success with *Never Come Morning,* insists that publishers will take a book "dealing with any strata of any society so long as it is a true book"—not contrived but drawn from the real world and written "with conviction of both feeling and thought." As long as one avoids falsity and the temptations of the "How-Did-He-Get-Rid-of-the-Corpse market" to write "honestly, for honest men"—"for the milkman, for the janitor, for the street-car conductor"—one's work, Algren avers, will last. Such writing is "confessional" insofar as it reveals one's "own inmost feelings" and is what is meant by "doing it the hard way."[4]

The Neon Wilderness might, then, be considered the exemplification of such ideas about effective writing as Algren was elsewhere elucidating. If his novels are mirrors in which contemporary American society might see its own tarnished image, the twenty-four stories comprising *The Neon Wilderness* are a shattered mirror reflecting as many small scenes of life among the permanently down-and-out. Written over the course of fourteen years—the collection includes the very early "So Help Me" (1933) and "The Brothers' House" (1934)—the stories, individually and collectively, point in several interpretive directions.[5] They have been read as existential glimpses into the abyss, as gospels of amorality, as explorations of the disastrous ends awaiting those who betray love.[6] Perhaps a useful point of entry is the epigraph, taken from "The City" by David Wolff:

> matchless city, terrible . . . and all, all
> I see are innocent; not walls nor men
> brutal, remote, stunned, querulous, weak, or cold
> do crimes so massive, but the hideous fact
> stands guilty: the usurpation of man over man.[7]

"The Captain Has Bad Dreams," which opens the collection, offers an introduction to the sort of men and women about whom the epigraph speaks. An instance of a recurring scene in Algren's work, the lineup interrogation, the story parades before an audience of middle-class victims of crime a holding cell's worth of "querulous, weak, or cold" souls.[8] For the most part, they are small-time recidivists (thieves, brawlers, addicts, prostitutes, homosexuals), all presumed guilty when grilled by the police captain, whose sarcastic interrogation habitually ends with the suggestion that the suspect put an end to his life: "Why don't you take a good belt of cocaine and jump out a twenty-story window?" the captain asks one man; "Have you tried gas?" he asks another (21, 24).

Finding himself increasingly "haunted" by those appearing before him week after week, the captain finds he "didn't always have the heart to point the unwavering finger of guilt" (19)—not because he feels compassion but because he is weary with indifference and the futility of it all. "You couldn't drown them because they weren't cats," he muses, "and when you drove them off they found their way back home anyhow" (19). Unable to accept the fact that the city is home not only for those he is paid to protect but also for those he polices, the captain languishes in bafflement despite daily intercourse with thugs and stewbums, pickpockets and deviants. What can it mean, the captain wonders, to be accused by an addict of throwing money at him "all the time" (society's stereotypical response to social problems) (33)? And why does another addict stand "as though impaled, an agonized Christ" (27) if not because he is somehow a sacrificial scapegoat for society's sins?

The stories that follow are not, however, united by a singular urban focus. "Depend on Aunt Elly" is set in Texarkana, "El Presidente de Méjico" in Texas, "He Couldn't Boogie-Woogie Worth a Damn" in southern France, "Kingdom City to Cairo" on the road. The notion of "the neon wilderness" must be understood rather as a metaphor that captures those particular manifestations of the "usurpation of man over man" that typify life in the 1940s for those, as Algren would later put it, "forced to choices too hard to bear."[9] It is any place where the disinherited live: an "unpossessed twilight land" (22), "the true jungle" (251).

Wherever life and Algren find them, the characters in these stories are people from the lineups: men and women who would

The Neon Wilderness / 55

do right if they could and who do wrong because they can. Perhaps they feel as does Rocco ("He Swung and He Missed"), a small-time boxer shortchanged all his life, who agrees to throw a fight because "he had earned the right to sell out" (159). They are people whom nobody really knows—like Mary ("Design for Departure"), ignored by her drunken father and the equally uncaring woman he has brought into their home, on her own since she was a teenager and eventually brought to wonder if anyone would ever "find out who, after all, she *really* was" (255).

Significantly, nine of these stories are told in the first person, for the neon wilderness is populated by those desperate to have their stories known, to assert themselves, to find some way of buttressing their shaky pride and tottering self-respect. Each longs to be seen and understood—like Tiny Zion ("Million Dollar Brainstorm"), walking drunkenly down the street and "boasting to the darkness" (212), or Rudy Sobotnik ("Poor Man's Pennies"), "always trying to prove he isn't a bum before anyone even says he is" (119). In "No Man's Laughter," to take a third example, Gino Bomagino makes a name for himself as the most daring car thief in Chicago because, as he tells his girl, it is only behind the wheel of a stolen car that he feels as though he has "got the world beat" (223), adding that "mostly I'm a guy like this: I don't like gettin' laughed at" (224). A loner with a strong belief in himself, Gino is drafted into military service during World War II, achieving a crazy hero's end when he crashes his single-seater scout plane into a Japanese cruiser he has dogged through the Aleutians until out of fuel, enjoying "the feeling of being, just this one time, the hunter instead of the hunted" (227).

Pride and belief in oneself motivate many in these stories: Rocco, "double-cross[ed]" by pride (162), attempts to win the fight in which he has agreed to take a fall because he refuses to go out a loser; the teenaged Bruno ("A Bottle of Milk for Mother"), being fitted for a murder rap after shooting a man to prove he "wasn't just another greenhorn sprout like [the man he shot] thought" (79), nevertheless brags boyishly to the police about his baseball and boxing prowess and has at one point the ludicrous impulse to remove his shirt so they might admire his build (84).[10] In "The Face on the Barroom Floor," Railroad Shorty—a legless man "of endless versatility and unfailing resources" (131) who gets around on a wheeled platform—beats the harmless bartender Fancy to "a paste of cartilage and blood" (139) because Fancy has suggested that Shorty is being supported financially by his girlfriend.[11] Again, in "Pero Venceremos," O'Connor, a veteran of the Spanish Civil War, retells the same war stories he has recited for a decade because the experiences they contain are the sole source of pride for this "poor boy doin' the best he can" (220).

In a world that gives them few breaks, these men and women know they must believe in themselves—and in luck and bluff. Thus in "Katz" a young man, having lost his bankroll in a poker game, returns to the game pretending to have more money than he does because he "believed in himself" as much as he believes in "lucky bucks, fast money" (232). His bluff called and unable to cover his losses, Katz is roughed up and thrown down the stairs, yet leaves hurling insults, his sense of self and faith in his luck unshaken. In "Kingdom City to Cairo," a defrocked minister boasts to a hitchhiker of his affair with his brother's wife and of the bedbug-infested hotel he has turned into a profitable bordello. In "Is Your Name Joe?" a deranged woman retains a sufficient sense of her own worth, despite protestations to the contrary after years of abusive relationships with men, to explain that she continues to fight because she "ain't *that* bad. *Nobody's* that bad" (44). The alternative, to lose one's belief in oneself, is the dead-end choice of death and damnation—like Mary, sunk so low that she craves only the release of nonexistence by overdose, or the woman narrating "Please Don't Talk about Me When I'm Gone," whose life has brought her only shame and the desire to be forgotten.

No one in these stories is immune from abuse, neither women nor children, honest working stiffs nor enlisted men: all are likely to meet defeat and humiliation. Not surprisingly, victimization is served up in heaping portions by those representing authority and charged with enforcing society's laws. Beyond the cynical, manhandling police of "The Captain Has Bad Dreams" and "A Bottle of Milk for Mother," there is the corrupt sheriff of "El Presidente de Méjico." Having jailed the Mexican Portillo (a newlywed with a child on the way) because the man is suspected of running a still, the sheriff releases him after having enlisted two other inmates, Jesse and Wolfe, to "pump the Mex" (172) regarding the still's whereabouts. Followed when he returns to his still, Portillo is shot, brought back to jail, and left to die. Further abuses of official power reside in the fates of Jesse and Wolfe. The former, a white Texan jailed for killing a Mexican, is soon released and given Portillo's sombrero; when last seen, he is again "a respectable citizen" (178) of his west Texas town. Wolfe, on the other hand, a Jew from New Jersey arrested for breaking into a shed while working on a government relief project, is sentenced to "four years on the pea farm at Huntsville" (177).

Equally corrupt is the criminal-justice system presented in "Depend on Aunt Elly." Here, corrections officer Elly Harper furloughs incarcerated women in return for monthly payoffs—

among them Wilma, arrested for prostitution after losing her job in a defense plant, whose marriage and dreams of respectability are destroyed when her husband discovers one of Elly's demands for more cash. As indifferently self-interested is the juvenile justice system as sketched briefly in "A Lot You Got to Holler" (116) and in greater detail in "The Children." The reformatory boys of the latter story are subjected to noxious platitudes, walls hung with "holy pictures" (203), and the wildly ineffective good intentions of "the ladies of the Polonia Women's Federation," who have decided the boys should put on a Thanksgiving Day play. Overseen by a guard who despises and fears them, the boys lie fearfully abed at night, filled with visions of revenge.

"That's the Way It's Always Been" and "The Heroes," two war stories, document flagrant abuses of power wielded by officers over enlisted men. In the former, the officers are presented as incompetent drunks and womanizers, ready to seize any privilege at the expense of the men they command. The officers, Algren writes, "would have sent out their mothers with detectors before putting a foot on mined earth themselves. They were all heroes on the bar front—but in the zone, no" (190). The men are required to pay for alcohol rations that were supposed to be free; to watch as the chaplain sells on the black market the cigarettes, candy, and soap he should have been distributing to them; and to listen politely while the colonel enjoins them to "act like white men just for once" (196) before he departs to sleep off a hangover with one nurse or another. Through it all, the chaplain offers what is to him sufficient explanation for such unfairness: "That's the way it's always been . . . so that's how it got to be" (199). In "The Heroes," the narrator, speaking on behalf of the enlisted men, explains that "our war was with the second lieutenants, the MPs, and the cooks" (267) as he recounts what seems to be a comic tale of circumventing authority in a search for alcohol until the story ends with his coconspirator stepping on a landmine.

If official authority is lambasted for the way it treats what it considers riffraff, Algren is equally intent here on showing how the sometimes brutal poor victimize each other—because most of the time they can get at only one another. Bruno, after all, has been arrested for shooting a neighborhood drunk; Fancy is beaten not by the law but by the cardsharp Railroad Shorty; David in "So Help Me" is robbed, conned, forced to participate in a holdup, then murdered by two older grifters; the boy paroled in "The Brothers' House" is unwelcome in his own home. Just so, Tiny Zion, although brain damaged, is kept in the ring by his ostensible friend and manager Myer although Tiny is no longer able even to take care of himself and must live with his mother, who "had always expected the worst and had never been disappointed" (214). At the story's end, Tiny in an unbalanced fit of pique, flings his cat out a second-story window as Myer walks off musing that "it ain't none of Myer Salk's business no more" and reflecting unconcernedly that Tiny will "be throwin' the old lady out the winda next. . . . Or jumpin' outa it hisself" (216).

Elsewhere, Augie's life of crime ("A Lot You Got to Holler") is attributed to the fact that his callous father left the boy's mother for her sister, raising Augie to believe that the sister was his mother and that his mother was his aunt—then banishing the "aunt" (the only person who has ever shown Augie any affection) from the home when the boy is eight. Augie's dysfunctional home life leaves the boy starved for affection and eager to retaliate against his father in whatever way he can.

Again, in "Please Don't Talk about Me When I'm Gone," the female narrator and her accomplice, Doc, attempt to con a naive young immigrant, first getting him hooked on dope, then killing him. The story ends with the narrator, fearing Doc's mistrust of her, beating him to death with a baseball bat.

If the poor and those outside the law victimize one another because they can, these stories make clear that those likeliest to suffer are the most defenseless: women, children, minorities, the mentally disabled. In these stories, Wilma and Augie; Portillo and the punched-out Tiny Zion; Wolfe and Mary, who sinks downward to darkness imagining herself to be the Virgin Mary and whose rosary beads are the barbiturates she consumes: "Veronal. Allonal. Luminal. Veronal" (257).[12] Yet just as often, these are people guilty of victimizing themselves: Katz, who having lost his bankroll, attempts to cheat at a game where getting caught means certain punishment; O'Connor, unwilling or unable to move past his war experiences; the nameless narrator of "Is Your Name Joe?" who keeps coming back for more punishment with yet another man poorly chosen. In "Stickman's Laughter," Banty Longobardi manages to win a bundle shooting dice, only to lose it all when, finding his wife out for the evening, he can think of nothing better to do than drink and gamble some more. Again, in "Poor Man's Pennies," habitual crook and liar Rudy Sobotnik (who anticipates Solly Saltskin of *The Man with the Golden Arm*) cannot refrain from looking for trouble even on the night before his marriage to Gladys, a saint of patience who is willing to overlook his numerous faults and to do whatever she can to keep him out of jail.

"Stickman's Laughter" and "Poor Man's Pennies" both end well. Banty may fear what his wife will say when she learns he has again lost his pay, but he falls asleep in her arms, his apologetic tears drying in "the shadowed valley of her breasts," his worried mind comforted by the knowledge that "nothing important had been lost after all" (72). Similarly, the last the reader sees of Rudy, he has been with Gladys and out of jail for ten years. There are other characters who beat the odds, who enjoy at least momentary victories over defeat and loss: Rocco, losing the fight he has refused to throw only to discover that his wife has bet all they have on his winning, can grin at this proof of her confidence in him, and Gino in "No Man's Laughter" dies as he imagines "coasting downhill at last, toward a land where he'd be unpursued forever" (229). In "He Couldn't Boogie-Woogie Worth a Damn," PFC Isaac Bailey is hiding out in Marseilles with an Algerian girl after having gone AWOL at war's end and risking arrest by selling stolen army supplies on the black market. Yet the story concludes cheerily enough with Bailey successfully avoiding capture by the military police and preparing to leave with his girl for a life in Algeria.

However, although some of these stories end happily, and others are told comically, the victories are gauzed with loss, and the humor muffled by sorrow. As Bailey's story ends, he hears the tolling of a bell "full of sorrow" (103)—for his escape to Algeria is not a homecoming, for his home remains America, where, alas, there is no future for a black man who refuses to shine shoes and who cannot box or sing or "boogie-woogie worth a damn" (99). Similarly, Tiny Zion may walk along joking loudly to himself, but he remains a derelict boxer vomiting on a city street to the disgust or indifference of passersby. And if Mary escapes her nightmare existence at the end of "Design for Departure," her surcease of pain comes only through a deliberately lethal overdose lovingly administered by her boyfriend, Christy, a "Christ" who saves by destroying.

"How the Devil Came down Division Street," perhaps Algren's most anthologized story, exemplifies how the humor of *The Neon Wilderness* is wrapped around a core of sorrow even as it is itself enwrapped in tragedy. Roman Orlov, asked how he came to be "the biggest drunk" on Division Street (35), explains that it all began when his family (mother, father, four children) moved into a tenement too small to permit all of them to sleep at once—a problem that was not a problem as long as Papa stayed out all night playing his accordion in local taverns. Yet when a knocking begins to be heard in the closet, the Orlovs learn their home is haunted by the ghost of a man who killed his girlfriend and then hanged himself. Shortly thereafter, Papa ceases his nocturnal serenading, the family prays for the unhappy dead man, and the ghost finds peace, thereby bringing the Orlovs fame and good fortune: Papa becomes "the best janitor on Noble Street" (40), Mama receives a blessing from the priest, sister begins to excel at school, and the twins stop their constant bickering. However, with nowhere to sleep now that Papa is home and sister therefore forced into the twins' bed, Roman begins haunting the taverns. Thus, as Mama admits, she regained "a worthless husband" at the cost of "a good son" (41), who has now been "drunk so long," the narrator observes, "that when we remember living men we almost forget Poor Roman" (35). The tragedy of a murder-suicide thus drives a comic tall tale that ends in the damnation and living death of Roman.

In offering his stories of "the usurpation of man over man," Algren is often tragic or pathetic when not as painfully matter-of-fact as a newspaper account of an unimportant arrest. If it is the humor that most requires explanation, perhaps it is sufficient to say that the stories are sometimes humorous because humor can be found in these people's lives as in everyone's. As

Algren later remarked of James Leo Herlihy's *The Sleep of Baby Filbertson and Other Stories,* which likewise explored the world of "the useless and unzipped, the loveless and defrauded," Herlihy erred in not realizing that, "even in the eons of endless rains, there [are] moments of sun" when even the defeated are "purely rocked with laughter."[13] Or perhaps what Algren writes of Corporal Hardheart in "The Heroes" is true of himself as well: "when he was joking he was most in earnest" (265). As Studs Terkel would have it, because we live "in a clownish time" in which no one can be taken seriously unless "he clowns as well," Algren is "the funniest man around" and therefore "the most serious."[14] What Algren was serious about was making readers see, as vividly and compassionately as possible, the sorry absurdity of the way things often are for those who inhabit America's "neon wilderness."

Although sparse, reviews of *The Neon Wilderness* were sympathetic. Algren's friend Jack Conroy wrote that "beneath each sordid and brutal [story] beats the comprehending and compassionate heart," and Charles Poore, characterizing the book as "a collection of stark tales from the murky depths," insisted that "the thing to say about stories like these is, always, that they're not pretty. Well, they're not pretty. But they generally ring true."[15] If John Woodburn found the book "both monotonous and uneven," its characters "feral and instinctual," he also felt the stories showed "Algren's power, the magnificent anger and indignation with which he articulates the lives of these ruined and invalidated people." Algren, Woodburn concluded, "is deeply and pitifully concerned with [such people], and he is determined that we should be aware of them." Similarly, while finding Algren "a definite apostle of amorality," Catherine Meredith

Brown praised his "perfect" dialogue and the "precision of the writing," which "must be both remembered, and admired."[16]

In 1996, Kurt Vonnegut suggested that, in writing about "dehumanized Americans," Algren was doing no more than saying, "Hey—an awful lot of these people your hearts are bleeding for are really mean and stupid. That's just a fact. Did you know that?"[17] Yet a close look at the stories comprising *The Neon Wilderness* reveals that they say more than that: they are indictments of an indifferent society and a mirror in which the reader (and the writer) may behold his own distorted face. As Algren writes elsewhere, articulating what he called "the Yogi concept," "if a man comes to your door, go and meet yourself." Or as he observes of Kenneth Millar's *Blue City*—a novel that "fetch[es] us monsters out of the city deeps . . . without indicating their origins"—the novelist needed to show that such human beings "are what they are because there was nothing else for them to become."[18]

Reviewing Edmund Fuller's *Man in Modern Fiction* more than a decade after the appearance of *The Neon Wilderness*, Algren was still fighting to have the humanity of society's least-fortunate members sympathetically recognized. He notes with dismay that "Fuller flatly refuses an old friend of mine, Frankie Machine [*The Man with the Golden Arm*], because he is a frightening character, without alternatives" and insists that Frankie's lack of options "was the very reason I wrote about him." Criticizing Fuller's refusal to grant "compassion and mercy" to those he finds undeserving, Algren insists that those about whom he has written "were men and women like men and women everywhere, with a little less luck than most." Then Algren poses a question: "Doesn't Christ preach forgiveness of sins?" If so, "Shouldn't the modern artist forgive too?"[19]

The Neon Wilderness / 65

To help readers understand why possibly frightening men and women such as those congregated in *The Neon Wilderness* were nevertheless deserving of empathy and forgiveness was central to the task Algren set himself in his next novel.

CHAPTER FIVE

The Man with the Golden Arm

In 1947, nine months after *The Neon Wilderness* appeared, Algren published a poem that would eventually serve as the epitaph for *The Man with the Golden Arm* (1949).[1] In the poem, Frankie Machine (minus his morphine addiction) is introduced as a man who "with a deck or a cue . . . had the touch" but who "crapped out" nonetheless. Carried over from the pages of *Poetry* magazine to close the novel, and located after a most prosaic transcript of the coroner's inquest following Frankie's death, the poem suggests that Algren considered Frankie first and last a poetic subject, as though the novel's agenda were an attempt to show how life's sorriest prose might become or contain poetry, or how the lowliest Skid Row gambler partakes of the same mythic qualities possessed by American folk heroes (or antiheroes) such as John Hardy and Stagolee, Willie the Weeper and Billy the Kid—alienated, brutalized (and brutalizing) men living out doomed lives that are made to matter because of how their stories are told:

> For it's all in the wrist with a deck or a cue
> And if he crapped out when we thought he was due
> It must have been that the dice were rolled,
> For he had the touch, and his arm was gold:
> Rack up his cue, leave the steerer his hat,
> The arm that held up has failed at last.

The Man with the Golden Arm / 67

> Yet why does the light down the dealer's slot
> Sift soft as light from a troubled dream?
> *(A dream, they say, of a golden arm
> that belonged to the dealer we called Machine.)*[2]

The novel that, in a sense, grew from this poem began as Algren enjoyed the modest success of *The Neon Wilderness*: generally sympathetic reviews; good sales in his hometown of Chicago; a television appearance in which he was interviewed by his friend the novelist Jack Conroy; and invitations to speak at literary events around town.[3] His hopes for the new book—which he was variously calling "The Dead, the Drunk, and the Dying," "The Weaker Sheep," "Hustler's Heart," or "Night without Mercy"—were high, even if he was having trouble finding a novelistic focus.[4] He recalled rewriting the book "a dozen times," with some sections passing through forty drafts. "It comes in lumps," he wrote later, describing his composing process, "and each lump has to be smoothed and grained down and then, when it's just so shining and smooth and you read it aloud to yourself and love the sound of every perfect word, you find you can't use it."[5] His uncertain progress toward his masterpiece is perhaps indicated by the fact that it began as a war novel set in Marseilles before the focus shifted to a GI just returned from the war to Chicago's Division Street; the drug-addiction angle that made the book something of a cause célèbre came late into the story and despite Algren's fears that it might prove too sensational.[6]

If his hopes were large and unflagging, this was because he was willing at the time—as he later claimed he would never be again—to "put in the three, four, five years to turn out a book

68 / Understanding Nelson Algren

that has a chance of enduring."[7] His biographer writes that, as the novel took shape, Algren was obsessed "with greatness and the desire to say something new"—and optimistic as always about the possibility of "dent[ing] the thick armor with which the middle classes shielded themselves from seeing the 'civilization' they supported."[8] For a while following the book's publication, such hopes seemed justified and its author poised to join the ranks of America's premiere twentieth-century novelists.

Consider the world of Frankie Majcinek, better known on the street as Frankie Machine or "Dealer." Returned from the war with a Purple Heart, the shrapnel that earned him this medal also serving to introduce him to morphine, Frankie lives in the dismal Division Arms Hotel (when not to be found in Antek "Owner" Witwicki's Tug and Maul bar downstairs) with his pathetic and spiteful wife, Sophie (Zosh), whom he never really loved—not enough, not in the right way—but whom he married when she thought she was pregnant. When just back from the war, Frankie gets drunk the week the atomic bomb is dropped on Hiroshima and crashes his car into a light standard, putting Sophie in a wheelchair.

Although she recovers physically, Sophie becomes a psychological cripple, using a wheelchair to keep Frankie tied to her with chains of guilt. Since that disastrous week (that is, for more than a year before the novel opens in the fall of 1946), Frankie has endured this guilt along with Sophie's scorn and relentless demands, meanwhile understanding that, as his drug dealer Nifty Louie Fomorowsky will eventually tell him, he is "one of the weaker sheep" (61), his only skill a machinelike ability to deal cards, his only close friend the slightly unbalanced "punk" Solly "Sparrow" Saltskin, a shoplifter, seller of stolen dogs, and philanderer—a habitual offender in the eyes of the law, too

The Man with the Golden Arm / 69

crazy to walk the streets but not crazy enough to put away for good. Working as a dealer for Zero Schwiefka's poker games and entertaining pipedreams of becoming a drummer in "a real band" (36), Frankie drinks, kibitzes, and yearns for Molly-O (Molly Novotny), the "girl with the heart-shaped face and the wonder gone out of her eyes" (30). She is Drunkie John's punching bag and meal ticket, and the one Frankie thinks could return him to himself, help him kick the junk for keeps, and give him a new life of love and tender honesty.

Eventually, life gets to be too much, and Frankie starts using again until, ashamed that he has been trapped in a net of quarter-grain hits of morphine, he impulsively (and largely accidentally) kills Louie following an argument over a poker bet. Soon, increasingly unsure even of who he is, Frankie goes on the lam, trying again to get the monkey of addiction off his back with Molly's help, until Sparrow and Frankie's need for a fix betray him. Molly, who has already fallen from the position of hostess at the Club Safari to that of stripper in a black nightclub, is left bereaved and looking at jail time. Sparrow, too, is headed for a long stretch in prison, tricked by Blind Pig (Division Street's new dealer) and the police into delivering Frankie's morphine: a setup to force the punk into fingering the Dealer. As for Sophie, Frankie's sudden disappearance has left her insane, and the last the reader sees of her, she is institutionalized and lost in a private world of remorseful fantasies.

The novel's plot is interrupted with great frequency by lengthy, sometimes digressive vignettes, poetic descriptions of setting and meditations on the characters' inner lives, lists and streetwise repartee, and a lineup's worth of character sketches (Meter Reader, DeWitt, Umbrella Man, Poor Peter, Blind Pig, Sgt. Kvorka, Little Lester, Applejack Katz)—a panoramic view of the urban underclass.[9] The novel, like its characters' lives, swings wildly between deepest gloom and defeat on the one hand, and comically triumphant "little things done in simple fun" as well as "the big things done for love" on the other (188). Ultimately, it is a novel riddled with guilt and loneliness, love sought and almost found, unlikely dreams deferred, and the compassionate bonds forged from mutual suffering and powerlessness, all of which serve to contextualize and thereby explain Frankie's addiction, thus providing the brief for indicting those responsible.

Algren would not elaborate his dissatisfaction with midcentury America until *Chicago: City on the Make* (1951) and *Nonconformity: Writing on Writing* (1950–53; published 1996). However, a short piece written for the *Chicago Sun Book Week* in 1947 offers a key to help unlock Frankie's story as social protest. In this slight essay, Algren laments the city's hollow laughter, diminished hopes and ambitions, spiritual ill health, and the essential loneliness of its citizens, each indifferent to the fates of anyone else and intent on pursuing only the crassest conceptualization of the American Dream. The essay ends with lines from an unattributed poem that suggest the consequences of such a stultifying social climate: "The young return—but cold, with skin-tight mask, / Seeing the city honors the most false."[10]

Indeed, as *The Man with the Golden Arm* opens, a young man—wearing the mask that conceals his morphine addiction—has just returned to the quicksand of Division Street, where the falsity of others and his own falsity (to himself as much as to others) has already begun to suck him under for keeps. Certainly, Frankie's story is one of self-imposed punishment of a sort worse than anything the police are dishing out. His guilt and shame lead him down a low road of drink and the needle, petty crime, and the shelving of dreams toward self-destruction and the gradual erasure of identity. He can brag all he wants—he is "the kid with the golden arm," who "drives like he deals, deals like he lives 'n he lives all the time" (9, 68), proud of his skill with dice and deck, cue and drumsticks—but Frankie is a broken machine, and what fixes him (the morphine that deadens the guilt) is also what keeps him broken and brings him down.

The Man with the Golden Arm asks its readers to consider the degree to which Frankie's failures—and those of the rest of the characters—result from bad choices made and flaws of character, and the degree to which he and the others are victims of circumstance, of forces beyond their control. It is easy to blame Frankie (and those whom he represents). For instance, Frankie "chooses" to go back on dope, yet his introduction to morphine (recovering from a war wound) was none of his doing, and one perhaps has to believe this admittedly weak sheep when he says of trying to kick the habit that "nobody can stand getting' that sick 'n live," that "there ain't no 'will power' to it like squares like to say" (262). Similarly, if he chooses to shoplift at Niebolt's department store, he does so because in his world there are only so many ways, most of them unwise in one way or another, to distract himself from his worries—and he needs distraction badly. Life with Sophie has grown bleaker by the day, and every day more and more people in the neighborhood seem to know who killed Louie—an act to which Frankie was driven because of the power Louie has wielded over him by virtue of being Dealer's dealer. And to come full circle, Frankie has needed what Louie dealt because Frankie inhabits a life where freedom is narrower than the stairway leading from the holding cell to the street.

Frankie, raised by a foster mother with whom he has lost touch, has less than a grammar-school education and has been in trouble since he was a boy. Powerlessness characterizes his situation: "Ain't nobody scared of me my whole life," he bemoans early in the novel (23). He has a criminal record and a habit, just as the police have a habit of picking him up whenever Zero Schwiefka is late with the payoffs or whenever Frankie finds himself just "a wrong guy in a wrong neighborhood out at the wrong hour" (20). The only fun he knows involves sex or monkeyshines, a pool cue or a deck of cards, a beer and a shot. He is surrounded by and socializes with "mush workers and lush workers, catamites and sodomites, bucket workers and bail jumpers, till tappers and assistant pickpockets, square johns and copper johns; lamisters and hallroom boys, ancient pious perverts and old blown parolees, rapoes and record-men, the damned and the undaunted, the jaunty and condemned" (197). Toughness and cynical savvy are his crowd's prized possessions. Everyone in a position of authority is corrupt, from Doc Dominoes (a quack turning three-dollar medical tricks with his "electric blood reverser" [76–79]) to the ward super, who pressures the police to find Louie's killer only because it is an election year.

In Frankie's world, honest work means primarily and most probably menial physical labor. Those who find the exits from Division Street are hardly inspirational and little more than guys who have pulled off a successful scam: Shudefski, a bartender who joins the Marines only to avoid having to marry the barfly Lily Splits; Zygmunt the Prospector, ambulance-chasing lawyer disbarred three months after "put[ting] out his shingle" (72). Zygmunt exemplifies what is a truism on Division Street: business as conducted in a white collar is a de facto con game. As Sparrow explains, "A businessman is a hustler with the dough to hustle on the legit 'n a hustler is a businessman who's either gone broke or never had it" (104).

Although Sparrow might put in any number of hours organizing peeping-tom tours of the neighborhood for pay, a conventional job is for squares, and anyone working on the square deserves to be ridiculed—as Vi mistreats and browbeats her husband, old Stash, whose hard-earned pay is squandered by his wife on her boyfriend Sparrow. Similarly Sparrow brags that he has trained the dog Rumdum to harass "all uniformed toilers . . . everyone, indeed, who didn't smell of beer or unemployment" (54). As a last example, when Vi takes up with Jailer Schwabatski and gets "all squared up"—the two of them saving their money, sending Jailer's mentally disabled son Poor Peter to "a school for tardy children," and doing everything they can to make it into the middle class—Frankie and Antek can understand such odd behavior only as a result of the couple being "in a tailspin on some religious kick" (323).

This sense of pandemic dishonesty licenses the immorality to be found behind the doors of Frankie's tenement house—a dissoluteness as ineradicable as the paper daisies Poor Peter is forever planting down the stairway. One cannot be too delicate or too particular in taking pleasures wherever they can be found: in the shots of "Old Fitz, Old Crow or Old McCall" that make "everything seem just the way everything ought to have been" (43, 128), in a little lovemaking with Sparrow while the string from the piece of Polish sausage he has just consumed still dangles from his mouth (140), in Molly's bed just down the stairs from the room in which Sophie sits brooding and mooning.

A poor man without skills or an education who identifies with a roach drowning in a jail-cell water bucket (21), a man soiled by guilt and shame, Frankie could be excused, perhaps, were he to agree with the inscriptions he finds scrawled on his cell walls: *"Everybody shut up. If you were any good you wouldn't be in here*" and "We're all victims of circumstance" (184, 185). He can be forgiven if, lying on his cell cot, he wonders if finding a million dollars would "really [make] a difference in the end" (187). He has heard the middle-class witnesses snicker with nervous rectitude during the lineup interrogations (197) and has a right to his thin conviction that "if there had been no war at all, if he hadn't volunteered, if there had been no accident, if there hadn't been this and there hadn't been that, then everything would certainly have turned out a lot better for Frankie" (112–13). Sophie may wonder how anyone could "make a fellow like that ashamed of himself" (63), but Frankie is plenty ashamed. If asked to justify his life, he could perhaps do no better, given its sundry impediments, than to tender the answer of another busted junkie: "I'm just the type *got* to have it, that's all. It's how I'm built. Don't ask me *why*—how do *I* know? It's just *something*, cousin. It's *there*" (206). Indeed, Frankie does no better when, explaining to Molly why he takes such chances with his life, he simply says, "Some cats just swing like that, Molly-O" (320).

The Man with the Golden Arm makes clear, however, that culpability is not limited to any particular social class. As Algren paints the scene, what ails Division Street is what ails midcentury America. In *Nonconformity,* for instance, which he began in 1950 as one writer's state-of-the-union message, Algren attributes social significance to the phenomenon of drug addiction in postwar America. The country was in such dismal disrepair, Algren argued, its ideals in tatters and so many of its promises broken, that scapegoats were needed: "Something is gnawing, so somebody has to be punished." In this context, Algren believes that "the addict's revolt has a special grace. When he shoves a needle into his vein it is, in a sense, to spare others. Somebody had to be punished all right—and he's the first who's got it coming. Things are going wrong in the world, so, in a sort of suicidal truculence, he impales himself."[11]

Just as scapegoated are those unwilling or unable to participate in a rat race whose prize for all successful American Dreamers is consumer goods in abundance—and the prestige and respect that accompany all such tangible symbols of status. Thus, early in the novel, Algren introduces readers to "the Republic's crummiest lushes" in the Saloon Street police station lockup: failures caught between a system that has little use and less concern for them and their own inability to make it in any way society is prepared to acknowledge or respect. These are men who "no longer felt they had been born in America" and who have been charred by guilt, "the great, secret and special American guilt of owning nothing, nothing at all, in the one land where ownership and virtue are one" (17).

The poor may have been with us always, but for Algren there is something new about equating ownership and virtue, and this newness is part of the change sweeping postwar America. That things are changing is an observation made by any number of characters throughout the novel—"We got all kinds of new ways of doing things since you come back," is how Sparrow explains it to Frankie (15)—and that the changes are seldom for the better is equally clear. Describing Vi's first days of married life, Algren locates them in a time "before the whole world started acting clandestinely" (139), and Frankie can lash out at Sparrow, "You know who I am? You know who you are? You know who *anybody* is any more?" (257). Throughout this autumnal story there is a sense of things running down and time running out "in a world gone wrong, all wrong" (98), a sense that everyone is expecting "the rain of that far-off night when his name would be the name of nobody at all, as the name of one who had never lived" (168).

Similarly, "the old days" obsess everyone as a better time when, as Frankie recalls, "the worst thing the neighborhood bucks got pinched for was strongarming and no one fooled with anything deadlier than whisky" (116–17). Just so, Sophie remembers a less vicious, less deadly time "when people who did right were rewarded and those who did wrong were punished. . . . God weighed virtue and sin then to the fraction of the ounce, like Majurcek the Grocer weighing sugar" (62). Nowadays, she can only believe that "God has forgotten us all" (99).

As Sophie looks out on the world from her wheelchair, she finds that "the city too was somehow crippled of late. The city too seemed a little insane. Crippled and caught and done for with everyone in it. No one was really any better off than herself" (96). The accident that left her convinced she is a cripple occurred after Frankie had had a few too many of Antek's "A-Bomb Specials" (triple instead of the usual double shots of whisky) during "a week when every tavern radio was blaring triumphantly of what a single bomb had done" and the jukebox had played "one last sad bar of the final song of a world that had known neither A-bombs nor A-Bomb Specials" (67). Since that week of stupendous changes in the world's prospects, "Everyone had become afraid of closing time everywhere, of having the lights go out in the middle of the dance while the chimes of all the churches mourned" (97).

This shared national anxiety is one source of connection between the ostensible "them" of the novel and the rest of "us." These weak sheep are just that: in one fatal way or another, the weaker members of society. Yet when Jailer explains to himself why Frankie and Sophie are always fighting ("They want to love each other—but they don't know how" [32]) or when Frankie finds how difficult it is to be himself, when Sparrow gets so lonesome that he wishes the police would pick him up "so that he could feel, for ten minutes, that he was going *somewhere*" (120), when Vi cheats on Stash or someone starts hitting the bottle too hard—the reader is encountering nothing that requires a visit to Division Street. Neither guilt nor sin, remorse nor self-pity, Algren implies, is a respecter of persons. Fortunately, neither are joy and tenderness, compassion and pride, friendship and loyalty, love and hope and poetry.

The vitality that is everywhere to be found in *The Man with the Golden Arm* accounts for (and is in large part conjured by) the humor that does so much not only to alleviate the book's darkness but to humanize its characters. The humor of Algren's first two novels is infrequent and often cruel; it repeatedly sneers with the self-satisfaction of one character triumphing at least verbally over another or winces slightly when a brave face is needed to conceal pain or defeat. Here, the humor is both more frequent and more various: the comic burlesque of the Great Sandwich Battle between Vi and Stash or Sparrow's absurd shoplifting expeditions; Algren's sly insertion of himself into the text in the scene in which Frankie tells his cell mate, Applejack Katz, about a guy he once saw in a bar who "wrote in a little book-like, everythin' that was goin' on" and never touched his beer (216). The characters seem to take as much pleasure in their witticisms as does their author, as when Frankie explains to police captain Record-Head Bednar that Sparrow isn't a moron: "He's a moroff. You know, more off than on" (5).

Perhaps the most important function of the humor in *The Man with the Golden Arm* is, as William J. Savage has argued, to reveal to the reader whose side he or she is on, for if laughter is a means of bonding character to character and character to reader, it accomplishes such ends depending on when, how, and at what or whom the reader laughs.[12] An exchange between Record-Head and a man picked up for breaking and entering illustrates this function of the novel's humor. Telling the man that "for a quarter you'd steal the straw out of your mother's kennel" (191), Bednar jokes for the benefit of the middle-class witnesses at the expense of the arrested: to erect a wall between himself and the witnesses and the grilled. To laugh with Record-Head is to laugh at, not with, the anonymous lost; to laugh more readily at the man's rejoinder ("What I'd do for a quarter you'd do for a dime" [191]) is, willy-nilly, to find oneself at least momentarily on the wrong side of the law.

Record-Head—the novel's most detailed representative of middle-class values—is crucial to understanding *The Man with the Golden Arm*. Grilling a "defrocked" preacher, the glib Bednar is brought up short when told, in a paraphrase of St. Paul, "We are all members of one another" (198)—a revelation as incomprehensible to Record-Head as Sparrow's conviction that "everybody's a habitual in his heart. I'm no worse'n anyone else" (276).[13] Both contentions cut in close for the captain, who is prepared to acknowledge that "every man was secretly against the law in his heart" (297). Indeed, Bednar has of late become perplexed by the fact that "the guilty felt so certain of their own innocence while he felt so uncertain of his own" and baffled "that men locked up by the law should laugh while the man who locked them there no longer felt able even to cry" (295). Neither, Bednar notices, do the middle-class witnesses at the lineups do more than snicker. Experiencing "a suffocating need for absolution" (296), unable to get the monkey of his own guilt off his back, Bednar self-medicates with a dose of "I only done my honest copper's duty" and salves his conscience by assuring himself that Sparrow "wasn't nothin' to nobody, the punk" (296). Yet Bednar still feels he has "done traitor's work all his life" and that, in setting up Sparrow, he has "sold out a son" (296). Even if everyone he sent to prison was "guilty to the hilt," Bednar also knows in the dark night of his soul that he is the guiltiest one of all because, although he never hated any of them, neither had he "loved any man at all" (297).

Bednar is suffering, but he resists the bonds of suffering that make us "all members of one another." As Sophie puts it in an imagined jab at Frankie, "If Jesus Christ treated me like you do I'd drive in the nails myself" (66). Molly, however, is willing to accept the pain of trying to love and redeem Frankie because she believes he is finally "worth something" (141). One night, Molly lays out the truth about his life for him: he is scared; he is beating himself up over Sophie when the sad, simple fact of the matter is that he just never fell "in love with her the way she wanted [him] to, the way she was in love" (142) and that ever since he has blamed himself, has assumed the entire burden of guilt, and has broken his life into pieces in the process. Molly treats Frankie with honesty, love, and encouragement, and even though a lifetime of hustling and of being chiseled has made him wary, he understands that Molly is someone to trust, is his chance to "talk straight to somebody at last." After all, as Frankie asks rhetorically, "how does any man keep straight with himself if he has no one with whom to be straight?" (143).

In *The Man with the Golden Arm* Algren wished to talk straight and, like Molly, to make an emotional investment in discarded souls. He wished to redeem the fallen world of Division Street, not by urging upon readers any social program for improvement or any vision of the disinherited as worthier of love than anyone else but by presenting the broken and defeated as fully human, and their world, as seen through their eyes, as a place of unexpected, woebegone poetry:

> It was New Year's Eve on the El, it was New Year's Eve down Division Street, it was Happy New Year's Eve for the boys from the Tug & Maul and the girls hustling drinks at the Safari. It was Happy New Year in Junkie Row at Twenty-sixth and California. . . .
>
> It was Happy New Year everywhere except in Molly Novotny's heart; neither her heart nor her nest gave sign of the season. The stove was smoking again and she thought carelessly, "we get the ones the landlords buy up for old iron," of both the stove and her heart. The day comes when both feel past throwing heat. (163)

Algren's emotional investment has frequently left him open to charges of being a sentimentalist—that is, a writer who indulgently bestows on his subjects heartwarming emotions in excess of what those subjects might seem to deserve. It is a charge to which Algren readily pled guilty. As he told H. E. F. Donohue, for him, sentimentality is the indulgence of the hope that "men and women [will] be good to one another" and a quality of writing without which "you don't get a true picture of people." He added that he saw sentimentality as "a kind of poetry, it's an emotional poetry, and, to bring it back to the literary scene, I don't think anything is true that doesn't have it, that doesn't have poetry in it."[14] What can be added to this expressed commitment to sentimentality is that it leaves Algren, a professed nonbeliever, forwarding a decidedly Christian understanding of his world.[15]

The Man with the Golden Arm is shot through with Christian imagery, and there are those who see in Frankie a "suffering god," his suicide "an act of rebellion, if not atonement for the sins of the faceless masses."[16] But if Frankie is a Christ figure, he is a failed and fallen Christ, those who loved him (with the possible exception of Molly) not redeemed but imprisoned or driven insane. Yet it is also worth noticing that as Frankie prepares to hang himself, he offers "a bit of a prayer for Molly," and that his last thought is of Sophie: "Have a good dream you're dancin,' Zosh" (337). Algren's penultimate paragraph also remembers Sparrow—for once designated by his proper name, Solly Saltskin (337)—thus bringing together in imaginative communion on the novel's final page the three people most important to Frankie.

God's eye, in the words of an old spiritual, is always on the sparrow, and so, even in Frankie's extremity, is Algren's. Solly Saltskin (a Jew among Poles) may be, as Christ expressed it, "one of the least of these my brethren," yet as Christ also promised, although sparrows are cheaply bought and sold, "Not one of them is forgotten before God."[17] Like Christ, Algren expressed a preference for social outcasts and a reluctance to side with anyone ready to cast the first stone at the accused. Algren's Sparrow, hearing a girl cry out as she is brought into jail, "Ain't anyone on *my* side?" can only answer silently, "Nobody, sister. Not a soul," for "he knew not one man on the side of men" (287). Algren wished to be that man, to urge upon his readers Christ's second great commandment: to "love thy neighbor as thyself." After all, "He that loveth not his brother whom he hath seen, how can he love God whom he hath not seen?"[18]

Readers would have to wait for *Chicago: City on the Make* and *Nonconformity: Writing on Writing* for the full story on the historical and social circumstances Algren felt victimized too many

Americans. If *The Man with the Golden Arm* dented the middle class's armor, the damage was slight and quickly repaired—at least if one judges a novel's ability to influence social change by its direct connection to the passage of new legislation (as Upton Sinclair's *The Jungle* led to the passage of pure food laws) or its ability to rally readers in great numbers against a particular social injustice (as Harriet Beecher Stowe's *Uncle Tom's Cabin* persuaded many readers of the evils of slavery). It is more difficult to chart the subterranean influence a book such as *The Man with the Golden Arm* may have had on its culture. At the time of its publication, the novel certainly attracted attention. Nominated for a Pulitzer Prize, the novel won the first National Book Award for fiction and remained on the *New York Times* bestseller list for nineteen weeks (October 2, 1949, to March 5, 1950). It went through five printings in its first year of availability and soon attracted the attention of Hollywood, resulting in a 1955 movie that broke the film industry's ban on the depiction of drug use.

Ernest Hemingway, in a letter to Nelson Algren providing a quotation to help promote the book, proclaimed that "this is a man writing and you should not read [him] if you cannot take a punch. . . . Mr. Algren can hit with both hands and move around and he will kill you if you are not awfully careful. . . . Mr. Algren, boy, are you good."[19] Reviewers were also impresssed. Although the *New Yorker* felt the novel might prove "too strong for most stomachs," *Time* magazine called the book "a true novelist's triumph."[20] Hollis Alpert observed that "Nelson Algren seems to be about the only one willing and capable enough to carry on a tradition" of "social and poetic realism." Praising Algren's "passionate warmness" and "bawdy humor," Alpert judged "this richly vivid novel" to be "unforgettable."

Similarly, A. C. Spectorsky, acknowledging that "there will be those who object to the sordidness of background, and the unrelieved starkness" of the novel, insisted that such readers "will be missing much, for it has a kind of dedicated and comprehending honesty out of which a crucial truth emerges": that people such as Frankie are as much the products as the victims of their environment.[21]

Carlo Rotella has recently demonstrated that *The Man with the Golden Arm* said important things about postwar urban change. Barry Miles has suggested that the novel's depiction of drug addiction paved the way for the publication of books such as William Burroughs's *Junkie* (1953), and Howard Zinn, activist and author of *A People's History of the United States*, has described the "powerful impression" the novel's depiction of "an American underclass" made on him early in his career.[22] Yet such claims do not perhaps add up to much, given Algren's hopes.

What can be said is that with *The Man with the Golden Arm* Algren had made his point: respectable citizens, confronted with reports of "the utterly doomed" (312) and the corrupt political/economic system that seals that doom, care too little about America's underclass to do more than read, then turn away. More horrifying than the "unlucky brothers with the hustlers' hearts" (197) wandering through these pages is the fact that a reader can emerge from *The Man with the Golden Arm* unhorrified in any profound way. Or, as the epigraph that opens the novel puts it, "All the horror is in just this—that there is no horror!" (2).

CHAPTER SIX

Chicago: City on the Make and *Nonconformity: Writing on Writing*

Following the success of *The Man with the Golden Arm,* Nelson Algren, still in his early forties, was suddenly famous and feted. Yet the world was a powder keg. The Soviet Union tested its first atomic bomb in 1949, and North Korean forces crossed the 38th parallel into South Korea in June 1950. At home, the Red Scare had the House Un-American Activities Committee investigating communist infiltration of labor unions, government, and Hollywood, and Senator Joseph McCarthy was waving lists he claimed contained the names of known traitors working for the State Department. The atomic spies Ethel and Julius Rosenberg were in prison awaiting execution for espionage while the McCarran Act of 1950 authorized the internment of subversives in the event of a national emergency. America was turning into a country of loyalty oaths, blacklists, and timid conformism.

Judging the nation to be gripped by political hysteria and paranoia, Algren wrote two pamphlet-length essays: *Nonconformity: Writing on Writing* (which he first called "A Walk on the Wild Side," and later "The State of Literature") and *Chicago: City on the Make*. Both were risky pieces of work, given the temper of the times. Indeed, his publisher, Doubleday, reneged on plans to publish *Nonconformity* after being told by FBI informants that Algren was a Communist, and the essay did not see print until 1996 after having been discovered among Algren's papers at Ohio State University and edited for publication by

Daniel Simon.[1] The FBI's charge was not a difficult one to make in this season of witch hunts: Algren had been associated with Communist/leftist groups since the 1930s, had published early work in leftist periodicals and signed open letters criticizing the government, and in 1952 served as honorary chair of the Chicago Committee to Secure Justice for the Rosenberg Case.[2] As a result, the FBI file on him was growing.

It was at just such a moment, however, that Algren felt the state of the union most needed to be assessed. America was experiencing a failure of conscience, and Algren could not keep silent. If his subject matter in these two essays remains what it had always been—the dispossessed and disinherited victims of American callousness and hypocrisy, denial and indifference— he seemed to understand that his advocacy must take a new, more urgent form.

Chicago: City on the Make

Chicago: City on the Make is a prose poem to the exhilarating nightmare he found Chicago to be and a text that portrayed the city, in the words of novelist Budd Schulberg, as "a kind of American annex to Dante's Inferno."[3] A perennial "frontier town" and "infidel's capital" yet the "most radical of all American cities," Algren's Chicago is a place to which one cannot belong because it fails to unite its citizens in any common purpose save hustling and then moving on.[4]

Understandably disliked by many Chicagoans as much as *Never Come Morning* had been disliked by Polish Americans, *Chicago* is in fact a bittersweet jeremiad, a song of both love and hate. Although disgusted by the current scene and dismayed by much of the city's history, Algren cares deeply about Chicago, regretting its autumnal decline while finding much in its past to admire: its reckless boisterousness and arrogant gullibility, its ability to take a punch and never give up. Although in Chicago it is "every man for himself," Algren can still aver that "once you've come to be part of this particular patch, you'll never love another. Like loving a woman with a broken nose, you may well find lovelier lovelies. But never a lovely so real" (23).

A place of "nightshade neon" and "carbarn Christs punching transfers all night long," of newspapers blowing under "the yellow salamanders of the El" and "nuns studying gin-fizz ads in the Englewood Local" (72), Chicago under Algren's gaze is a "place built out of Man's ceaseless failure to overcome himself" (73). He points with pride to those who, for a moment, have managed to pull the city "half an inch out of the mud" (57): novelists Theodore Dreiser and Richard Wright, poets Carl Sandburg and Edgar Lee Masters, reformers Jane Addams and Eugene V. Debs, jazzmen King Oliver and Bix Beiderbecke, Chicago White Sox outfielder Shoeless Joe Jackson and Cubs pitcher Grover Cleveland Alexander. Even the city's most reprehensible citizens get paraded by in a sort of literary police lineup that often smacks of approval: Mickey Finn, inventor of the knock-out drink that still bears his name; Hinky Dink Henna, corrupt ward alderman; John Dillinger, the FBI's first Public Enemy Number One; tycoons Cyrus McCormick (inventor of the mechanical harvester) and George Mortimer Pullman (inventor of the railroad sleeping car). Perhaps what redeems these hustlers and "coneroos" (confidence men) is the gusto and laughter with which they went about their often shameful business, the "spiritual good health" (75) that even their sinning brought them.

Acknowledging the efforts of "Do-Gooders" who have periodically taken on the city, Algren opines that "they only get two outs to the inning while the hustlers are taking four" (14)—a state of affairs unchanged since the first settlers arrived "looking for any prairie portage that hadn't yet built a jail" (10) to cheat the Pottawattomies (the Native-American tribe that inhabited the area) out of everything they had before nightfall. Created by the same sort of men and women among whose descendents are the Cass McKays and Dove Linkhorns about whom Algren had written, Chicago in 1951 remained what it had always been: "a rigged ball game" (14), Hustlertown, U.S.A.

The difference is that by 1951 its hustle had somehow grown both more oppressive and less colorful, its rapines bloodier and "more legal" (18), more businesslike, its faces more "careworn" (67). It is not even a tough, broad-shouldered place anymore, just scared and cowed and corporate. Increasingly it is difficult to tell the hustlers from the squares, and despite civic concern over "harlots and hopheads . . . dips and hipsters and heavy-hipted madams" (22), it is the middle class out in the lush neighborhoods with their "immaculate pews" and "self-important bookshelves" (27) who are at midcentury the real predators. As the author's preface, added in 1961, and the poem ("Ode to Lower Finksville") added in 1968 make clear, for Algren the passage of twenty more years would change nothing except for the worse. Increasingly, the city seemed to offer less bang and more whimper for the buck:

> Giants lived here once. It was the kind of town, thirty years gone, that made big men out of little ones. It was geared for great deeds then, as it is geared for small deeds now. . . . Now it's the place where we do as we're told, praise poison, bless the F.B.I., yearn wistfully for just one small chance to prove ourselves more abject than anyone yet. (52)

In 1961, Algren credited European readers with keeping *Chicago* alive, but such interest as the book held for Europeans such as Jean-Paul Sartre (who translated excerpts for publication in *Les Temps Modernes*) had less to do perhaps with Chicago per se than with reading it as a synecdoche for America, the Second City's sins and sensibility a microcosm of America's. Algren encourages such a reading throughout, calling Chicago "the most American of cities" and no "tougher at heart than the U.S.A. is tough at heart, for all her ships at sea" (56, 58). Of the "two-timing bridegroom" to whom he compares Chicago, Algren asserts, "The guiltier he feels the louder he talks. . . . He isn't a tough punk, he's just a scared one. Americans everywhere face gunfire better than guilt" (58).

Indeed, if Carlo Rotella is correct in reading *Chicago* as a narrative of urban decline brought on by waning industrialism, changing demographics, the disintegration and reconstitution of white-ethnic neighborhoods—thus making Chicago an instance of what was happening in urban centers across the country—it is also the case that the city's decline was for Algren in part a function of the cold war mood of conformist self-interest that was settling over the country like red-white-and-blue smog.[5] He likens Chicagoans at midcentury to FBI informants (52), asserts that the country is being turned into "an arsenal" inhospitable to art and culture, and compares the Korean War to the Mexican War of 1846–48 (58). In the essay's third section, "The Silver-Colored Yesterday," he recounts his family's 1920 move from the south to the north side and the need to defend his boyhood hero Swede Risberg (one of the White Sox players implicated in the Black Sox scandal of 1919) to the neighborhood "sprouts" like someone dragged before some "local loyalty board" to have his patriotism questioned: "What kind of American *are* you anyhow?" he recalls being asked. The effect of such enforced conformity at home and militarism abroad is, Algren contends, to sap the young of any desire to be artists, doctors, or engineers by brainwashing them into believing in nothing except "the uses of the super-bazooka against 'gooks'" (59). In this context, the essay's final image of all that Chicago will someday leave behind "for remembrance"—"one rusty iron heart" (77) from some abandoned forge or diesel engine—evokes the aftermath of the nuclear Armageddon so fearfully anticipated during the cold war.

As a diagnosis of American ills circa 1951, *Chicago* moves back and forth between personal anecdote and slangy character sketch, metaphoric reverie and the fragments of an argument perhaps too painful to do more than adumbrate, touching on issues of class and race, love and religion, business and politics, sport and culture—each of which is boosted cynically while corruption or indifference flourish. Wherever he turns, Algren finds that the country "forever keeps two faces, one for winners and one for losers; one for hustlers and one for squares" (23). If everybody is on the make in this land of opportunity—and anything goes, Algren believes, as long as it pays and thereby wins "the cheapest grade of praise" (57)—how could it be otherwise than that the "buck alone lend[s] purpose to the lives of the anonymous thousands living in anonymous rows along anonymous streets, under an anonymous moon" (22–23)?

Perhaps, Algren suggests, Chicago—and by extension, America—simply grew up too fast, too soon, and should not be expected to have any worthier aims than financial gain, celebrity, the avenging of "bone-deep grudges" (62), or the pride of ending up champ of the no-holds-barred battle to see who is fittest to survive. There is no room here for compassion or the consideration of any higher values: "How much did he *have*, is what we demand to know when we hear good old Joe Felso [Algren's name for the average Joe] has gone to his reward. Never what *was* he in human terms" (75). Yet "the masses who do the city's"—and the country's—"labor also keep [its] heart" (68). The squares and the losers, "lost and unloved for keeps and a day" (68), matter because they are no less human—no more immoral or less possessed of dignity—than anyone else. "However do senators get so close to God? How is it that front-office men never conspire?" (39), Algren asks, and his implicit answers are that they are not and they do not. And while the nation's attention is focused on "the big soap-chip and sausage-stuffing tycoons" (58), the trapped and the broken shuffle beneath "the miles and miles of high-tension wires servicing the miles and miles of low-pressure cookers" (68), waiting to "take their revenge" (67). Attention, in short, must be paid, and Algren pays it with humor, admiration, and regret.

Defending his essay in 1961, Algren offered his most often-cited definition of literature: "I submit that literature is made upon any occasion that a challenge is put to the legal apparatus by conscience in touch with humanity" (81). He adds that *Chicago* "was written out of an awareness that multitudes live among us who share the horrors but not the marvels of our split-level Bedlam"—and if these "castaways" are growing restless, it is not on orders "from the devils in the Kremlin . . . but from the instruction of the hearts of men everywhere where men wish to own their own lives" (90, 106).

The book, then, is in part a cautionary tale, a word of warning about the social and spiritual consequences of continued neglect and scapegoating of our fellow Americans. It is also a salvage operation, the attempt to redeem the lost from anonymity and slander. To accomplish such redemption, Algren employs a prose style that would redeem with poetry a nation quickly being turned, in his opinion, into a fortress of military might, realpolitik, and indifference to those who cannot or will not conform. Points are made not via reasoned argument or facts but through charged language, poetic imagery.[6]

On issues such as Algren writes about here, emotional appeals and poetry are more persuasive than facts or rational argument. And in *Chicago* Algren identifies poetry as a radical act—"both poet and working stiff being boys out to get even" is how he puts the matter at one point (63)—and so employs what was in 1951 the radical form of the prose poem ("radical" because at the time the prose poem existed as a marginalized form that rejected the poetic tenets of the literary establishment). A home for fugitive content and marginal viewpoints, the prose poem is an oxymoronic hybrid genre that allows one to say the otherwise unsayable because it inhabits a space free from both readerly expectations and the writerly conventions governing verse poetry, on the one hand, and prose, on the other.[7] Further, to bestow poetry on material that might seem unlikely to reward (or deserve) such poetic treatment is in itself a manifestation not merely of tour-de-force writing but of compassionate advocacy and identification of self with subject—the means by which "the color, the complexity, and the light" that escape mere "sociologically accurate accountings" are attained.[8]

Why Nelson Algren chose to bring his unconventional thoughts to bear in the unconventional form of the essay-as-prose-poem is clarified if *Chicago* is read in the context of the equally poetic essay Algren was also drafting in the early 1950s, *Nonconformity: Writing on Writing*.

Nonconformity: Writing on Writing

Worked on between 1950 and 1953, *Nonconformity* unpacks the motive and method of *Chicago* while making the entire

American scene its explicit target. If the Windy City represented all of America, in *Nonconformity* the writer stands in for all Americans, the writer's dilemmas and obligations everyone's. In *Chicago,* the cold war context of the book's composition surfaces only sporadically; in *Nonconformity,* the crisis at midcentury assumes center stage as Algren attacks Americans' willingness to sell out, to conform, whatever the cost to one's spirit or one's fellow Americans. The critique was powerful enough to cause his publisher, Doubleday, to refuse to publish the book and to prompt critic Maxwell Geismar, a friend to whom Algren had earlier showed the essay, to write that "this will be one of the first books they will burn: congratulations."[9]

As Algren told the *Daily Worker* in 1952, in his opinion the Rosenbergs were "being put to death for nonconformity," yet as *Nonconformity* makes clear, the wages of conformity are also a kind of death.[10] Opening with the observation that the writer's lot "is never a happy one," Algren alleges that the home-front climate of conformity (enforced by laws and kept alive by fear) makes it almost impossible for young writers to explore what William Faulkner termed "the problems of the human heart in conflict with itself" because, Algren explains, writers know "enough of the heart to know it cannot conform" (4).[11] If the risk of following the heart is nonconformity, and if nonconformity is dangerous, why not try rather "to keep one's nose clean"? As a result, Algren asserts, only cynicism and hypocrisy prevail, and truth is not wanted (5).

Marshalling support from a host of writers, Algren insists that the country is being conned, asked to pledge allegiance to "napalm and thunder-jet," "the closest American Legion Post," and a "capacity to wage technological warfare across another people's soil" as proofs of American superiority (12–13). Ignoring

John Quincy Adams's nineteenth-century assurance that "America does not go abroad in search of monsters to destroy," America is now beating the bushes for threats to national security while "monsters enough roam in the woods at home" (11–12). We have, Algren charges, sold our birthright for a mess of conformism and repression, and the only winners are "our business brass" in partnership with the government and the military—what President Dwight Eisenhower would soon be terming the "military-industrial complex." With piety and patriotism masking paranoia and self-interest, with the Bill of Rights in danger, and "nobody investigat[ing] the men who are trading off our freedoms" (10), what is needed is "out-loud" (12) doubting: the raising of adversarial, questioning voices.

The writer's choice, then, is between engaging with the issues of the day, asking uncomfortable questions, and speaking truth to power, or refusing such obligations, perhaps making aesthetic or "professional" excuses for one's decision. Dismissing as disingenuous writers who have proffered such excuses, Algren insists that it is the writer's task "to relate mankind to the things of the earth," to be willing to be seen in "shabby company," and to identity oneself even with the objects of one's horror because "there is no way of becoming a serious writer in the States without keeping shabby company . . . without becoming a victim" (18–19). As it was for Whitman and other writers Algren admires, the choice is between the people and the power elite, between uncomfortable, soul-draining life, on the one hand, and a profitable, cozy "denial of life," on the other (20).

On one side are the writers who have taken the risk of speaking the hard truths they have made their own: Twain and Whitman, Poe and Stephen Crane, Jack London and Vachel

Lindsay, Joseph Conrad and Franz Kafka. On the other side are writers who approach their craft with the desire to please and whose failure to risk much or to stand for much ensures they will be forgotten: Louis Bromfield, Frank Yerby, Booth Tarkington. The kind of writer Algren admires and feels is needed is not interested in pleasing anyone, in being the literary equivalent of a first-rate bellhop: "No book was ever worth the writing that wasn't done with the attitude that 'this ain't what you rung for, Jack—but it's what you're damned well getting'" (20–21).

Algren contends that a real writer is necessarily at odds with his culture, willing to swim "against the tides of his own time" (22) and to risk himself in his pursuit of truth, as Algren felt F. Scott Fitzgerald so spectacularly had. Although not typically seen as part of that tradition of socially conscious writers with whom Algren identified himself, Fitzgerald, Algren argues, refused to report on the world from a safe distance, instead spending himself "by coins of pity and love and pride, into spiritual bankruptcy" (28), preferring to serve rather than to be served by the lives about which he wrote and ready to pay the psychological costs of such a choice.

Should such "emotional sharing" (27) seem too softly sentimental, Algren adds that, along with compassion, it is also necessary to possess vindictiveness, ruthlessness, and an alienated desire "to get even": "If you feel you belong to things as they are, you won't hold up anybody in the alley no matter how hungry you may get. And you won't write anything that anyone will read a second time either" (34). American literature, Algren believed, must stop trying to be polite and politically correct; it must (as Algren did throughout his career) tell the stories of those among us who pass "hand-to-mouth hours without friendship or love" (35), whose "names are the names of certain dreams from which the light has gone out" (37), and who, "between rest by day and play by night, do the little deals" (39). The otherwise unrecorded lives of such displaced and disinherited people must be told because they make up the majority of humankind, who live on the "unswept streets where most of humanity has always lived" (41). It is among such lost and forgotten souls, from working stiff to soup-kitchen habitué, that one catches life undisguised in all its depth and human reality; it is among such men and women that "the true climate of the human condition on the home grounds may best be gauged" (41).[12]

Algren's America is, then, what sociologist David Riesman in 1950 dubbed a "lonely crowd."[13] It is a country, Algren writes, that is riddled with guilt and "spiritual desolation" (45), where the desire to be of real use finds no greater gratification "than the promotion of chewing gum" (45) and where too many who might make a difference are too "right-minded" to get "personally involved" (57). Living lives of gum-snapping desperation, Americans have become moral cowards, trading conscience for soporific comfort: "From the coolest zoot-suit cat getting leaping-drunk on straight gin to the gentlest suburban matron getting discreetly tipsy on Alexanders, the feeling is that of having too much of something not really needed, and nothing at all of something needed desperately. They both want to live, and neither knows how" (47).

While scapegoating drug addicts, juvenile delinquents, and other damaged souls (whose lives are symptoms, not causes, of the current social malaise), while blaming everything from comic books to Communists for what is wrong, the country fails to see that it is the middle class that is really the guilty party. Society is complicit in individual wrongdoing and suffering because it is corrupt, allowing the conditions that breed poverty and vice to remain unredressed and denying far too many people access to its stores of justice, mercy, and fair play. Thus, as Algren reads the social scene, the roles of victim and criminal are reversed:

> When one walks into a courtroom where women are being tried, it begins to seem that they are the innocent ones. That it is His Honor, the arresting officers and that little man who stands beside His Honor whispering, "She was up before you on the same charge last week, Your Honor," as well as the indifferent spectator, who are the guilty parties.
>
> Guilty of indifference. Guilty of self-righteousness. Guilty of complacency. (58–59)

Because conformity points an accusing finger at all who will not conform, and because all who are accused are presumed to be guilty of something, Algren argues that now more than ever the writer's function "is to champion the accused" (65).

For Algren, America at midcentury was "a laboratory of human suffering" (73) wherein too many Americans were willing to be lied to by the media and by leaders both secular and religious, where too many were afraid of "coming alive to something more than merely existing," and the country itself seemed diseased, the symptoms of which included "insanity, criminality, alcoholism, narcoticism, psychoanalysm, homicide and perversion in sex as well as in perversion just for the pure hell of the thing" (75). The indictment is painful in its continuing pertinence more than half a century later:

> On the back streets and the boulevards of Palm Beach and Miami, on Fifth Avenue in New York and Canal Street in New Orleans, on North Clark Street in Chicago, on West Madison or South State or any street at all in Los Angeles: faces of the American Century, harassed and half-dehumanized, scoffing

or debauched; so purposeless, unusable and useless faces, yet so smug, so self-satisfied yet so abject—for complacency struggles strangely there with guilt. Faces full of such an immense irresponsibility toward themselves that they tell how high the human cost of our marvelous technological achievements has really been. (74)

If *Nonconformity* is Algren's credo, as Daniel Simon suggests, its plea is for writers to stand up for those truths (otherwise known as "the problems of the human heart in conflict with itself") and for all of those who have been broken and beaten by the ways of a world that pretends the heart's conflicts are not felt by everyone or do not matter if those hearts do not beat in wholesome middle-class breasts outfitted in a gray flannel suit or a day dress at least as nice as those carried by Sears.[14] Algren witnesses for the trapped and broken in whose hearts, he felt, these ancestral conflicts were writ large: "Theirs are still the defeats in which everything is lost, theirs victories that fall close enough to the heart to afford living hope. Whose defeats cost everything of real value. Whose grief grieves on universal bones" (77).

Algren's unconventional essay is, like *Chicago,* a formal enactment as well as an articulation of the nonconformity he calls for—not least in his implicit agreement with the words of one of his personal heroes, the labor organizer and socialist leader Eugene V. Debs, who famously said that "while there is a lower class I am in it, while there is a criminal element I am of it, and while there is a soul in prison I am not free."[15] This is the lesson that almost saves Record-Head Bednar in *The Man with the Golden Arm*—a lesson taught by a writer who, as the 1950s unfolded, had to struggle to keep alive his own belief that to deny another is to betray oneself.

CHAPTER SEVEN

A Walk on the Wild Side

Mao Tse-tung once taught that "the revolutionary moves among the people like a fish in the sea." If so, then by the mid-1950s, Nelson Algren was a fish out of water. The FBI considered him "a potentially active enemy agent," and his publisher, Doubleday, had recently backed away from the controversial *Nonconformity*.[1] A photo-essay on Algren by Art Shay that was to have appeared in *Life* magazine was killed after being delayed for six months, and a picture book about Chicago to be written by Algren, illustrated by Shay, and published by Doubleday also quickly came to nothing. Meanwhile, his biographer writes, Algren was growing deeply troubled by General Douglas MacArthur's "heroics" in Korea, fearing MacArthur's actions would lead to a new world war, and disturbed by the country's cold war hysteria and "atmosphere of conformity."[2] Algren would find himself increasingly at odds with the literary scene as well.

As early as 1953, Algren had observed to novelist Millen Brand that "you can't be a good writer in the States anymore," and by 1955, despite the best-selling *Man with the Golden Arm* and the commercially successful film made from the book, Algren was $8,200 in debt.[3] "Entrapment," the novel he had said he wanted to write for Simone de Beauvoir, languished with their affair.[4] Furthermore, not only was his personal life troubled, but his status as a serious writer was being challenged on two fronts. Although it would require the publication of *A Walk on the Wild Side* to bring the first challenge fully to light, influential cold war critics (Leslie Fiedler, Alfred Kazin, Norman Podhoretz) were poised to dismiss Algren as a writer who sentimentally valorized society's bottom dogs in the outmoded manner of literary naturalism. Thomas Hill Schaub has demonstrated how the demise of 1930s radicalism and the chastened liberalism of the cold war affected literature, causing a wholesale rejection of exactly the sort of fiction Algren was writing, a state of affairs that would leave Algren too far left-of-center until the 1960s exploded.[5]

Algren might have weathered such sniping; indeed, he counterattacked relentlessly—in his 1960 introduction to *The Neon Wilderness*, in *Notes from a Sea Diary*, *The Last Carousel*, and in interview after interview. Yet he was also filled with self-doubts, which constituted the second challenge to his ability to write seriously. The angry reaction of Polish Americans to *Never Come Morning* or of some Chicagoans to *Chicago: City on the Make* might have energized Algren: these were, after all, proofs that he was being heard and taken seriously. However, his confidence was shaken following his encounters with Otto Preminger and Hollywood regarding the filming of *The Man with the Golden Arm*. Algren felt he had been cheated financially and treated with disrespect by Preminger, who bought the rights to the novel and directed the film. But as important, he took what was done to his novel as it was transformed into a celluloid vehicle for Frank Sinatra to be proof that serious work such as his was not wanted. "The book should really have been used seriously," he explained in one of his countless rehashings of the debacle, because it was "a real cry of anguish." Instead, the "movie was used to make this cry of anguish something that could be sung on a jukebox, that Sinatra could perform to, and that was its whole meaning."[6] Thus, by 1954, a year before the film even appeared, Algren was insisting that the days of serious writing were over and that, like everyone else, "I'm hacking too."[7]

William Brevda characterizes Algren's situation in the mid-1950s poignantly: "In the real dark night of [his] soul, Algren turned his back on the three great loves of his life—Chicago, Simone de Beauvoir, and serious fiction—because he felt they had turned their back[s] on him."[8] Whereas the never-completed "Entrapment" was envisioned as a serious book, Algren approached *A Walk on the Wild Side* as, in his words, a "reader's book," in which one must always have "one ear to the audience for yaks."[9] Perhaps his bitterness and doubts regarding a sympathetic readership determined the course he took with *A Walk on the Wild Side,* its often comic absurdity a mockery of his own earlier earnestness. Or perhaps Algren imagined that it would not matter if his novel were not taken seriously if what he seemed to be offering was itself unserious. However, as the novel progressed, it became in fact a complex tragicomic interweaving of emotions, as comically serious as anything he ever wrote. Like the novel's Hallie Breedlove, *A Walk on the Wild Side* smiles precisely because it is so very sad.[10]

A Walk on the Wild Side was, at any rate, an accidental novel undertaken to make money when, asked for permission to reprint *Somebody in Boots* to capitalize on the success of *The Man with the Golden Arm,* Algren agreed on the condition that he be permitted to make changes—changes so numerous and far-reaching that the result was something entirely new. Although often described as a comic version of his first novel, this is a misleading characterization. In the first place, *A Walk on the Wild Side* is much more than a stylistic revision of *Somebody in Boots* that omits the explicit Marxism. Although Algren was a constant recycler—of arguments, favorite quotations, images, lines of dialogue, character types, dramatic situations, even entire narratives—with novels-in-progress mined for stories and essays cobbled together to make books, *A Walk on the Wild Side* quickly moved into terrain all its own despite appropriating material not only from *Somebody in Boots* but also from the stories "So Help Me," "El Presidente de Méjico," and "The Face on the Barroom Floor."

Even when *A Walk on the Wild Side* most resembles the earlier novel, Algren has made significant changes: unlike Cass McKay of *Somebody in Boots,* Dove Linkhorn of *A Walk on the Wild Side* is shrewd, self-satisfied, and sexually precocious. Dove's time on the road prior to settling in New Orleans is relatively painless and not at all traumatizing, and his father, Fitz, is neither hated nor feared by his neighbors, who enjoy the old man's drunken hellfire sermons, delivered weekly from the courthouse steps; unlike Stubby McKay and Cass's brother Bryan, whose hostile relationship ends with Stubby brutally beating his son, Fitz and Dove's brother Byron argue amicably about theology, Fitz half drunk and Byron high on marijuana. Numerous other differences between the two novels could be noted.

Neither is it entirely accurate to describe *A Walk on the Wild Side* as simply a comic novel, although it is often humorous. It is less horrified jeremiad than an often-outrageous burlesque of the American Dream and of notions of the self-made man. From his creative misuses of the English language, irrepressible optimism, and good-natured gullibility to the absurd situations in which he finds himself, Dove possesses the comedy of the innocent abroad. He is Henry Fielding's Tom Jones, Voltaire's Candide, Mark Twain's Huck Finn: a comic figure trapped in a tragic, often horrible world, the comedy arising at least in part from the humor of the pratfall—funny insofar and only so long as the fallen rebounds unscathed.[11] Yet the novel is laced with sorrow; its characters are often plagued by feelings of guilt, shame, and loneliness, and a fair number of them are ultimately defeated by life. Indeed, *A Walk on the Wild Side* is shot through with the consequences of poverty and stupidity, violence and depravity, societal indifference and the exploitation of the defenseless (especially of women). Its most poetic passages are its most wistful, its most leaflessly autumnal:

> And the moon that could never wane dimmed down to no more than a gas lamp's leaning glow. Drinkers and dancers, gaffers and gamblers, all had gone. . . .
> And a little wind went searching in circles to ask, Where had those lovers gone before the dance was done?
> All was well. They had breathed each other's breath. All was well: they had drunk of each other's lips.
> All was well, for what was dust had when living been loved. (21)[12]

A Walk on the Wild Side presents familiar Algren character types: grifters and mental "defectives," pimps and prostitutes, perverts and junkies, and those otherwise down on their luck. Set in the early years of the Depression (spring of 1930 through the spring of 1932), Algren's episodic novel takes Dove Linkhorn from the small town of Arroyo, Texas, to New Orleans. In the manner of *Never Come Morning* and *The Man with the Golden Arm,* the main plot is frequently interrupted: more than fifty pages are devoted to the Perdido Street brothel where Dove will eventually perform public sex acts for the voyeuristic pleasure of paying customers; thirty pages detail the stories of those with whom Dove spends five months in jail; and minor characters such as Cross-Country Kline, Rhino Gross, and Achilles Schmidt are provided with detailed biographies.

Having forced himself on Terasina Vidavarri, the Mexican woman who runs the town chili parlor and with whom he had earlier had consensual sexual relations, sixteen-year-old Dove hits the road unsure of "what kind of great I'm bound to be" but convinced he is "a born world-shaker" (56). His adventures—hopping freight trains, committing robbery with seventeen-year-old runaway Kitty Twist (whose life he saves and whose favors he enjoys before leaving her behind in the hands of the law)—take him to San Antonio, Houston, and lastly New Orleans. Dove remains there, finding shady odd jobs as door-to-door salesman and manufacturer of O-Daddy condoms and shadier friends before encountering the pimp Oliver Finnerty and commencing his career as a professional deflowerer of phony virgins —a career move that leads to a brief romance with prostitute Hallie Breedlove and a vicious beating at the hands of Hallie's legless lover, Achilles Schmidt, that leaves Dove blinded and heading for home.

Many of Dove's experiences are played for laughs, as when he cannot understand the jim crow laws that prevent him from using a "colored only" restroom, or when he does not grasp that the woman baring her breasts as she sells him overpriced Coca-Colas is attempting to interest him in something else entirely. Throughout, Dove remains the same childlike soul he was as an illiterate boy who had never been to a dance or seen a movie and who delights in the playground he and Kitty stumble on in Houston. Like the decapitated turtles he watches clamber over one another on their way to becoming soup, Dove never realizes that there is always "room for one more at the bottom" (114). Yet as with the comic stories of *The Neon Wilderness* and the comic scenes in *The Man with the Golden Arm,* the comedy here enwraps and is enwrapped by something else entirely.

The New Orleans through which Dove moves is a city filled with "lonesome monsters" (216) so defeated by life that they are bent on "getting even on somebody" (231)—and almost anyone will do. Consequently, Algren's "comic" walk on the wild side does not yield endearingly romanticized portraits in the manner, say, of John Steinbeck's *Cannery Row* or *Tortilla Flat* because the novel's humor is not the sort that merely charms but the kind that exposes people's basest deeds and desires, those otherwise unspeakable truths that can perhaps be given voice only in seeming jest. The comedy here causes readers to drop their guard, then comes in for the kill as it bluntly reveals the tragicomic absurdity of life—as inherently laughable as it is appalling.

Although a joker, the third-person narrator possesses what is ultimately a depressed and pessimistic vision of the world through which the novel's characters move: all people are unclean (160), and in every face "[hangs] the sense of impending defeat" (110). It is on any city street that "the wildest beast of all roamed free" (279), and, in the end, no matter to whom they belonged, "all bones [bleach] the same" (110). Just so, many of the characters have reached equally bleak, idiosyncratic conclusions about life. For Dove's father, this means a combination of racism, angry distrust of labor unions, and a brand of Christianity that is particularly attracted to death. For Achilles Schmidt, wisdom resides in needing no one (254), and for Kitty Twist comfort is found in believing that "anything that happens has a right to happen, so what does it matter who it happens to?"—a rhetorical question the answer to which (that it does not matter at all) leads to the "logical" conclusion that it is therefore best not to "care for anything or anyone" (298). "Everyone gets what's coming to them, that's my philosophy," propounds the prostitute Reba (208), whereas Rhino Gross finds that the secret of success is never to trust anyone, especially a woman—because trust "leads to *giving*," which is "the worst of a bad lot" (180).

The world Algren's characters inhabit is corrupt and often indifferent to suffering, a reality the novel often exposes without humor in scenes of violence, alienation, shame, and loss: in the story of the prostitute Hallie Breedlove, a schoolteacher until she is discovered to have black blood, and in the description of the sadistic beating Dove receives at the hands of Legless Schmidt, himself then destroyed by those who had gathered to watch the fight. Nor is there humor in many of the descriptions of Perdido Street, where "anything could happen to a woman available to anyone"; where hookers "died of uselessness one by one, yet lived on behind veritable prairie fires of wishes, hoping for something to happen that had never happened before"; and where the girls' customers are "dull boys whose joy expired in one piggish grunt" (216–17).

If what Voltaire's Candide should have learned by the end of his story is that all is not for the best in the best of all possible worlds, this is a lesson Dove has by heart: "'I feel like I been everywhere God got land,' Dove thought, 'yet all I found was people with hard ways to go. All I found was troubles 'n degradation. All I found was that those with the hardest ways of all to go were quicker to help others than those with the easiest ways. . . . Sports of the world, poor bummies, poor tarts, all they were good for was to draw flies I was told. You could always treat one too good, it was said, but you never could treat one too bad'" (332–33). Yet however flawed the world in which they find themselves, Algren's men and women are capable of acting honorably and selflessly, driven by pride and a desire for dignity, desperate for knowledge and acceptance, love and redemption. They possess a joie de vivre and moral awareness; they are admirably resilient and persistent. And they are, as Algren once described such people, "less hypocritical," less phony, than "the 'good' people" who run the world.[13]

What Algren once remarked of *Never Come Morning* applies to *A Walk on the Wild Side* as well: that what is implied by the story is that "society carries the embryo of its crimes in its womb and the criminal becomes society's tool."[14] Thus, the novel blames "the city fathers, Do-Right Daddies and all of that, Shriners, Kiwanians, Legionaires, Knights of this and Knights of that" who decry prostitution (and much else) but who have "to kick loose of home and fireside now and again . . . and ball with outlaws" (108):

> Later [Daddy] had to be purged of guilt so he could sleep with his wife again. That was where the pulpit came in. There had to be something official like that to put the onus on the women. The preachers, reformers, priests and such did this work well. Some girls were just naturally bad, they explained. Others were made bad by bad men. In no case was it ever the fault of anyone who profited by the shows. Daddy, you can go home again. (109)

Similarly, Algren faults policies that dictate "self-reliance for the penniless and government help to the rich" (97) and describes the Perdido Street prostitutes as women "who would have been safely married" had it not been for such "Old Guard economics" (189).

As the prostitute Reba explains, the panderer Oliver "didn't invent his trade no more than we invented ours. I never heard of a pimp being elected mayor nor even of one who bothered to vote, so why blame *them* for the way things are? They weren't the ones who made the laws that let the trade go on. If nobody wanted there to be pimps, honey, there wouldn't be no pimps" (203–4). As Algren has written elsewhere, "I can no more believe that the human soul is nourished by squalor into a many-splendored flowering than I can believe it is nourished by possession of a hidden hi-fi and wall-to-wall carpeting," adding that no one ever acknowledges "that there is also a spiritual squalor, and that the seamy side of American life doesn't begin on Chicago's west side [that is, in the slums] but in the squalor that lives in the waterish hearts" of the middle class.[15] Or as Dove's jail mates profess, everyone is "innocent of nothin'! Guilty of everythin'!" (328).

It is an insight such as Reba expresses in the preceding paragraph that underwrites the novel's burlesque of the American Dream. As Dove concludes near the end of his story, "All I found was two kinds of people. Them that would rather live on the loser's side of the street with the other losers than to win off by theirselves; and them who want to be one of the winners even though the only way left for them to win was over them who have already been whipped" (332–33). Thus, the novel travesties the Jeffersonian promise of "life, liberty, and the pursuit of happiness" as it skewers notions of self-reliance, survival of the fittest, and America as the land of opportunity. Just as myths of progress are parodied by Algren's description of the degenerate American West of the early 1930s—"The road West now led only to a low, dark and battered chili parlor" (19)—so, too, does the novel mock the stories Americans love to tell of hard work, self-reliance, and rugged individualism:

> In less time than it takes to say God with your mouth open, the go-getting door-to-door canvasser became the backbone of the American economy. He went to work for Realsilk Hose or Hoover Vacuum long enough to go-get himself a dozen pair of Realsilk hose or a second-hand sweeper by stealing it part by part. There was also small change, milk money and such, left lying about on shelves and sills while housewives studied one proposition or another. Change-snatching too came under the heading of go-getting. (118)

While preaching "room at the top for one more" (111) and making boys such as Dove believe that "it's the boys who were willing to work just for the experience [who] got to be millionaires" (129), society instills in the Dove Linkhorns of the world the fear that "by highways dry and highways wet everyone but himself was getting to be a captain of something or other" (165). Yet in the summer of 1931, Algren's sarcastic avowal that "New Orleans offered almost unlimited opportunities" is quickly qualified by his observation that those with the most sense chose to work their way not up but *down* the "Ladder of Success . . . that route being faster" (117).

The novel mocks the successful: "Brokers and buyers, efficiency experts with private means, personnel managers from banking families, men who had been born to ownership of ships or banks or mines or wells . . . who yet wanted to know of life—'What's the answer?' Without pausing once to wonder what was the question" (233). These are the ones who frequent the Spider-Boy Court prostitutes and whose sexual desires are most perverse; they are also the ones whose success turns on the same sorts of manipulation of others and callous indifference to what is right that characterize a pimp like Oliver Finnerty and a punk like Dove. It is Finnerty who believes a working girl cannot be trusted "until she had forgotten it was money she was working for" (198) and who keeps his employees in line with intimidation and violence while Lothario-for-hire Dove, whose job mocks the notion of being a "hard worker," brags that although he could not read his name "were it wrote a foot high on the side of a barn," he nonetheless "make[s] more in a single day than some educated fools earn in a month" (245).

A Walk on the Wild Side ridicules the stupidity of "keeping up with the Joneses"—a typical housewife, the door-to-door salesman Smiley tells Dove, would "sooner risk the black death than have her next-door neighbor own something she didn't" (123)—and the gibberish of "official" economic analyses meant to boost confidence: "Times weren't as hard as some people grew fond of pretending. All that had happened really was a withdrawal from abnormal prosperity with business progressing on a downward grade toward new planes of normality and increasing equalization of opportunity" (119). Rejected as well is the inherent immorality of competition:

> "It don't do no good for a man to rise these days, son," was Country Kline's curious philosophy, "for that can't be done any longer except on the necks of others. And when you make it that way, all the satisfaction is taken out of it. . . . There's no trick in not going down the drain if you don't live in the sink." (322)

Thus, on several related fronts, *A Walk on the Wild Side* retains the critique of capitalism that had informed *Somebody in Boots*.

On the dust jacket of the first edition of *A Walk on the Wild Side,* Algren had explained his novel's intentions by remarking that "the book asks why lost people sometimes develop into greater human beings than those who have never been lost in their whole lives. . . . Why the laughter of old survivors rings more true than those whose laughs have to be bought." Certainly, the laughter of Algren's survivors is crucial here, for whatever the failures of these men and women, they have not failed to find the humor in their lives—humor that perhaps makes tolerable the horror and defeat and that permits Algren to say what might otherwise be too painful to hear. The strategy here can be illustrated by what are possibly Algren's most frequently quoted words of advice, delivered in *A Walk on the Wild Side* by Dove's cell mate, Cross-Country Kline: "Never play cards with a man called Doc. Never eat at a place called Mom's. Never sleep with a woman whose troubles are worse than your own" (312). Just as Kline conceals a hard truth behind its humorous presentation, so the hard truths of *A Walk on the Wild Side* are swaddled in dismissive humor of various kinds: black humor and slapstick, gentle whimsy and good-natured exaggeration, bitter mockery and surreal absurdity, risqué jokes and over-the-top satire, wordplay and ungrammatical dialogue.[16]

Whatever the sort of humor employed, it is never without point. Thus, for instance, Algren's decision to name the small black boy who lives in the brothel "Warren Gamaliel" jokingly plays with the long-held suspicion that Warren Gamaliel Harding, the twenty-ninth president of the United States, had some black blood flowing in his veins to make the point that racial categories are arbitrary and revelatory of little.[17] Again, when Dove, visiting the zoo, jokes that a male monkey "banging his knuckles on his girl friend's skull" (276) reminds him of Oliver and Reba, he exposes the brutality of such human relationships and the animal lust that makes both prostitution and pandering profitable. A final example is Dove in his role of peep-show deflowerer of the demented prostitute Floralee, who immediately strips and begins singing a bawdy song. Algren writes that "nobody could make [Floralee] understand that that wasn't at all how lovely reluctant virgins carried on" (246): a comment that wraps in a laugh both the depravity of the peep show and the brokenness of the forlorn Floralee.

A Walk on the Wild Side understands that ridicule and comic exaggeration are among the few effective ways of criticizing a national psyche as depraved and deprived as Floralee's. The novel understands further that refusing to treat the American Dream seriously is in itself a radical act of judgment and rejection. Such humor is part of what makes *A Walk on the Wild Side* a tour de force, a mature handling of apprentice material that now presents our world in all of its emotional complexity and roundedness, the humor as various as the wider range of emotions informing the novel—its anger and disgust, sorrow and wonder, hope and despair, guilt and pride. As slapstick yields to horror, beauty to ugliness, pathos to scorn, depravity to poetry, the reader is ravished by a world seized whole and as emotionally complete as the reader's own.

Is *A Walk on the Wild Side* finally comic or tragic? The story can certainly be read as ending unhappily enough: the boastful, naive Dove, beaten and blinded in a horrific fall from grace, returns to Arroyo, seeming to have learned little from his year's adventures, his one hope being that Terasina will welcome him. The novel's tone as it concludes is subdued, ultimately elegiac: "That was all long ago in some brief lost spring" (346). Yet the novel does not, finally, offer an exclusively tragic vision, and not merely because of its passages of clownish absurdity or because of its treatment of "low" characters in an often less-than-lofty style. *A Walk on the Wild Side* is finally tragi*comic* because it holds out the long-shot promise of a new beginning and hence the hope that all will be well that ends well. Dove, after all, is last seen enjoying feeling of "strange content" in "the big Rio night" while thinking optimistically that "if God made anything better than a girl. . . . He sure kept it to Himself" (346).

The title of Algren's fourth novel and the world that title connotes have become part of American culture.[18] At the time, some reviewers found Algren's politics, style, and subject matter out of step with cold war America: Leslie Fiedler, for instance, labeled Agren "the Last of the Proletarian Writers" and dismissed the novel as "escape literature," its politics "largely sentiment" and its "morality pure corn"; Norman Podhoretz complained that, as a "protest novel," *A Walk on the Wild Side* had nothing to protest, offering instead "boozy sentimentality" and "a lyric rhapsody on the theme of bums and whores."[19] Novelist James T. Farrell, on the other hand, praised Algren as a writer whose "talent is . . . definite and unmistakable"; James Kelly found the novel "a better-made book than any [Algren] has written before," applauding its "raw poetry" and warning that it may prove "too rough for frail" readers; and Maxwell Geismar found the book "refreshing" at a time when America's "other big-name writers have turned so sour." *A Walk on the Wild Side,* Geismar concluded, "is filled with brilliant little profiles . . . with comic interludes of a Rabelaisian hiliarity . . . and with passages of inimitable dialogue."[20]

A Walk on the Wild Side appeared on the *New York Times* bestseller list for fifteen weeks (June 10 to September 23, 1956). A musical version (with lyrics by Algren and Fran Landesman) was staged in St. Louis in 1960; and in 1962 the novel was made into a movie starring Laurence Harvey and Jane Fonda. The author himself knew what he had accomplished, telling one reviewer that, compared to *The Man with the Golden Arm* (often regarded as his masterpiece), "*A Walk on the Wild Side* is by sixteen furlongs and eleven lengths the better book. . . . It is a kind of novel that, so far as I know, has never been written before. It is an American fantasy, a poem written to an American beat as true as *Huckleberry Finn*."[21]

CHAPTER EIGHT

Who Lost an American? and *Notes from a Sea Diary*

Following the publication of *A Walk on the Wild Side,* Nelson Algren turned his back on the novel. He was disillusioned. He was being dropped from college reading lists and anthologies; he sneered at those (such as the Beats) who might have been his comrades; and his feelings about his place in American letters were growing increasingly bitter, as when he responded with dismissive rudeness in 1959 to a question from the National Book Award committee asking what the award had done for him: "If you are in touch with any person interested in purchasing the first plaque awarded by your committee, I should be pleased to dispose of it!"[1] His friend and fellow novelist John Clellon Holmes felt that Algren "was exhausted by his efforts to maintain with some degree of purity the vision of his youth" and came gradually to fear he was "written out." Even the politically explosive, psychedelic 1960s would, Holmes added, provide no home for an old 1930s radical such as Algren.[2] Bettina Drew, Algren's biographer, reports that by August 1956, Algren had been diagnosed as suffering from depression, and an emotional breakdown soon left him briefly hospitalized. In December, he wrote to Simone de Beauvoir "that a light had gone out of him," and on New Year's Eve he almost drowned when, out walking, he fell through the ice while crossing a frozen Lake Michigan inlet—an event several of his friends read as an attempted suicide.[3]

However, if Algren had lost enthusiasm for "Entrapment," his novel-in-progress, he was hardly "written out." He continued to write for the magazines, where the money came more readily and more dependably. Between 1956 and 1965, he published more than forty book reviews and as many stories, essays, and poems in periodicals ranging from *Atlantic Monthly,* the *Kenyon Review, Nation,* and the *Saturday Evening Post* to men's magazines such as *Cavalier,* the *Dude, Gent, Playboy,* and *Rogue.* The bulk of this output (all but eight articles) eventually found its way into *Who Lost an American?, Notes from a Sea Diary,* and *The Last Carousel.* In 1962 he lent his name to *Nelson Algren's Own Book of Lonesome Monsters,* a collection of short fiction he selected and to which he contributed an introduction and story, and in 1964 a lengthy series of interviews conducted by H. E. F. Donohue appeared as *Conversations with Nelson Algren.*

Throughout these years, Algren's subject matter and perspective on America remained what they had been. "The Strange Sleep" offered a vignette of life among drug users, and "The Daddy of Them All" reworked the condom-making episode of *A Walk on the Wild Side* to tell of Dingdong Daddy and the two female "heroin-heads" who serve as Daddy's assistants. The story's mood is one of bleak black humor as the three prey upon each other in a sealed-off apartment where "it did not matter ... whether the world would go on for a million years or blow up tomorrow" and "junk is like God."[4] Lighter in mood are "How the Man with the Record One Eighth of an Inch Long Was Saved by a Bessarabian Rye" and "Say a Prayer for the Guy," the former telling of a man constantly picked up by the police because he always looked guilty of something, the latter a comic account of a man who drops dead while playing poker with four nonplussed but not terribly upset friends.[5] Similarly, Algren's essays cover ground he had long since made his own. "Down with Cops" argues that the police are people who hide feelings of inferiority behind a badge as they administer society's "vindictiveness"; "Moon of the Backstretch: Still and White" sketches racetrack life"; and "G-String Gomorrah" visits the strip clubs of Calumet City, Illinois—dens of iniquity that will never be cleaned up because they are "the town's economic jugular. You don't fool around with jugulars."[6]

As a glance at such stories and articles reveals, Algren's sense of vocation remained what it had been: conducting tours of life's wild side, defending society's bottom dogs, and critiquing the ills of a society that, among other things, refuses to acknowledge its complicity in the fates of America's lost and larcenous citizens. Throughout the late 1950s and into the 1960s, he delivered such messages with impatient insistence. In a 1959 interview Algren explained that the disease affecting all Americans is an alienated disconnection from one another, "which affects Americans from penthouse to tenement" and causes the afflicted to "suffer from [an] inability to love, fear of sex and dread of joy." Again, speaking at a 1961 symposium on American literature sponsored by *Esquire* magazine, Algren insisted that "there is a vast multitude of Americans who are not recognized, who don't belong to American society, and it's my particular self-appointed function to keep saying that they are there," adding that his "only purpose is to express my horror of what I see around me, whether it's the murderous treatment of drug addicts as though they were criminals, which they are not, [or] of prostitutes as criminals, which they are not . . . my purpose is to react."[7]

Elsewhere, Algren detailed piecemeal his disenchantment with America. In "The Mafia of the Heart," he rails against respectable society's "complicity in vice," and he takes the occasion of eulogizing novelist Richard Wright to observe that when truth is wanted, one does well to consult not the respectable but "the born-to-be-doomed."[8] Harsher still are his comments on foreign policy. Contributing a statement to a small book entitled *The Race for Space!* Algren dismissed the need to beat the Soviet Union to the moon and emphasized instead the need to right the wrongs occasioned by cold war hysteria, observing that "when the innocent man must prove his innocence or stand convicted on the word of an unseen accuser, though we own the moon, we are lost." Insisting to H. E. F. Donohue that America is "an imperialist son-of-a-bitch" that controls other countries for the benefit of American business and labels anyone who objects a Communist, Algren contends elsewhere that "we must recognize that, in the eyes of the world, the C.I.A. is now reversing the meaning of what it once meant to be an American."[9]

What was new about Algren's writing during these years was an increasingly international perspective and the manner in which the message was often delivered. Having burlesqued his earlier earnestness with the tragicomic realism of *A Walk on the Wild Side*, Algren throughout the late 1950s and into the 1960s was in search of a new style. Certainly, in the material assembled to create *Who Lost an American?* and *Notes from a Sea Diary,* Algren was flirting with a kind of writing that would eventually be labeled "postmodern": writing that rejects realism and the complexity of much modernist prose; that is self-referential, playful, and nonlinear; that replaces psychological depth with a sometimes cartoonish surface; that collapses genre distinctions,

118 / Understanding Nelson Algren

erases the line between fiction and nonfiction, juxtaposes fragments, and mixes seemingly antithetical voices; that prefers collage and performance to selectivity and polished artifact.[10] *Nelson Algren's Own Book of Lonesome Monsters* was the first to anthologize Thomas Pynchon, and Algren was soon praising the then unconventional and comically irreverent fiction of Bruce Jay Friedman, Joseph Heller, and Terry Southern, perhaps because the work of these writers both encouraged and vindicated what he was himself attempting.[11] As Kurt Vonnegut has recalled of Algren in 1965, he "appeared to want to modernize himself somehow."[12]

Who Lost an American?

Dedicated to Simone de Beauvoir and readable as a sometimes parodic imitation of her *America Day by Day* (both books cataloging a tourist's observations and meditating on national psyches), *Who Lost an American?* (1963) is an often flippant, philippic-laced account of the author's travels through Europe that closes with four chapters devoted to Chicago past and present—the connection to the European chapters being that "anyone in Chicago can now become an expatriate without leaving town."[13]

The book begins in absurdity—perhaps because, as Algren insists, "In an absurd society all men are absurd except the absurd man" (206)—with an improbable explanation of why Algren, on the advice of his lawyer (who also had him sign over to her his house and stamp collection), embarked on his travels: to avoid enemies who have discovered that he "marched in a demonstration protesting the bombing of Ethiopia in 1936" (10). Thus, Algren mocks both his FBI-propagated reputation as a dangerous subversive and the woes attendant on his lawsuit against filmmaker Otto Preminger.[14] An account of his bon voyage party provides an occasion for skewering fellow novelists James Baldwin and Norman Mailer (here dubbed "Giovanni Johnson" and "Norman Manlifellow"), after which nose-thumbing adieu to the venal New York literary scene, Algren narrates, in the book's equally absurd second chapter, his sea passage to Europe. This chapter offers cartoonish sketches of his fellow passengers and, as throughout the book, ridicules middle-class self-regard: "The waiter returned with good news for everyone—a lobster was just putting in his death throes under the auspices of the chef, after having gotten the latter's promise that he wouldn't be served to any but a first-class passenger" (43).

The following eight chapters follow Algren around Europe: to Dublin, where he meets writer and revolutionary Brendan Behan (*The Hostage, Borstal Boy*) and encourages the IRA to blow up a statue of Lord Nelson; London, where he recalls his war experiences and picks up Sandy, the Birmingham whore; Paris, where he lampoons Americans abroad and recalls Simone de Beauvoir, Jean-Paul Sartre, and their circle. Three chapters take the reader to Spain, where Algren lambastes dictator Francisco Franco, turns bullfighting into a silly joke, and sympathizes with the country's poor. In Crete, Algren joins a fishing crew on their night run and spoofs antiquity before leaving for Istanbul to satirize waiters, guidebook authors, taxi drivers, and the city as the historical meeting point of Christianity and Islam.

Throughout, dismay competes with amusement, sorrow for the lot of the poor with scorn for almost everything else. In Algren's hands, nothing is momentous, and much is outrageous or ridiculously disappointing. The chapters are as meandering as the peripatetic tourist-author who wrote them, each rambling

120 / Understanding Nelson Algren

from topic to topic, from sights seen and people encountered to biographical reminiscence and reflections on global politics, as though no sustained or coherent view is possible, as though the parts cannot make a whole. The method can be illustrated in brief with the following paragraph, part of a sketch of a Barcelona prostitute:

> She asked me to come to her room to help her count her clothes, as she had recently lost track. I went with her and, what do you know, that girl really *does* have fourteen dresses and six pairs of shoes! I counted twice to make sure. Then we went back to the café because I wanted to take her picture while there was still a good light. She seemed puzzled about something. My father was born in San Francisco and raised in Black Oak, Indiana, which was at the time hardly more than a village. Later a rich vein of silver tinfoil was discovered there, so the town has now entirely disappeared. (130–31)

Nonsense and non sequitur often characterize Algren's account. European history, for Algren, is a tale told by idiots, filled with irresponsible violence, poverty, ignorance, and bad faith. Mockery is the fittest response: of London businessmen, "Isn't the end product of the square who gets squarer and squarer, a fascist?" (79); of Franco's Spain, "There is a fisherman in the port of Barcelona who can eat fire, and other fishermen say Franco taught him how: once you swallow Franco you can swallow anything" (127); of the ruins of the ancient city of Gortynia in Crete, "Candidly, all I could see was a hill with a lot of good stonework gone to hell" (192).

Frequently sarcastic and often charmingly nonchalant, *Who Lost an American?* uses slapstick and whimsical ridicule to catch readers off guard, then vituperates against life-destroying injustice and stupidity. Thus, for Algren, big business everywhere, like General Motors in the United States, has "price fixing" as its "end product" (79); the "degradation of Spain's young womanhood" is the work of France, England, and America, each of which "preferred a fascist state to a democracy" (157); the progress of history comes down to a shift from "no man is an island" to "I'm getting mine" (157). Informed in Istanbul that Turks consider themselves "members of the White Race," Algren admits that "that's how I got my start" but wonders why "someone wants to wait till the last possible minute to join a losing organization," adding that both Turkey and Greece are "great democracies" only because "if they know what's good for them they'd better be" (201, 204).

In the process of being Americanized—"We don't want your Coca-Cola culture around here," Algren reports being told in Dublin (50)—everyone is caught by the cold war struggle between America and the Soviet Union for the hearts and minds of the world's peoples, an idea Algren satirizes when describing a starving cat wandering the streets of Istanbul:

> She was a cat caught in the worldwide struggle between Democracy and Communism, so it was my duty as an American to liberate her because we invented milk. Now we have a surplus we want to donate to undernourished peoples unconditionally in return for airbases and affection. If you don't love *us* more than *them,* you can't have *our* nice milk. But this was a Commie cat; she told me Keep Your Goddamned Milk. (215)

The intimate connection between America—as purveyor of everything from pop culture to milk, airbases to ideology—and the rest of the world returns Algren in his four concluding chapters to Chicago (seen here, as in *Chicago: City on the Make,* as a microcosm of America) to dissect exactly what the country is intent on exporting besides *Playboy* magazine, Diners' Club cards, and Coca-Cola.

For Algren, America circa 1963 is "a country that never needed spoofing more" (258), its most comfortably situated citizens so economically and morally self-satisfied "that [their] sense of relationship to the rest of the world is severed in a torpor akin to funk" (319). Claiming that "multitudes" inhabit America "like expatriates who never left town" and without any sense of who they are or what their lives mean, Algren insists that the "American bourgeois lives in a dream world wherein he sees the representation of himself pictured in *Time,* film, and so on, as his actual self"—a situation with international implications insofar as the average Joe, having bought the media's image of himself, is prepared to understand "people pitch[ing] tomatoes at Eisenhower" as a personal attack and to back foreign-policy decisions as in his personal best interest (320). Citing James Baldwin's contention that "if you don't know my name you don't know your own," Algren extends the idea: "If you don't know your own[,] you can't know your own country's name" (320).

Thus, because Americans do not know who they are or what their country is, they cannot recognize that what the Americanization of the world portends is the spreading of fear, insecurity, spiritual impoverishment, a materialistic "cult of money" (331), immoral self-interest, virtues of convenience, and a disdain for the dignity and worth of those unlike themselves—all of which Algren playfully enacts in *Who Lost an American?* Much that is wrong with America, Algren feels, stems from a crippled masculinity, a contention developed in the final Chicago chapter by way of an examination of the success of Hugh Hefner, the "Playboy of the Midwestern World" (303) and creator of *Playboy* magazine and the Playboy Key Clubs.

In the other Chicago chapters, Algren reprises complaints he has made elsewhere (indeed, the second and third Chicago chapters are difficult to distinguish from the introduction he wrote for the 1961 edition of *Chicago: City on the Make*): America is in decline, having betrayed its ideals; it is in the hands of corrupt businessmen and clergy, police and politicians, judges and newspaper columnists; what is wanting is men of conscience, particularly writers who do more than play cynically with ideas. Against such a disappointing present, Algren places his initial Chicago chapter, which fondly recalls an idyllic childhood and a father who worked hard with his hands all his life to make that childhood possible. As in the anecdote in which Algren recalls how his mother made him send a valentine to the only black girl in his grade-school class, Algren suggests that in his upbringing and in those times long gone can be found values that might redeem the malaise of early 1960s America just as that upbringing instilled in him the compassion he now feels for children living in caves above Almería and women forced into prostitution in London or Barcelona, for hungry little girls peering into restaurant windows in Seville and kids without a future on the streets of Chicago.

Locating himself within what he terms "the antilegalistic tradition toward society which had distinguished Chicago writers since the early years of the century" (273)—that is, writers who took the side of the downtrodden against those in power—Algren laments that there are no longer readers for such work. Rather than wanting "to feel there shall be no difference between himself and the rest," what the "new reader" wants is that "the difference between himself and the rest be officially recognized by the federal government" (273). What Algren gives such readers in *Who Lost an American?* is mockery of their need to see themselves as different from the world's children of darkness shot through with moments in which those Others (those hungry Spanish children, that long-dead father) step forth in all their moral dignity. It is a book that moves uncertainly into and out of genres (travel book, social commentary, memoir, farce, postmodern tall tale) and that possesses a vacillating tone because the world it pictures is itself uncertain, unstable.

Who Lost an American? may seem finally a slapdash effort dominated by impatient scorn, recycled outrage, and anything-for-a-laugh observations—making it, in Algren's mind, a real "reader's book": a book filled with clowning and aimed at aimed at readers who, Algren felt, perhaps did not deserve better.[15] Perhaps he felt that nothing he had to say would make a difference anyway. In an apostrophe to Chicago, he recalls how "you gave me your gutters and I gave you back gold" (285)— and what thanks had he received?

Notes from a Sea Diary: Hemingway All the Way

Although *Who Lost an American?* appeared in May 1963 to mixed reviews, Algren was soon transforming his travels of the previous year—the Far East by tramp steamer—into *Notes from a Sea Diary: Hemingway All the Way* (1965).[16] Again employing a variety of narrative voices, *Sea Diary* combines anecdotes of life aboard ship and stories of adventures in various ports of call (Pusan, Kowloon, Bombay, Calcutta) with social commentary and a running if frequently interrupted defense of Ernest Hemingway against dunderheaded critics bent on misunderstanding and undervaluing him. Two chapters scornfully recount meals shared with boorish literary types; another is devoted largely to recalling a neighbor from Algren's childhood who practiced walking a tightrope in his backyard. A comic account of Algren as a look-at-me buffoon visiting a convalescing Hemingway in Havana resides between the same covers housing a chapter offering an apologia for the prostitutes of Bombay in the form of eighteen brief biographies delivered in self-effacing prose.

The often comic episodes taking place ashore or aboard the cargo ship *Malaysia Mail* (a recurrent highlight are the improbable, self-serving stories of Able Seaman Gary "Crooked-Neck" Smith) are among the book's most appealing passages for the general reader, although the picture of the officers and crew that emerges is bleak. As Algren explained to Donohue, these were "very submerged men. I mean, they're like men in prison . . . there were men on that ship who never got off." He added that the ship represented "what the United States is like . . . what was wrong with the ship was, I think, what was wrong with the United States," mentioning the men's isolation, contempt for those encountered in port, and readiness to exploit those financially dependent on the American presence in the Far East.[17] The resentment the crew provoked represented for Algren the resentment smaller countries around the world felt toward America.

Telling stories of violence, drunkenness, crime, whoring, lying, and mutual distrust among the ship's men, Algren presents the *Malaysia Mail* as a microcosm of the American psyche; the attitudes of officers and crew are America's, as when ship's purser "*Mister* Manning" (who will eventually commit suicide after being caught dealing in contraband) informs Algren, "These people [Asians] aren't like us . . . they steal everything they can get their hands on."[18] Similarly, the exploitation of undeveloped countries by the United States, attributed to America's "increasing indifference to the suffering of others" (137), mirrors America's indifference to the exploitation and suffering of its own citizens. For successful Americans, as for the ship's men, "Property and prestige were more real than love and death." Both middle-class America and the seamen of the *Malaysia Mail* have created "a dream-world more real to them than the world of struggle going on in the streets" (162)—whether of Calcutta or Los Angeles, Pusan or Detroit—and both are deaf to "a whole night-universe begging Americans for their lives" (138).

Whether he writes of being hassled by the Korean pimp Slicky-Boy or of buying transistor radios in Kowloon to sell on the black market, of spending a week with the Calcutta prostitute Martha or of living among men satisfied by "a pint of cheap gin and a girl by the clock" (42), of visiting Pusan whores listening to twelve-year-old American pop songs on records whose labels they cannot read (51) or of watching a loincloth-clad Indian "standing in cowdung" while waiting to deliver messages for Western Union (116), Algren's point is in part to expose the unfortunate consequences of America's presence abroad. Thus, a "woman naked to her waist and breast-feeding an infant" while "toting a bucket of suds in her free hand" through the streets of Pusan receives this summary interpretation: "Slopwater is by courtesy of the American mess hall, *chapeau* by the Quartermaster Corps. Shod by Firestone, employed by nobody, impregnation courtesy of the American P.X." (47). Rejecting a prostitute's offer and refusing to give her a handout, Algren endures her brief abuse before concluding, "I'd done it again. Every time anybody in Asia tried improving his difficult lot, there I'd be throwing my weight against his chances. I was certainly going out of my way to foul people up" (129). Offered as a comic defense of his personal innocence, the remark is anything but comic when Algren is seen as a representative of America abroad.

If it is not difficult to see how the travel material connects to the book's interest in the world's underclass, a question remains: what has all of this to do with Hemingway? *Notes from a Sea Diary* is subtitled *Hemingway All the Way*. Yet of the book's twenty-two chapters, only nine consider Hemingway, and some of these only slightly: one chapter for only four of its nineteen pages, another for only a page and a half, and a third for the space of two paragraphs. A fourth chapter mentions Hemingway only in its concluding sentence. Additionally, much of the talk in the chapters concerned with literature is devoted primarily to ridiculing the current literary scene with special attention to the inanities of academic critics, particularly those who have failed to do Hemingway justice. (Several of these critics number among those who also failed to appreciate Algren.)[19]

Yet what gets said about Hemingway's critics is central to understanding the connection between the Hemingway material and the rest of *Sea Diary*. The critics, Algren contends, are nothing more than servile apologists for "the Establishment" (14) who peddle mediocrity and sterility and whose inherent inferiority is revealed when they consider their own lives in the light of Hemingway's: "To men whose self-doubt put them in need of formal respect from others, the ease with which Hemingway earned the informal respect of workaday men and women felt like an accusation" (88). In short, what ails America, at home and abroad, is what ails both the *Malaysia Mail* and (in spades) Hemingway's critics: a fear-riddled resentment of the world caused by not having really lived their lives, not having made any genuine human connections or achieved any important self-insight.

Hemingway's fiction reveals that he had plumbed the emotional and imaginative depths of a fully lived life. His critics, having failed in this endeavor, cannot countenance his success and must insist on seeing him as a failure, as nothing more than "an athletic young man" (90) overly fond of big-game hunting, bullfights, and war, a celebrity thanks to the discovery of some stylistic tricks that made his books best-sellers. For men who do not know how to live their lives, Hemingway's life is an affront, for he knew that, if "the proper study of mankind is man," this "doesn't mean to annotate Man but to live like one. The critic's resentment here is that which the small shopkeeper has always felt for the restless wanderer. What business does anyone have, he is asking, following bullfighters from arena to arena when he could be having a rich, full life teaching young women iambic pentameter?" (104). Like the middle-class readers of *Playboy,* like American women who no longer know "that the vagina was intended for *use*" (137), and like the desperately carousing men of the *Malaysia Mail,* the critic does not know how to live seriously and authentically in the often risky world in which he finds himself, and such failure leaves him slightly unreal and alienated, begrudged and indifferent to others. Indeed, "Hemingway's life," Algren avers, "could be told solely in terms of his hostility toward the *petit bourgeois* demand that neither love nor death be real. . . . He began with *Nada* [that is, "nothing"], he ended with *Nada:* but he knew those ports-of-call where life conflicts with death. He made the voyage" (105).

Algren ships out on a tramp steamer to record his thoughts on Hemingway to emphasize that he, too, made the voyage and "knew those ports-of-call where life conflicts with death"—hence the book's climactic account of the knife fight between Algren and Second Mate Danielsen, followed by the news that

Manning is dead largely because no one "cared, in the slightest degree, whether the man lived or died" (249). Algren wishes to emphasize the fact that he is not some closeted belletrist but rather, like Hemingway, a "restless wanderer" adventuring in the world of men. Algren wishes to underscore the fact that his work, too, is grounded in the harsh realities of lived experience and has earned the respect of "workaday men and women."

In the chapter "Rafts of a Summer Night," Algren tells a story that must have held special significance for him (he told it twice more—once as a newspaper column, again in *The Last Carousel*). It concerns Greener, a young man who had practiced his tightrope walking in the backyard next door to the young Algren, who took from the experience of watching Greener this lesson: "A man had but to be foolishly daring and the world was changed, from sunlessness to sun, for everyone" (99). Here, in this otherwise extraneous and perhaps fictitious reminiscence, can be found the crux of Algren's admiration for Hemingway, who had also changed the world for the better by daring to live as he did and by finding the means of making that life matter to others. Thus, Algren believes that "of many American writers who represented their own times, Hemingway alone made his times represent him" (105).

The secret of Hemingway's success resides in "the risks he took," which were both "literary and personal" (105). As far as the literary is concerned, the risk was stylistic. However, as Algren defines "style," the literary is quickly subsumed by the personal: "Style is that force by which a man becomes what he most needs to become. When this need is one common to multitudes and the man's force suffices, we call him an artist, because in saving himself he saves others" (89–90). Thus, it is not Hemingway's "syntax, but the man inside the prose" (93) that finally earns Algren's praise, for in Hemingway, Algren discerned a man who, because not divorced from his conscience, achieved "light and simplicity" for everyone "enduring a murky complexity" (171), a man who confronted death many times and returned to tell about it, to "[note] how many letters littered the field where the Austrian dead lay face-down in the sun with their hip pockets emptied" and to imagine himself "the English girl dreaming herself dead in an Italian rain" (251).

> Hemingway had felt his life fluttered like a pocket-handkerchief by the wind of death. In the watches of the night he had heard retreat beaten. Out of dreams like Dostoevsky's, endured in nights wherein he had lost his life yet had not died[,] Hemingway forged an ancestral wisdom in terms usable by modern man: that he who gains his life shall lose it and he who loses it shall save it; into a prose magically woven between sleep and waking. (91)

Having found in Hemingway what he believed too many others in the world were running from fearfully—the wherewithal to risk oneself in the pursuit of fully human existence—Algren would have his own life's voyage understood as "Hemingway all the way." Had not Algren himself, as he writes of Hemingway, "identified himself with the victims of America; as though those most unworthy of love were the most worthy of it" (169)? Had not both men forged styles that, by enabling them to find and thereby save themselves, might redeem others? Had not both rejected the idea of "abstracting life from the poetry of living" (102) and of preferring "the Meaning of Man" over flesh-and-blood men and women? Had not both been accused of an inability to think by people who believed "that literature derives from other books rather than from life" (102–3)?

Had not both rejected fakery, striven to find "the courage to speak directly" (177), and understood that "the novelist, grown remote from people who don't read, becomes untrue to those who do read" (105–6)? And is Algren not describing himself when he locates Hemingway in that tradition Algren had already claimed as his own, a tradition that sees literature "made upon those occasions when a challenge is put to the legal apparatus by a conscience in touch with humanity" (163)?

The answer to the question "Who lost an American?" was that too many Americans had—because they had lost touch with themselves and with one another. Or as Algren said a few years later of a Vietnamese peasant executed after throwing a bomb into an American PX, "Unless we know who this boy on the bike is, we do not know who we are" because "to live a lifetime in the same house [that is, in the same world] with another human being without admitting his reality is to fail to find one's own true self."[20] Hemingway, that lion among hyenas, had turned his back on neither himself nor others, Algren believed, and to go with Hemingway "all the way" meant to refuse alienated isolation and to welcome compassionate involvement in the world. To stand with Hemingway meant accepting the risk involved in learning the names of the disenfranchised everywhere. It meant accepting the need "to earn one's death in order to become alive" (167), in order to stand any chance of finding a "chasmed love, with thighs that locked so sure" that it "makes the world come true" (253).

For Algren, restless and frustrated at the age of fifty-six and trying, according to his friend Dave Peltz, "to get over what he had done with his life, what he had done with [the] great opportunity that he [had] had," these were for Algren more than pretty things to think; they were a necessary vindication of his own life and work.[21]

CHAPTER NINE

The Last Carousel and *The Devil's Stocking*

Conrad Knickerbocker concluded in 1965 that if Algren did not publish another novel, it would not be because he no longer cared "to bear witness" but because "life is short" and Algren "no longer in the mood for all-or-nothing investments" of his time and emotions.[1] As Algren himself described his unwillingness to write another novel, "If you're going to let your life be dominated every day for three or four years," then it has "got to be writing for posterity. When you are 20, you can do it—but not when you're 64. Four years is a long goddamn time. My life is for my own benefit."[2]

Algren would write another novel, and more surprising still to those who knew him, he would leave Chicago to do it. But before moving to New Jersey in late 1974 (first to Paterson, then to Hackensack) to be close to the story that came to obsess him (the arrest, conviction for murder, and retrial of boxer Rubin "Hurricane" Carter), he spent ten quietly eventful years following the release of *Notes from a Sea Diary* traveling and writing from his Chicago base. In the mid-1960s, he tried his hand at teaching (at the University of Iowa's Writers' Workshop) and took a second run at marriage. Neither venture was a success.[3] In 1967 he was arrested for possession of marijuana, and in December 1968 he left for six months in Southeast Asia (where he was badly beaten up while black marketeering). He made television appearances and lectured, remarking in 1973 that "I live on book reviews and by giving talks."[4] For a few months in 1970, he wrote a column for the *Chicago Free Press,* and that same year he bought a racehorse, which his friends nicknamed Algren's Folly. But whatever else he was doing, Algren was also turning out essays, stories, and poems, many of which found their way into 1973's *The Last Carousel.*

Although one can read most of *The Last Carousel* with little sense that the explosive 1960s had taken place (the essays about Vietnam are the exceptions), other occasional writing and the interviews he granted made clear his positions on issues of the day. He referred to Vietnam as "the Crime of the Century" and expressed contempt for the conduct and rationale of the war; he labeled Chicago's mayor Richard Daley the greatest threat to the city's well-being and described the beating of protesters during the 1968 Democratic Convention as something that "could not be witnessed without a disgust: a disgust with Daley and his police."[5] In a 1974 interview he noted that because America consumes "30 percent of the world's energy and goods," and because "we're committed to keeping it that way," future wars are inevitable.[6] He again praised Richard Wright as a "voice of multitudes," mourned in verse the fates of Asia's and America's poor, and eulogized James T. Farrell as that rarity, a novelist whose work has lasted because, despite its artistic shortcomings, it "changed readers' lives."[7] In 1975's "Requiem," Algren bid a last farewell to Chicago and to a lost way of life that had made virtue and achievement possible.[8]

Elsewhere, Algren provided additional glimpses into his work and its motivations. In an essay on the paintings of Edward Hopper, for instance, he echoed part of his argument in *Notes from a Sea Diary* when he observed that art is "a solitary search for one's true self." Again, insisting that he does "look at things seriously," Algren explained to *Publishers Weekly* that "you've got to pretend it's all a big laugh. You never get any attention by finger-shaking at people." In a reassessment of once-ballyhooed World War II novels, he implicitly justified his own prose style when he concluded that Joseph Heller's *Catch-22* is the best of the lot because only Heller's prose contains poetry.[9]

A short piece entitled "On Kreativ Righting" offers one final assault on writing workshops as tools of the establishment meant to produce writers cut off from the real world and work intent on "sustain[ing] the reader's conviction that his own society is the best of all possible societies." In 1977, Algren defended the worth of *A Walk on the Wild Side* against its critics by reporting that hookers and pimps with whom he had spoken claimed he had got their stories "just right," adding, "I'm perfectly satisfied that I'm a good writer. . . . Oh, when it comes to technical skill and literary manipulation, I couldn't touch [Saul] Bellow or [John] Updike. But I'm a more enduring writer, and I'm more in touch with real life."[10]

The appearance of *The Last Carousel,* Algren's ninth book and a repository of signature themes and obsessions, offered further reasons to believe that Algren was indeed a writer who would endure.

The Last Carousel

The Last Carousel is Nelson Algren's longest book: 435 pages of poems, essays, and stories, all but six of which were written during the 1960s and early 1970s. Although twenty-eight of the book's thirty-seven selections are acknowledged as having previously seen print, in fact thirty had already been published elsewhere (including four pieces deriving from the recent *Notes from a Sea Diary*), several of them more than once. Most of the remaining selections will remind careful readers of other work by Algren. The recycling, in short, is extensive. For instance, the scene from *A Walk on the Wild Side* in which Dove Linkhorn helps Rhino Gross make condoms, which was first revised into the story "The Daddy of Them All" (1964), appears here, reworked again and fresh from a 1969 appearance in *Commentary* magazine, as "The Mad Laundress of Dingdong-Daddyland."[11] Similarly, versions of the poem "Tricks Out of Times Long Gone," which closes the collection, had appeared in the *Nation* (1962), *Who Lost an American?* (1963), and as the conclusion to "Ode to Lower Finksville" (added by Algren to the 1968 edition of *Chicago: City on the Make*).

An amalgam of twice- and thrice-told tales, *The Last Carousel* was clearly not conceived as a "best of" sampler, but neither is it simply a miscellany if by that term is meant a collection of unrelated works. If the book is more than the sum of its thirty-seven parts, it coheres as a symbolic portrait of the artist—a catalogue raisonné of the imaginative and emotional contents of Nelson Algren's voyage through the first sixty-four years of his life, what might at the time have seemed a swan song reprising the people and concerns that had long obsessed him.

The combination of first-person (and often quite personal) essays and stories for the most part told in the first-person (even when the first-person narrator is largely invisible in the unfolding story) encourages reading *The Last Carousel* as an apologia if not a valedictory. Algren's life, the collection suggests, has been inextricably interwoven with his work, and the line separating fiction from nonfiction, oneself and others, is here as easily crossed as the line dividing poetry from prose. Thus, just as an essay (for example, "Ballet for Opening Day") or story ("Watch Out for Daddy") can suddenly break into verse, *The Last*

Carousel itself commingles the essayistic and the fictional, memory and imagination. "The Mad Laundress of Dingdong-Daddyland," for instance, now draws on Algren's criticism (in *Who Lost an American?*) of Hugh Hefner and the American male's fear of women to turn the story's main character, Daddy, into a reader of *Playboy*. Algren has this to say about him in the story's denouement:

> The passion that, in him, had been transformed by fear of woman into deep need of something to love *safely*—a paper doll or a girl wearing a bunny-tail—curiously overlapped that of lives equally barren yet more affluent. . . .
>
> For he shared a secret fury with the world: a hatred of all birth that comes from love of man for woman.[12]

Just as the stuff of Algren's essays sometimes materializes in a story, essays are sometimes difficult to tell from fiction (for example, "The Cortez Gang"). Throughout, the book is punctuated by the autobiographical: from "Otto Preminger's Strange Suspenjers" (Algren's final assault on the filmmaker, so improbable in the telling it seems fictitious) through "Poor Girls of Kowloon" (a travel piece that suddenly shifts focus to recollect the author's father and grandfather) to "The Last Carousel" (the events in the summer of 1932 that indirectly led to Algren becoming a writer).[13]

"Previous Days" is perhaps the linchpin piece when viewing *The Last Carousel* as a book that both transforms the author's life into literature and suggests that his fiction is the proper window onto that life. Appearing at the book's midpoint, "Previous Days" begins with recollections of Algren's childhood before metamorphosing into a series of verbal snapshots indistinguishable from and possessing the creative flare of novelistic vignettes as Algren sketches, among others, a heroin-addicted hooker and the "small begoggled outcast" (215) who pimps her, a hotel desk clerk who can (he claims) guess which guests plan to check out by leaping to their deaths, and the legendary dadaist comic Lord Buckley.

Several essays, in addition to "The Last Carousel," take the form of memoirs. "Merry Christmas, Mr. Mark" and "Everything Inside Is a Penny" retell stories of Algren's childhood. "Different Clowns for Different Towns" offers a comic account of his early efforts to find a position with one or another Chicago newspaper and thereby provides the occasion to criticize the irresponsibility of journalists. The largely comic "Brave Bulls of Sidi Yahya" uses a 1949 trip across North Africa from Marrakech to Médenine to paint an unflattering portrait of his former lover, Simone de Beauvoir. "The Ryebread Trees of Spring" finds Algren taking an early morning walk, while a series of seven travel pieces describes the author's 1969 trip to the Far East: "I Know They'll Like Me in Saigon" (Algren sketched San Francisco while waiting for his ship to sail), "Airy Persiflage on the Heaving Deep" (comic account of life aboard ship), "No Cumshaw No Rickshaw" (pictures of Japan), "Poor Girls of Kowloon" (notes on Macao, other ports of call, and his infatuation with one Maria Chan). Three essays in this sequence—"Letter from Saigon," "What Country Do You Think You're In?" and "Police and Mama-sans Get It All"—treat Saigon (now officially Ho Chi Minh City) during the American occupation.

Other essays concern miscreants of various sorts and degrees of villainy: Otto Preminger, the personification of Hollywood venality ("Otto Preminger's Strange Suspenjers"); White Sox owner Charles Comiskey, who won the public's sympathy while eight of his poorly paid players took the fall for throwing the 1919 World Series ("Go! Go! Go! Forty Years Ago" and "Ballet for Opening Day"); Clyde Barrow and Bonnie Parker, "children of the wilderness whose wilderness had been razed" and the "only American outlaws, other than Jesse James, who achieved an aura of the supernatural" (176, 177) ("After the Buffalo"); Gregorio Cortez, another desperado who, wrongly accused in 1901 of horse stealing, shot a sheriff and then evaded capture while the posses in his pursuit killed eight Mexicans while wounding and falsely arresting many more ("The Cortez Gang").

"Come In If You Love Money" finds Algren betting the horses and playing poker in Butte, Montana, a place where those who own the mines are "too big to beat" and victory for the workers "consists in snatching a draw out of the jaws of certain defeat" (86)—an observation that leads to reflections on the brutality with which mine owners early in the century had responded to the efforts of union organizers and to an account of the August 1917 murder of organizer Frank Little. Miscreants of a different stripe can be found in "Tinkle Hinkle and the Footnote King," which targets for abuse the well-known critic Alfred Kazin (among whose sins was the failure to appreciate Algren's work); "Hand in Hand through the Greenery," which offers a powerful indictment of the philistines in control of the current literary scene; and the absurdist "Could World War I Have Been a Mistake?" which mocks the avant-garde and the "integrity of art" (20).

The essays join Algren to the subjects of his compassion: Saigon prostitutes and kids turned into outlaws, the girl forced to make her living as "Hannah the Half-Girl Mystery" (403) at the Jim Hogg County Fair ("The Last Carousel") and the black girl who never received a valentine in Algren's otherwise all-white grade-school class ("Everything Inside Is a Penny"), "an old blown bum" (254) dispensing religious cards for a nickel ("The Ryebread Trees of Spring"), and the author himself, victim of malicious critics, Hollywood moguls, Depression grifters, and an attractive French intellectual. Algren has lived among underdogs because, as he explains to Preminger, "When I live around other [respectable] people they turn out to be such [bad] people, that I go back and live around just *such* people," adding that he in fact does "like some people who are under, but not *because* they're under. Under is just where they happen to be" (24).

The essay "The Last Carousel" ends with a Ferris wheel within an arriving dust storm "sinking . . . forever downward into dust" (428). The collection then concludes with the poem "Tricks Out of Times Long Gone" in which those about whom Algren has written—"All those whose lives were lived by someone else" (429)—return as "unremembered" ghosts "to claim / What never rightly was their own" (429). It is an appropriate double conclusion for an autumnal book that is everywhere riddled by endings—and nowhere more so than in the collection's eleven short stories. Thus, "The Mad Laundress of Dingdong-Daddyland" closes when Daddy finds in death the "kick greater than H [heroin]" (61) while beyond his window a neighborhood and an era fall silent, and "The Passion of Upside-Down Emil" ends with Emil giving up tightrope walking, first for a factory job, then for alcohol, and thereby causing "some magic that had been in the world" (228) to disappear.

In "Dark Came Early in That Country," journeyman boxer Roger Holly gives up his career and his dreams of being a champ to open a diner, and although the story concludes with his woman, Beth, still at his side, the last the reader sees of Roger he is still reciting the places where he once boxed and acknowledging that "a Vaseline jar and half a bottle of liquid adrenalin" are all he has to show "for getting my face punched in for fourteen years" (17). The comic "I Never Hollered Cheezit the Cops" ends with the arrest of a washed-out jockey turned inept bookie (another bookie at the end of his career appears in the poem "Ode to an Absconding Bookie"). Also comic in tone are "I Guess You Fellows Just Don't Want Me" (about a man who will never go anywhere in life except to jail) and "The Leak That Defied the Books," which began as a short story in the men's magazine the *Dude* (March 1962) and, revised, appeared in *Notes from a Sea Diary* as one of the tales told by Gary "Crooked-Neck" Smith. The latter concerns a man who works for Some People's Gas sniffing out possible gas leaks and who may be responsible for the explosion that kills his two-timing wife.

Two hard-bitten stories of racetrack deceit—"Bullring of the Summer Night" and "Moon of the Arfy Darfy"—treat the end of jockey Hollie Floweree's career and its pathetic aftermath, while "A Ticket on Skoronski" offers a much darker version of "Say a Prayer for the Guy" (1958), in which a man's death from a heart attack while playing poker with friends provokes so little in the way of concern or sorrow that the friends' callousness (picking the man's pockets, making jokes, using the death as an opportunity to request free drinks) becomes ghoulishly surreal, especially insofar as events are played out before a mysterious stranger looking on from a dark corner of the barroom whom no one but the narrator can see. "Watch Out for Daddy" follows two addicts—a pimp and his hooker girlfriend—through their codependent days and dysfunctional nights, the story eventually fading to black as Beth-Mary resignedly reflects, "I was sixteen when he came by and became a sickness in my heart. I'm going on twenty-four and he's a sickness to this hour" (396).

What *The Last Carousel* offers start to finish are stories of "times long gone" and the concomitant loss of love, hope, dreams, possibility, life itself: what Algren elsewhere termed "the defeats in which everything is lost."[14] From Vietnam to Montana, Chicago to San Francisco, North Africa to East Texas, dreams become nightmares while people do what they can to hold onto their dignity as they sink downward to darkness.[15] Thus, "Moon of the Arfy Darfy" concludes,

> *Through sunlight bright as seconal*
> *Through twilights swept by snow—*
> *Can't you see by the gloom*
> *Of a blue paper moon*
> *These are Christ's poor damned cats*
> *Who'll never see home?* (366)

From the whores of Médenine to Bonnie and Clyde, from naive writing students purchasing "painless creativity . . . based on a self-deception" (77) to striking miners, from Algren's grandfather inventing the "Father & Son Cigar" (246) to the "mad laundress of Dingdong-Daddyland" helping to manufacture "the condom of tomorrow" (48), from Shoeless Joe Jackson and Swede Risberg of the Chicago White Sox to Upside-Down Emil and Hollis Floweree, from the "mama-san" Giang trying "to hold onto her own" (139) to Nelson Algren—all are being cheated out of what ought to be theirs, and for each of them, life as it once was has ended, and what might have been is no longer possible.

Although Algren may insist that "when you come to the end it's the end that's all" (366), each time he looks back on what was or glances around him at what is, he feels not dispassion but rather "a gentle *whoof,* like someone had touched [his] heart" (369). Consequently, it is perhaps no accident that the cacophonous late 1960s and early 1970s should be largely absent from the pages of *The Last Carousel,* for what the thirty-seven pieces comprising this volume proffer instead are times and people "too dear for losing" (425).

The Devil's Stocking

The title *The Last Carousel* might have promised a last ride for Algren's readers, but a new novel, again combining story and essay, fact and fiction, eventually grew from Algren's obsession with the story of Rubin "Hurricane" Carter, a contender for the middleweight boxing crown until convicted in 1967 for a triple murder in a Paterson, New Jersey, bar in June 1966. Published posthumously, *The Devil's Stocking* is the fictionalization of Carter's story, a reworking of Algren's book-length documentary account that had begun as a magazine article—an exercise in investigative journalism that, following a 1976 retrial that failed to exonerate Carter, generated no interest among publishers.[16]

From Bruno Bicek (*Never Come Morning*) to Roger Holly ("Dark Came Early in That Country"), Algren, who had a pair of boxing gloves tattooed on one arm and used a punching bag for diversion when working, had written often about prizefighters. In *The Devil's Stocking,* this passion for the fights combined with longstanding concerns (regarding racism, middle-class hypocrisy, and the corruption of the American criminal-justice system) to yield a novel that illustrated perfectly Algren's definition of literature as that which "is made upon any occasion that a challenge is put to the legal apparatus by conscience in touch with humanity."[17] What makes the novel different from earlier Algren work is the extent of his use of the Carter material, the presence of an intelligent, articulate protagonist, and the specificity of Algren's social criticism.[18]

A roman à clef, *The Devil's Stocking* transforms Rubin Carter into Ruby Calhoun, police lieutenant Vincent DeSimone into Vincent De Vivani, and Judge Samuel Larner into Judge Turner. Many of the details surrounding the Carter case are carried over into the novel—from the perjured testimony of two excons, Arthur Dexter Bradley and Alfred P. Bello (here, Dexter Baxter and Nick Iello), to celebrities rushing to Carter's defense. Like Carter, Ruby is a black kid who gets into trouble early, seems to like it, and stays there—until he discovers boxing while in the army. Ruby's promising career as a professional boxer is detailed fight by fight until the murder of three whites in a bar leads to Ruby's arrest and conviction. Algren then charts Ruby's life behind bars (including his role in a prison riot modeled on the Rahway Prison uprising of 1971 in which Carter was unavoidably involved) and his lawyers' efforts through the mid-1970s to secure Ruby's release. Algren leaves Ruby, following a detailed account of his retrial and reconviction, alone in a one-man cell, estranged from his family, abandoned by the media and his erstwhile celebrity supporters, and "subsist[ing] on canned foods, brought to him once a month by some devoted fan" (302).[19]

The Devil's Stocking, however, diverges from the Carter story in significant ways.[20] Focusing on the racism that he believes explains Carter's conviction, Algren slights such facts as the committee (which included prominent politicians) formed in 1975 to assist in Carter's defense, appeals that same year from more than a dozen elected officials calling on the governor of New Jersey to reopen the case, and a petition drive to demand that Carter be set free.[21] Also omitted is Carter's alleged accomplice, John Artis (imprisoned in 1967, paroled in 1981), who is replaced in the novel by two prominent characters, Ed "Red" Haloways and Dovie-Jean Dawkins, who have no parallels in the Carter story. It is Red Haloways, Ruby's best friend, who, Algren implies, committed the murders for which Ruby takes the rap and who ends up an institutionalized "madman" (304). Haloways is the "the devil's stocking," someone "knitted backwards" (25) and consequently useless, unnatural, evil. Dovie-Jean, Ruby's occasional lover and Red's girlfriend, receives Algren's close attention not because she may help explain why Red betrays Ruby but because, turning to prostitution after she and Red flee New Jersey, Dovie-Jean provides an opportunity for Algren to revisit one of his favorite topics: day-to-day life in a brothel and the reasons why men are attracted to prostitutes and women to such a life.

Algren has, in short, bent the historical account to his own ends, which he described in a interview the day before he died as an attempt "to write about a man's struggle against injustice," a theme that ties the Rubin Carter / Ruby Calhoun material (with Ruby the victim not only of American racism, corrupt police, ineffectual legal counsel, a vindictive criminal-justice system, and hellish prisons but also of those closest to him) to the Dovie-Jean story (which paints the choice of prostitution and the harassment of prostitutes as the results of unequal social opportunities, social and familial dysfunction, and middle-class hypocrisy).[22]

Dovie-Jean—who believes "you're born somehow. You live somehow. You play out the hand that's dealt you somehow. Then you die somehow" (63)—is a young woman who grew up without "a name truly her own" (26) and who never, until she met Red, had a "chance to be kind to another person" (62). Similarly, Red is a man who does not know who or what he is: so light-skinned he can pass as white and so damaged by American racism that he has always "wanted to get away from niggers" (306), Red earns his living for a time lip-synching to songs by white crooners, and at one points stands before a mirror in which an image both "himself, yet not himself" fades until it disappears (274). The difficulty of securing a healthy self-identity and the risk of self-loathing provoked by living in a racist society are, then, among the injustices against which Ruby struggles and the novel rages.

Ruby refuses to allow himself to be defined by others. Thus, in prison, he insists on both his race and his innocence by wearing a dashiki and headband—"both against prison regulations"—because, as he explains, "I can't let myself be treated like a criminal.... If I let myself be treated like that, I'd begin to *think* like a criminal. Most of the men in here feel that what has happened to them *ought* to have happened. I don't. Dressing in prisoner clothes would be to acknowledge openly that I belong here. I don't" (144–45). To Barney Kerrigan, the state investigator from the public defender's office who is working to free him, Ruby explains that he knows he is a "threat" to those running the prison because "I remain uncrushed. I never acknowledge guilt.... I do no work. That would be an act of repentance and I have nothing to repent," adding that the imprisoned "are men like other men. Not, after all, monsters" (213). Like Flash, a minor character who dies after being sucker-punched by Red for refusing to pay for an overpriced drink in the bar where Red is working, Ruby also pays "dearly to preserve his dignity" (267).

The world in which Ruby struggles to remain true to himself is topsy-turvy. An innocent man, Ruby is locked away while the police and prosecuting attorney are lauded although guilty of playing the race card, of withholding and falsifying evidence, of intimidating witnesses, and of cutting deals with known criminals in which fabricated testimony is exchanged for lighter sentences and the promise of a cash reward. It is a world in which neither the National Association for the Advancement of Colored People (NAACP) nor the Southern Christian Leadership Conference (Martin Luther King's civil rights organization) will come to Ruby's aid until "sensing the political value of supporting" him (233); in which, as the hooker Fortune explains, pimps provide young women with the attention, however brutal, elsewhere lacking in their lives (121–22); and in which "masters of industry, politicians, clergymen Christian or Jewish, TV celebrities, members of the Bar, professors of ancient Greek, violinists with perfect pitch and editors of newspapers with a million circulation" all search for love "with fifty-dollar bills in their wallets" (120) while publicly condemning vice and immorality.

The NAACP will not touch Ruby for the same reason Red will let Ruby rot in prison: everyone is playing it safe, is looking out for "number one," in a corrupt and corrupting society. Thus, for instance, what the state has tried to do to Ruby—"reducing a man to a number" (299)—it has already done to his guards, who are described as men determined never "to get involved . . . with anything, or anybody, for any reason" and who seem "as fully prisoners of the establishment as were the prisoners" (301). Similarly, the celebrities who rush momentarily to Ruby's defense are, Algren believes, mostly hoping thereby to advance their careers; the media spreads lies indifferently to boost circulation or entice viewers to tune in; no-nothing professors pen jejune defenses of capital punishment as more humane than imprisonment; and those charged with upholding the law "commit a violation of the Constitution as heinous as the crimes" for which Ruby was convicted.[23]

Meanwhile, Ruby understands that "death isn't merely a matter of the body ceasing to breathe. Death comes to many before actual death sets in. I doubt, for example, that the professor [of the death-penalty article] has ever really been alive" (143). Giving voice to Algren's longstanding conviction that most Americans are afraid of life, Ruby understands further that America, operating on "the old tribal belief of an eye for an eye" (143), is a place where a lie—disseminated by the media or the police, a false witness or false friend—"covers the whole world by the time the truth can get its boots on" (212). Among the lies Ruby exposes are that those in charge of the American criminal-justice system have justice as a first priority, that in America change can best be effected by working within the system, and that the penal system cares about rehabilitation or the decent treatment of those it incarcerates. "People will believe anything that supports their prejudices," Ruby explains to Kerrigan, but the truth is that there "are no people more brutal, nor more cowardly, than those who control our prisons" (213). Understanding that the authorities will do whatever they think they can get away with, Ruby adds that the suppressed prison uprising in which he was involved taught him that there is "no way of bucking an administration from inside. So long as they have barbed wire and censorship they'll do whatever they want with you" (213).

More damning still is what Algren has Ruby learn about the powers-that-be: that those in power "can always handle violence" but cannot deal with reason, which is feared simply because "they don't live by reason themselves. When it pops up they reach for a gun" (214). Arguing that prisoners are human beings who do not need to be guarded like mad dogs, Ruby demonstrates the willingness to reason so feared by the state:

> Nothing is more dangerous than making the state feel useless. What if it became apparent that prisons themselves are unnecessary? What would happen to the contractors and politicians whose whole lives are invested in protecting society from criminals? What if it looked as if there were no real difference, no basic difference, between people inside the walls and people outside? God almighty, what a fright that would be, top to bottom. (214)

The Devil's Stocking is ultimately an indictment of America as a society in which there is no real difference between those inside the walls and those outside. As Algren writes of the official investigation into the prison uprising, regarding "the most heinous crime, that of demanding that men be broken to dogs, committed by society against the criminal, no mention [is] made" (210). Making clear that this heinous crime is likewise routinely committed against blacks, women, and the poor (whether guilty or innocent), Algren characterizes as corrupt both the state and those holding privileged status therein (its clergymen and politicians, professors and attorneys, masters of industry and media celebrities), thus reprising a charge he had made throughout his career: that those with the power to deny others a place at the table are themselves responsible for the crimes such disenfranchised persons commit. Why? Because "the human need to *belong*" is so strong that those denied the privilege of belonging will if necessary "kill for it."[24]

Perhaps the severest condemnation proffered by *The Devil's Stocking* comes not in what is explicitly said about police corruption, the win-at-all-costs vindictiveness of prosecuting attorneys, or the ease with which juries can be manipulated; the disingenuousness of celebrity activists, the need for penal reform, or the hypocrisy of an outraged middle class crying for law and order. Rather, Algren's portrait of America as itself a devil's stocking is most powerfully conveyed through the book's prose style, which for the first time largely withholds the poetry of Algren's compassion. Of Bob Dylan, who had organized benefit concerts for Rubin Carter and recorded the song "Hurricane" to tell Carter's story, Algren writes that Dylan's "poverty of spirit could be sensed in the emptiness of his voice" (234). What Algren heard in Dylan's voice he also saw rampant in the America in which he was living—and captured in the uncharacteristically flat, unadorned prose of his final novel.

Nelson Algren did not live long enough to see Rubin Carter released from prison in 1985 and the indictments against him finally dismissed in 1988. Indeed, Algren did not live long enough to see *The Devil's Stocking* published. If he died still searching for new ways to tell the story of "man's struggle against injustice," it is difficult not to conclude that Algren died believing that (in the closing words of his final novel) "all is changed," yet somehow "everything remains the same" (308).

CHAPTER TEN

Conclusion

Nelson Algren suffered a heart attack on Christmas 1979. At 6:05 on the morning of May 9, 1981 (according to his watch, which broke when he fell), Algren died of a second heart attack. This was just a few days before he was to have been inducted into the American Academy and Institute of Arts and Letters and at a time when, in the words of his friend Joe Pintauro, "Everything he had mourned as lost seemed on the brink of coming back again."[1] His final short fiction, "Walk Pretty All the Way," appeared the next month to tell the story of two runaway fourteen-year-old girls headed for lives on the wild side. July saw the publication of his final essay, "So Long, Swede Risberg"—a last look back at childhood and the 1919 Black Sox scandal first broached in his 1942 poem "The Swede Was a Hard Guy."[2]

In 1992, *America Eats,* the study of midwestern cuisine Algren wrote while working for the Illinois Writers' Project during the 1930s, was published by the University of Iowa Press as part of its Culinary Arts Series.[3] In 1995, the University of Texas Press gathered eleven previously published pieces under the title *The Texas Stories of Nelson Algren,* and in 1996 *Nonconformity: Writing on Writing* was salvaged from Algren's archive at Ohio State University, edited, and finally published.

By 1987, Algren's principal achievements, *The Man with the Golden Arm* and *A Walk on the Wild Side,* were out of print,[4] and although he has yet to reclaim the place in American letters he held for a while following the appearance of *The Man with the Golden Arm,* by the end of the 1980s Algren was becoming available again, thanks largely to Daniel Simon, who began bringing Algren's work back into print as copublisher of Four Walls Eight Windows and has continued his efforts since founding Seven Stories Press in 1996—adding to these reissues both *Nonconformity* and a fiftieth anniversary edition of *The Man with Golden Arm.* In 2001 the University of Chicago Press published a fiftieth anniversary edition of *Chicago: City on the Make* and reissued H. E. F. Donohue's *Conversations with Nelson Algren.*

Algren still cannot be found in the standard anthologies used to teach American literature, but since the 1990s his work has appeared in perhaps unexpected venues. In 1993 the early story "He Swung and He Missed" was released in an edition aimed at young readers; an excerpt from *The Man with the Golden Arm* found its way into an anthology devoted to descriptions of drug experiences; the chapter "Festival in the Fields" from *America Eats* was reprinted in *The Penguin Book of Food and Drink;* and an excerpt from *Chicago: City on the Make* recalling the 1919 Black Sox scandal was included in the Library of America's *Baseball: A Literary Anthology.*[5]

Recent scholarship on Algren, although not voluminous, has been steady, sophisticated, and sympathetic. Leading the way were Matthew J. Bruccoli and Judith Baughman's extremely useful *Nelson Algren: A Descriptive Bibliography* (1985) and James R. Giles's *Confronting the Horror: The Novels of Nelson Algren* (1989), only the second book-length study of Algren's work and the first aimed primarily at scholars.[6] Bettina Drew's indispensable *Nelson Algren: A Life on the Wild Side* soon followed.[7] Whereas Giles was interested in locating Algren within the context of American literary naturalism and in showing

152 / Understanding Nelson Algren

how Algren's incorporation of existentialist ideas and absurdist humor rang changes on that tradition, thereby influencing younger novelists, in recent years, critics have found Algren useful for exploring specialized concerns that his work is seen to illustrate. Thus, Carlo Rotella has read Algren as a chronicler of the decline of the industrial city in the years following World War II; Thomas S. Gladsky has examined *Never Come Morning* for its images of Polish ethnicity; and Carla Cappetti has used the same Algren novel in an attempt to redeem from critical neglect the sociological novels of the 1930s.[8]

Algren scholarship is thriving—"Nelson Algren: An International Symposium," for instance, was held in 2000 at the University of Leeds—but Algren remains most alive, as is only proper, on the streets and off the campuses.[9] Recently, Wayne Kramer (founder in 1967 of Detroit's rock band, the MC5) has recorded an album that includes the song "Nelson Algren Stopped By," and Chicago's Frankie Machine Blues Band routinely performs their "Algren Street," written by Warren Leming, who in 1989 founded with Stuart McCarrell the Nelson Algren Committee, dedicated to keeping Algren's work, and the spirit of that work, alive.[10] The Nelson Algren Award for Short Fiction, created in 1982 by *Chicago* magazine, continues to be awarded annually; 2000 saw John Musial's *Nelson & Simone* open at Chicago's Live Bait Theatre and broadcast on WTTW; and in 2001 Chicago's Lookingglass Theatre Company staged *Nelson Algren: For Keeps and a Single Day*.

Algren has likewise been someone who has mattered to younger writers, from Russell Banks to Richard Brautigan, whose *Trout Fishing in America* pays homage to Algren in the figure of Trout Fishing in America Shorty and in references to Algren throughout.[11] The Beat writer and activist Edward Sanders has referred to Algren as someone he, "like hundreds of thousands" of other high school kids, read in the 1950s and recognized as "neglected by the poohbahs of literary officialdom," and novelist Richard Ford has recalled hitchhiking in the snow from Ann Arbor to Kalamazoo to hear Algren read in 1973.[12]

More significantly, Don DeLillo has suggested Algren's role in his formation as a novelist when he writes that Algren's work "extended the reach of [James T. Farrell's] Studs Lonigan trilogy, which was probably the first fiction I'd ever read that suggested that environments similar to my own . . . might produce material suitable for books." This is a point echoed by John Sayles, who recalls that Algren "jump-started" him as a writer simply because the fact of Algren's existence, and "the existence of [his] characters, the spirit of them, open[ed] up a possibility" in Sayle's mind. Chicago writer Stuart Dybek has written, "I don't think I ever quite looked at the city in the same way after reading *The Man with the Golden Arm*. All the attitudes one acquires without reflecting—acquires from street life itself—that permit a certain numbness toward the daily downtrodden . . . were called into question. Each had a story, meaning each had a soul."[13]

Algren, writes Rick Hornung in a 1990 reappraisal of Algren's accomplishment, "warned us of the society we'd created. No one listened, but he knew his novels were true and would come true."[14] Consequently, Algren remains a writer—like Richard Brautigan or Charles Bukowski—read most intently not by students, their teachers, or professional critics but by those to whom such hard truths matter. This man who was a tangle of contradictions—a Jew who kept silent about the Holocaust, who created empathetic portraits of women in his fiction yet could turn around and treat flesh-and-blood women shamefully, who raged against Simone de Beauvoir for years for having written about their affair yet kept her letters to him safe in a box in his home until the day he died—made himself a voice for the voiceless, a "conscience in touch with humanity."[15] He was a humorist of horrors, a sentimentalist of life's brutalities. He drank with the famous and dated actresses but never stopped writing of marginal Americans, accused or unaccused, eventually becoming himself one of the trapped and broken, the onetime giant of American letters whom Hemingway once ranked second only to Faulkner but who spent the last twenty years of his life doing mostly little deals.

Although he was fond of remarking dismissively that "every serious writer is interested only in expressing himself. He doesn't really care what the reaction is," Algren never stopped believing that literature was an occasion "to make a fight of whatever is left you of truth."[16] Speaking at a 1957 roundtable at Chicago's Roosevelt University, Algren insisted that Americans are no different from any other people in believing they are "the wisest, and the healthiest, and the happiest" who ever lived, and that this happy state of affairs would last forever. Yet he then imagined "one dissenting voice from under the floorboards" and concluded, "Time, it seems, has always been on the side of that voice."[17]

When the man Simone de Beauvoir described as "that classic American species: the self-made-leftist-writer" was buried in a whalers' cemetery in Sag Harbor, Long Island, his headstone arrived with his name misspelled. Algren would doubtless have found this amusing, and it did not matter anyway. The work remains, and in that work Algren had already written about how he wanted to be remembered:

Conclusion / 155

I'll be alright . . . though you look on the doorbell in the hall and find my name isn't there anymore. I'll be alright so long as it has been written on some cornerstone of a human heart.

On the heart it don't matter how you spell it.[18]

Notes

Chapter One—Understanding Nelson Algren

1. Art Shay, *Nelson Algren's Chicago: Photographs* (Urbana: University of Illinois Press, 1988), xvi.

2. The description belongs to Christopher Lasch, *The Culture of Narcissism: American Life in an Age of Diminished Expectations* (New York: W. W. Norton, 1979).

3. H. E. F. Donohue, *Conversations with Nelson Algren* (New York: Hill and Wang, 1964), 151; Leonard Cohen, "Democracy," *Stranger Music: Selected Poems and Songs* (New York: Pantheon, 1993), 369.

4. Donohue, *Conversations with Nelson Algren*, 94, 279; Algren, afterword to *Chicago: City on the Make*, Fiftieth Anniversary Edition, ed. David Schmittgens and Bill Savage (Chicago: University of Chicago Press, 2001), 81, 83.

5. The understanding of the biblical prophet's function articulated here comes from Walter Brueggemann, *The Prophetic Imagination* (Philadelphia: Fortress Press, 1978).

6. The indispensable source for biographical information about Algren is Bettina Drew, *Nelson Algren: A Life on the Wild Side* (New York: G. P. Putnam's Sons, 1989). Firsthand information can also be found scattered throughout the nonfiction and in Donohue, *Conversations with Nelson Algren*.

7. Quoted in Bettina Drew, "Introduction to the Texas Stories," *The Texas Stories of Nelson Algren*, ed. Bettina Drew (Austin: University of Texas Press, 1995), x.

8. In her biography, Bettina Drew writes that "a notation in [Algren's] not always accurate FBI file suggests he may have been associated with the Communist Youth League as early as 1931" (34). Herbert Mitgang, who obtained the dossiers of more than fifty writers through the Freedom of Information Act, reports that Algren's FBI file ran to 546 pages (including information supplied by army

and navy intelligence as well as by the state department), making it larger than the file of any other American writer surveilled by the FBI. See "Annals of Government: Policing America's Writers," *New Yorker,* October 5, 1987, 47 passim (material on Algren: 74, 76).

9. Algren later explained that the initial contact with Vanguard Press had been nothing more than a form letter. See Jim Gallagher, "Literary 'Exile' Is Pleasant for Algren," *Chicago Tribune,* March 29, 1977, sec. 2.

10. Walter B. Rideout, *The Radical Novel in the United States 1900–1954* (Cambridge: Harvard University Press, 1956), 287.

11. Malcolm Cowley, "Chicago Poem," review of *Never Come Morning,* by Algren, *New Republic,* May 4, 1942, 614; Ernest Hemingway quoted in Drew, *Nelson Algren: A Life on the Wild Side,* 143.

12. There is confusion among Algren scholars regarding when he entered the army, many giving 1942 as the year. However, his military service record (a copy of which can be found in the Algren archive at Ohio State University) indicates that Algren entered into active service on August 6, 1943.

13. "The Brothers' House" and "A Bottle of Milk for Mother" won O. Henry Awards in 1935 and 1941, respectively. "A Bottle of Milk," reprinted as "Biceps," was included in *The Best American Short Stories 1942,* ed. Martha Foley (Boston: Houghton Mifflin, 1942), and "How the Devil Came Down Division Street" was included in *The Best American Short Stories 1945,* ed. Martha Foley (Boston: Houghton Mifflin, 1946).

14. Maxwell Geismar, *American Moderns: From Rebellion to Conformity* (New York: Hill and Wang, 1958), 190; Tom Carson, introduction to *The Neon Wilderness,* by Algren (New York: Seven Stories Press, 1986), 7.

15. Drew, *Nelson Algren: A Life on the Wild Side,* 209; Stuart Brent, *The Seven Stairs* (Boston: Houghton Mifflin, 1962), 43.

16. Ernest Hemingway quoted in Drew, *Nelson Algren: A Life on the Wild Side,* 210.

17. Donohue, *Conversations with Nelson Algren*, 143.

18. Algren's affair with de Beauvoir lasted only four years although the two remained close by fits and starts (she was buried wearing his ring); their relationship strained when de Beauvoir fictionalized the affair in her best-selling novel of 1956, *The Mandarins*. More serious damage was done when, in 1965, the third volume of de Beauvoir's autobiography, *The Force of Circumstance (La force des choses)*, appeared with its unflattering analysis of the affair. Algren counterattacked with reviews in *Ramparts* (October 1965) and *Harper's* (May 1965) and an interview with *Newsweek* wherein he charged "Madame Yackety-Yack" with "fantasizing a relationship in the manner of a middle-aged spinster" ("I Ain't Abelard," *Newsweek*, December 28, 1964, 58–59). Sartre was France's premier postwar intellectual. Novelist and playwright, existential philosopher and Marxist, Sartre helped translate *Never Come Morning* and parts of *Chicago: City on the Make* into French.

19. Donohue, *Conversations with Nelson Algren*, 144, 288.

20. John William Corrington, "Nelson Algren Talks with NOR's Editor-at-Large," *New Orleans Review* 1 (Winter 1969): 130.

21. Norman Podhoretz, "The Man with the Golden Beef," review of *A Walk on the Wild Side*, by Algren, *New Yorker*, June 2, 1956, 132, 134, 137–39; Leslie Fiedler, "The Noble Savages of Skid Row," review of *A Walk on the Wild Side*, by Algren, *Reporter*, July 12, 1956, 43–44; Ralph J. Gleason, "Perspectives: Is It Out of Control?" *Rolling Stone*, August 6, 1970, 9.

22. Alston Anderson and Terry Southern, "Nelson Algren," *Writers at Work: The "Paris Review" Interviews*, ed. Malcolm Cowley (New York: Viking Press, 1960), 241.

23. Sheldon Norman Grebstein, "Nelson Algren and the Whole Truth," *The Forties: Fiction, Poetry, Drama*, ed. Warren French (Deland: Everett/Edwards, 1969), 299.

24. Hilton Kramer, "He Never Left Home," review of *Who Lost an American?* by Algren, *Reporter* June 20, 1963, 47; Conrad Knickerbocker, "Scraping the Barnacles off Papa," review of *Notes*

from a Sea Diary, by Algren, *Book Week,* August 15, 1965, 3. Reviews of *The Last Carousel,* which sold well, were largely positive: although Sal Maloff in *New Republic* complained about Algren's "overblown . . . lyricism" and dated prose style ("Maverick in American Letters," January 19, 1974, 23), Van Allen Bradley thought the book contained "some of [Algren's] finest writing" and "superbly [bespoke] the social consciousness, the acute perceptions, the infinite understanding and compassion of Algren as novelist and human being" ("'Last Carousel': His Best Book in 20 Years," *Chicago Daily News Panorama,* October 27–28, 1973, 3). James R. Frakes cheered the appearance of a new book by a writer "as sure-footed and fast off the mark as Nelson Algren" ("Something of Algren for Everyone," *New York Times Book Review,* November 11, 1973, 20).

25. The American Academy had in 1974 awarded Algren its prestigious Medal of Merit while neglecting to make him a member —further proof for Algren that, the award notwithstanding, he was not wanted.

26. The description a "documentary" novelist comes from Geismar, *American Moderns,* 192.

27. The writers Algren most admired were Louis-Ferdinand Céline, Anton Chekhov, Joseph Conrad, Charles Dickens, Fyodor Dostoyevsky, Ernest Hemingway, Henrik Ibsen, Franz Kafka, Alexander Kuprin, Jean-Paul Sartre, and Richard Wright. His heroes included socialist Eugene V. Debs, jurist Learned Hand, lawyer Clarence Darrow, and reformist governor John Peter Altgeld (Illinois, 1893–97).

28. Anderson and Southern, "Nelson Algren," 248.

29. Algren, preface to *Somebody in Boots* (New York: Berkley Medallion, 1965), 9.

30. See Studs Terkel, afterword to *The Neon Wilderness,* by Algren (New York: Seven Stories Press, 1986), 292–93.

31. Brent, *The Seven Stairs,* 39–40.

Chapter Two—Early Work and *Somebody in Boots*

1. Alston Anderson and Terry Southern, "Nelson Algren," *Writers at Work: The "Paris Review" Interviews,* ed. Malcolm Cowley (New York: Viking Press, 1958), 242.

2. Algren, "'Politics' in Southern Illinois," *New Republic,* August 1, 1934, 307.

3. Algren, "Call for an American Writers' Congress," *New Masses,* January 22, 1935, 20.

4. Algren, "For the Homeless Youth of America," *Masses* 12 (March–April 1934): 4.

5. Algren, "Within the City," *Anvil* 3 (October–November 1935): 8–9; "American Obituary," *Partisan Review* 2 (October–November 1935): 26–27.

6. Algren, "Holiday in Texas," *Anvil* 6 (May–June 1934): 23–26; reprinted in *The Texas Stories of Nelson Algren,* ed. Bettina Drew (Austin: University of Texas Press, 1995), 35–43. Parenthetical references are to *The Texas Stories.*

7. Algren does not identify the songs whose lyrics he quotes in this story, but they are "Dreary Black Hills," an old mining-camp song; "Hallelujah, I'm a Bum"; "Old Chisholm Trail"; and the Communist anthem "The Comintern."

8. Algren, "Lest the Traplock Click," *Calithump* 1 (June 1934): 21–30; reprinted in *The Texas Stories of Nelson Algren,* 5. Parenthetical references are to *The Texas Stories.*

9. Algren, "A Lumpen," *New Masses,* July 2, 1935, 25–26.

10. Algren, "So Help Me," *Story* 3 (August 1933): 3–14; reprinted in *The Texas Stories of Nelson Algren* and in *The Neon Wilderness* (New York: Seven Stories Press, 1986). Parenthetical references are to *The Neon Wilderness.* On anti-Semitism, Algren would write in the notebook kept while in jail in Alpine, Texas, that there were "two ways of cursing one unlike yourself: call him 'Jew'; call him 'fool.' I am alone, I am a Jew, in all the world I have no

home" (quoted in Bettina Drew, *Nelson Algren: A Life on the Wild Side*, 71–72). Although Jewish characters command center stage only in the story "Million-Dollar Brainstorm" (*Neon Wilderness*), Jews appear often in Algren's work: Creepy Edelbaum (*Somebody in Boots*); Snipes (*Never Come Morning*); Wolfe, Tiny Zion, and Sheeny McCoy (*Neon Wilderness*); Solly "Sparrow" Saltskin (*The Man with the Golden Arm*).

11. Algren, "Forgive Them, Lord," *A Year Magazine* 2 (December 1933–April 1934): 148. Parenthetical references are to this publication.

12. Algren, "The Brothers' House," *Story* 5 (October 1934): 22–25; reprinted in *The Neon Wilderness*. Parenthetical references are to *Neon Wilderness*.

13. Algren, *Somebody in Boots* (New York: Vanguard Press, 1935), n.p. Parenthetical references are to this edition. The novel is currently out of print; it was most recently available in paperback from Thunder's Mouth Press (New York, 1987).

14. Walter B. Rideout, *The Radical Novel in the United States 1900–1954* (Cambridge: Harvard University Press, 1956), 287; Maxwell Geismar, *American Moderns: From Rebellion to Conformity* (New York: Hill and Wang, 1958), 188.

15. Algren, preface to *Somebody in Boots* (New York: Berkley Medallion, 1965), 8–9.

16. Quoted in Drew, *Nelson Algren: A Life on the Wild Side*, 77.

17. See, for instance, Ian Peddie, "Poles Apart? Ethnicity, Race, Class, and Nelson Algren," *Modern Fiction Studies* 47 (Spring 2001): 118–44, and the concluding chapter of William J. Maxwell, *New Negro, Old Left: African-American Writing and Communism between the Wars* (New York: Columbia University Press, 1999).

18. Jon Christian Suggs, "The Proletarian Novel," *Dictionary of Literary Biography*, vol. 9, ed. James J. Martine (Detroit: Gale Research Company, 1981), 238.

19. Suggs, "The Proletarian Novel," 240.

20. Mary Ellen Lease quoted in Allen Nevins and Henry Steele Commager, *A Short History of the United States,* Modern Library edition (New York: Random House, 1945), 378. Scripture from Psalms 9:18. Regarding the Gospels, see for instance Luke 13:30: "behold, there are last which shall be first, and there are first which shall be last."

Chapter Three—The WPA, Early Poems, and *Never Come Morning*

1. Algren, afterword to *Somebody in Boots* (New York: Berkley Medallion, 1965), 256.

2. The *Galena Guide* was one of many such guides produced as part of the "American Guide Series." There is disagreement among scholars regarding the extent of Algren's involvement with this project. Algren may have written eight of the guide's brief chapters—as a copy annotated by Algren now in the possession of the Ohio State University library suggests—or only one chapter, as a second Algren-annotated copy, now owned by Kent State University libraries, indicates. The chapter Algren seems likeliest to have written, "A Middle-Aged Clerk in a Faded Army Coat," concerns the arrival of Ulysses S. Grant in Galena to help run one of his father's stores until the Civil War recalled him to the army. See Dean H. Keller, "Nelson Algren and the *Galena Guide,*" *Serif* 8, no. 3 (September 1971): 33–34; Matthew Bruccoli, "A Further Note on the *Galena Guide,*" *Serif* 9, no. 3 (Fall 1972): 47; and Robert A. Tibbetts, "Nelson Algren and the *Galena Guide:* A Further Note," *Serif* 9, no. 3 (Fall 1972): 48. See also Bettina Drew, *Nelson Algren: A Life on the Wild Side,* 105–6. The other projects mentioned are described in Drew, *Nelson Algren: A Life on the Wild Side,* 105, 109. One Algren-authored tall tale, "Hank, the Free Wheeler," was included in *A Treasury of American Folklore,* ed. B. A. Botkin (New York: Crown Publishers, 1944), 540–42. The story, polished to conform to the conventions of the tall tale, tells of the life and death of

an entrepreneur addicted to speed, efficiency, and automation. The Revolutionary War essay, "Salomon and Morris: Two Patriots of the Revolution," can be read in part in Kenneth G. McCollum, *Neson Algren: A Checklist* (Detroit: Gale Research Company, 1973), 87–107.

3. Algren, *America Eats*, Iowa Szathmáry Culinary Arts series, ed. David E. Schoonover (Iowa City: University of Iowa Press, 1992), 1. Further references are noted parenthetically.

4. Algren, "How Long Blues," *Poetry: A Magazine of Verse*, September 1941, 309; "Local South," *Poetry: A Magazine of Verse*, September 1941, 308–9; "Home and Goodnight" and "Travelog," *Poetry: A Magazine of Verse*, November 1939, 74–77; "Makers of Music," *New Anvil*, April–May 1939, 23.

5. Algren, "This Table on Time Only," *Esquire*, March 1940, 78–79; "The Swede Was a Hard Guy," *Southern Review* 7, no. 4 (1942): 873–79; "Utility Magnate," *New Anvil*, April–May 1939, 16–17; "Program for Appeasement," *New Anvil*, April–May 1939, 12. Perhaps because Algren was listed as managing editor for the issue of *New Anvil* in which "Utility Magnate" appeared, the poem was published under the pseudonym "Lawrence O'Fallon."

6. Algren, "Cinematic Novel of Life in the Carolinas," review of *Men of Albemarle*, by Inglis Fletcher, *Chicago Sun Book Week*, November 1, 1942, 31; omnibus poetry review, *Poetry: A Magazine of Verse*, January 1942, 221.

7. Carla Cappetti, *Writing Chicago: Modernism, Ethnography and the Novel* (New York: Columbia University Press, 1993), 168. Botkin is quoted by Cappetti on 168.

8. "Staff Conference in Industrial Folklore," "American Life Histories: Manuscripts from the Federal Writers' Project, 1936–1940," *American Memory: Historical Collections for the National Digital Library*, Library of Congress, February 21, 2003, http://memory.loc.gov (search "Algren"), September 30, 2003. Interestingly, when Algren applied (unsuccessfully) for a Guggenheim Foundation grant in 1940 to help fund the writing of *Never Come*

Morning, he emphasized his data-gathering skills (mentioning plans to gather material in "churches, poolrooms, taverns," and elsewhere) and personal contacts with prison inmates, social workers, policemen, and "an indicted alderman." He termed his approach the employment of "the methods of naturalism" (quoted in Drew, *Nelson Algren: A Life on the Wild Side,* 117).

9. This example is taken from Cappetti, *Writing Chicago,* 165–66. The interview with the prostitute is from an unpublished manuscript, "When You Live Like I Done," archived with the Federal Writers' Project files in the Library of Congress. The passage from *Never Come Morning* is on page 182 (New York: Seven Stories Press, 1996). Parenthetical references are to this edition. The novel, which has been often reprinted since first published in 1942, was translated into French by Jean-Paul Sartre as well as into more than a dozen other languages. The first edition contained an introduction by Richard Wright, and the 1963 Harper-Colophon paperback edition contained a preface by Algren (also included in the Seven Stories edition).

10. Chester E. Eisinger, *Fiction of the Forties* (Chicago: University of Chicago Press, Phoenix Books, 1963), 77.

11. For James R. Giles, Algren's prose is of such probing and nuanced complexity that it moves the novel beyond literary naturalism into existential questions of how *anyone* can create an authentic self and a meaningful life; see *Confronting the Horror: The Novels of Nelson Algren* (Kent: Kent State University Press, 1989), chapter 4.

12. Ernest Hemingway to his editor Maxwell Perkins, July 8, 1942, quoted in Drew, *Nelson Algren: A Life on the Wild Side,* 143.

13. Malcolm Cowley, "Chicago Poem," review of *Never Come Morning,* by Algren, *New Republic,* May 4, 1942, 613–14; Benjamin Appel, "People of Crime," review of *Never Come Morning,* by Algren, *Saturday Review of Literature,* April 18, 1942, 7.

14. James T. Farrell quoted in Drew, *Nelson Algren: A Life on the Wild Side,* 143; Philip Rahv, "No Parole," review of *Never Come Morning,* by Algren, *Nation,* April 18, 1942, 466–67.

15. Algren, preface to *Never Come Morning* (New York: Seven Stories Press, 1996), xv. In light of Algren's WPA interest in documentary realism, it is worth noting that he called the novel "a thinly fictionalized report on a neighborhood" and on "the lives of half a dozen men with whom the writer had grown up, as well as upon newspaper reports of the trial of Bernard 'Knifey' Sawicki" (xv). Sawicki, from whom Algren got the final words spoken by Bruno in the novel, was a nineteen-year-old who went on a killing spree in the summer of 1941; see Drew, *Nelson Algren: A Life on the Wild Side*, 134–35.

16. *Never Come Morning* is vague when locating present action in time. Many allusions can be dated to the second half of the 1930s (for example, Benny Goodman's 1937 hit "I'm a Ding Dong Daddy from Dumas"), but a reference to *Superman* comics, which began publication in the summer of 1939, suggests the story probably begins in the autumn of 1938 and concludes in November of the next year.

17. Algren, preface, xvi.

18. John Clellon Holmes, "Arm: A Memoir," *Representative Men: The Biographical Essays*, vol. 2 (Fayetteville: University of Arkansas Press, 1988); reprinted in *The Man with the Golden Arm*, Fiftieth Anniversary Critical Edition, ed. William J. Savage Jr. and Daniel Simon (New York: Seven Stories Press, 1999), 351–52.

Chapter Four—*The Neon Wilderness*

1. Algren, "Frontier History Takes on Semblance of a Road Show," review of *Sun in Their Eyes*, by Monte Barrett, *Chicago Daily News*, October 25, 1944, 24; "Satire on a Labor Hating Uplifter," review of *Gideon Planish*, by Sinclair Lewis, *Chicago Sun Book Week*, April 25, 1943, 2; "From Locusts and Tax Collectors to The Happy Land," review of *Syrian Yankee*, by Salom Rizk, *Chicago Sun Book Week*, January 24, 1943, 4.

2. Algren, "With Scruples as a Luxury," review of *Angry Dust*, by Dorothy Stockbridge, *Chicago Sun Book Week*, November 24,

1946, 27; "Small Things Turn Lyrical in Boy's Eyes," review of *Blue Boy*, by Jean Giono, *Chicago Daily News*, April 10, 1946, 3; "When G.I. Joe Comes Home, Will He Fit as a Civilian?" review of *They Dream of Home*, by Niven Busch, *Chicago Daily News*, December 27, 1944, 9.

3. Algren, "A Social Poet," review of *For My People*, by Margaret Walker, *Poetry: A Magazine of Verse*, February 1943, 635; "Literary Pen Balks Chance for Tragedy," review of *The Lost Men*, by Benedict Thielen, *Chicago Daily News*, May 1, 1946, 32; "Weariness, Danger and Pain," review of *The Voice of the Trumpet*, by Robert Henriques, *Chicago Sun Book Week*, March 14, 1943, 5.

4. Algren, "Do It the Hard Way," *Writer* 56, no. 3 (March 1943): 69, 68, 67.

5. "So Help Me" and "The Brothers' House" are discussed in chapter 2. Of the twenty-two remaining stories, six had previously appeared in periodicals: "A Bottle of Milk for Mother" (as "Biceps") (1941), "Stickman's Laughter" (1942), "He Swung and He Missed" (1942), "The Children" (1943), "How the Devil Came Down Division Street" (1944), and "The Face on the Barroom Floor," which appeared in *American Mercury* the month *Neon Wilderness* was released. Also worth mentioning is a 1947 story omitted from the book: "Single Exit," *Cross Section 1947: A Collection of New American Writing*, ed. Edwin Seaver (New York: Simon and Schuster, 1947), 217–24. In this story, a poor man in bed with his wife and child in their roach-infested one-room apartment dreams that he arises and leaves his family to enter a tavern at closing time, joining the sole remaining patron, a woman unknown to him, and revealing to her that he is naked beneath his coat. Awaking from his dream, the man lies brooding upon betrayal and cursing "his own humanity."

6. These interpretations are offered by John Woodburn, "People of the Abyss," review of *The Neon Wilderness*, by Algren, *New York Times Book Review*, February 2, 1947, 16; Catherine Meredith Brown, "Chicago without Tears or Dreams," review of *The Neon Wilderness*, by Algren, *Saturday Review*, February 8, 1947,

14; and George Bluestone, "Nelson Algren," *Western Review* 22 (Autumn 1957): 33–35.

7. Quoted in Algren, *The Neon Wilderness* (New York: Seven Stories Press, 1986), 15. Parenthetical references are to this edition. "David Wolff" was the pen name of Ben Maddow (see chapter 5, note 10). Translated into several languages, *The Neon Wilderness* went through three editions and various printings from its initial publication through the 1960s; the Seven Stories reissue is the first in many years. Two stories—"A Bottle of Milk for Mother" and "How the Devil Came Down Division Street"—have been frequently anthologized.

8. Lengthy line-up scenes occur in "The Captain Is a Card" (*Esquire*, June 1942), which was recycled in *Never Come Morning*, and "The Captain Is Impaled" (*Harper's*, August 1949), which was recycled in *The Man with the Golden Arm*.

9. Algren, introduction to *The Neon Wilderness* (New York: Hill and Wang, 1960), 14.

10. Substantially revised, this story was incorporated into book 2 of *Never Come Morning*.

11. The story bears virtually no resemblance to Hugh Antoine d'Arcy's famous 1887 poem with the same title.

12. A comparison of "Design for Departure" with Margaret Widdemer's poem "Modern Hymn for Grief," *Hill Garden* (New York: Farrar and Rinehart, 1936), reveals that, in addition to those techniques discussed in "Do It the Hard Way," Algren also found inspiration in other texts—details from which he was not hesitant to appropriate.

13. Algren, "The Sad Amphibia," review of *The Sleep of Baby Filbertson and Other Stories*, by James Leo Herlihy, *Nation*, January 31, 1959, 105–6. In an unpublished, undated essay, "The Chevalier of Vain Regrets," Algren again emphasizes the importance of humor to truth-telling, arguing that Ring Lardner is a better writer than Sherwood Anderson because, in part, Lardner, confronted by the corruption of early-twentieth-century America, knew

how to "put an antic disposition on" ("Miscellaneous Manuscripts," Midwest Manuscript Collection, Newberry Library, Chicago).

14. Studs Terkel, afterword to *The Neon Wilderness*, by Algren (New York: Seven Stories Press, 1986), 289.

15. Jack Conroy, "Tenderness and Skill in Nelson Algren's Writing," review of *The Neon Wilderness*, by Algren, *Chicago Sun Book Week*, February 2, 1947, 2; Charles Poore, "Books of the Times," review of *The Neon Wilderness*, by Algren, *New York Times*, January 25, 1947, 15.

16. John Woodburn, "People of the Abyss," review of *The Neon Wilderness*, by Algren, *New York Times Book Review*, February 2, 1947, 16; Catherine Meredith Brown, "Chicago without Tears or Dreams," review of *The Neon Wilderness*, by Algren, *Saturday Review of Literature*, February 8, 1947, 14.

17. Kurt Vonnegut Jr., introduction to *Never Come Morning*, by Algren (New York: Seven Stories Press, 1996), xx.

18. Algren, "Dreiser's Despair Reaffirmed in 'The Stoic,'" review of *The Stoic*, by Theodore Dreiser, *Philadelphia Inquirer*, November 23, 1947, 3; "Johnny Comes Marching Home," review of *Blue City*, by Kenneth Millar, *Philadelphia Inquirer*, August 17, 1947, 4.

19. Algren, "Author Bites Critic," review of *Man in Modern Fiction*, by Edmund Fuller, *Nation*, August 2, 1958, 57. It is perhaps worth noting that nowhere does Fuller directly say anything as specific about Algren's work as Algren would lead readers to believe.

Chapter Five—*The Man with the Golden Arm*

1. Algren, "Epitaph: The Man with the Golden Arm," *Poetry*, September 1947, 316–17.

2. Stagolee (or Stackerlee), John Henry, and Willie the Weeper are perhaps less well known than Billy the Kid unless the reader is also an aficionado of American folk music: John Hardy was "a desperate little man" who "carried two guns every day" and whose song tells of how he ran away after murdering a man; Stagolee was a homicidal "bad man" ("when you lose your money, learn to

lose"); Willie was a chimney sweeper and dope fiend ("he had the habit, boy, he had it bad"). Verse extract from Algren, *The Man with the Golden Arm* (New York: Seven Stories Press, 1996), 343. Parenthetical references are to this edition (pagination of which corresponds to that of the first edition). *The Man with the Golden Arm* has been frequently reprinted and reissued. The edition used here is a reissue of the 1990 edition from Four Walls Eight Windows Press. In 1999, Seven Stories released a Fiftieth Anniversary Critical Edition that is still available. The novel has also been translated into several languages, including French, German, Italian, Japanese, Portuguese, Spanish, and Serbo-Croatian. An excerpt from the novel, "The Captain Is Impaled," appeared in *Harper's* (August 1949).

3. See Bettina Drew, *Nelson Algren: A Life on the Wild Side* (New York: G. P. Putnam's Sons, 1989), 174–75, for details on Algren's growing literary acclaim following the publication of *The Neon Wilderness*.

4. Drew, *Nelson Algren: A Life on the Wild Side*, 190, 199.

5. "Letter to Joe Haas," in William J. Savage and Daniel Simon, eds., *The Man with the Golden Arm*, Fiftieth Anniversary Critical Edition (New York: Seven Stories Press, 1999), 345–47.

6. Drew, *Nelson Algren: A Life on the Wild Side*, 188.

7. H. E. F. Donohue, *Conversations with Nelson Algren* (New York: Hill and Wang, 1964), 144.

8. Drew, *Nelson Algren: A Life on the Wild Side*, 198, 203.

9. George Bluestone has argued that Algren's novels are punctuated by "frozen" moments "like a series of stills," digressions whose point is their pointlessness insofar as, in a novelistic world in which love is all that matters but is always betrayed, there is nothing to tell between betrayal and the destruction of the betrayer. See "Nelson Algren," *Western Review* 22 (Autumn 1957): 27–44.

10. Algren, "Laughter in Jars—Not as Sandburg Wrote of It: Two Poems Show How Chicago Has Changed," *Chicago Sun Book Week,* July 20, 1947, 2. The poem is "The City" by David Wolff

(Ben Maddow), *Poetry,* January 1940. See Jeff McMahon, "Nelson Algren's Secret: The True Story Behind 'City on the Make,'" January 29, 2003, *Newcitychicago.com,* http://www.newcitychicago.com/chicago/2230, August 27, 2003.

11. Algren, *Nonconformity: Writing on Writing,* ed. Daniel Simon (New York: Seven Stories Press, 1996), 48.

12. William J. Savage, "The Quality of Laughter: Algren's Challenge to the Reader," *The Man with the Golden Arm,* Fiftieth Anniversary Critical Edition, ed. William J. Savage Jr. and Daniel Simon (New York: Seven Stories Press, 1999), 417–22.

13. Compare Romans 12:5: "So we, being many, are one body in Christ, and every one members one of another."

14. Donohue, *Conversations with Nelson Algren,* 274. My definition of *sentimentality* is adapted from William Harmon and C. Hugh Holman, *A Handbook to Literature,* 7th ed. (Upper Saddle River, N.J.: Prentice Hall, 1996), 474–75.

15. Asked by H. E. F. Donohue if he was an atheist, Algren offered a simple "yeah" (*Conversations with Nelson Algren,* 159).

16. R. W. Lid, "A World Imagined: The Art of Nelson Algren," *American Literary Naturalism: A Reassessment,* ed. Yoshinobu Hakutani and Lewis Fried (Heidelberg: Carl Winter, 1975), 188; James A. Lewin, "Algren's Outcasts: Shakespearean Fools and the Prophet in a Neon Wilderness," *MidAmerica* 18 (1991): 110.

17. Matthew 25:40, Luke 12:6.

18. Mark 12:31, 1 John 4:20.

19. Ernest Hemingway quoted in Drew, *Nelson Algren: A Life on the Wild Side,* 210.

20. Review of *The Man with the Golden Arm,* by Algren, *New Yorker,* September 17, 1949, 98; "The Lower Depths," review of *The Man with the Golden Arm,* by Algren, *Time,* September 12, 1949, 106.

21. Hollis Alpert, "Fallen Angels," review of *The Man with the Golden Arm,* by Algren, *Saturday Review of Literature,* October 8, 1949, 22–23; A. C. Spectorsky, "Saloon Street, Chicago," review of

The Man with the Golden Arm, by Algren, *New York Times Book Review,* September 11, 1949, 8.

22. Carlo Rotella, *October Cities: The Redevelopment of Urban Literature* (Berkeley: University of California Press, 1998); Barry Miles, *William Burroughs: El Hombre Invisible* (New York: Hyperion, 1993), 57; Howard Zinn, E-mail to the author, September 1, 2003.

Chapter Six—*Chicago: City on the Make* and
                      Nonconformity: Writing on Writing

1. For a full account of the essay's history and editing, see Daniel Simon, afterword to *Nonconformity: Writing on Writing,* by Algren (New York: Seven Stories Press, 1996), 98–102; and also Bettina Drew, *Nelson Algren: A Life on the Wild Side* (New York: G. P. Putnam's Sons, 1989), chapter 15. It should be noted that excerpts from the manuscript-in-progress did find their way into print. The *Chicago Daily News* published a brief excerpt ("Great Writing Bogged down in Fear, Says Novelist Algren," December 3, 1952) that was reprinted in *Nation* (as "American Christmas, 1952" [December 27, 1952]). *Nation* also published two additional selections: "Hollywood Djinn with a Dash of Bitters" (July 25, 1953) and "Eggheads Are Rolling: The Rush to Conform" (October 17, 1953). In 1952 Algren published "Things of the Earth: A Groundhog View," *California Quarterly* 2 (Autumn 1952): 3–11, a condensed version of *Nonconformity*.

2. See, for instance, "Authors Defend Open Letter," *New York Times,* May 24, 1948, 18 (a public letter signed by thirty-two American artists protesting a United Press report on an exchange of letters between American and Soviet artists calling for world peace), and "What Are You Doing Out There?" *New York Times,* January 15, 1951, 9 (open letter calling on Americans to take a stand for freedom of thought and expression).

3. Budd Schulberg, "Heartbeat of a City," review of *Chicago,* by Algren, *New York Times Book Review,* October 21, 1951, 3.

4. *Chicago: City on the Make,* Fiftieth Anniversary ed., annotated by David Schmittgens and Bill Savage (Chicago: University of Chicago Press, 2001), 16, 22, 64. Parenthetical references are to this edition. The pagination of this edition matches that of the 1983 McGraw-Hill edition and the 1987 reprinting of that edition by the University of Chicago Press. Following the appearance of a version of the essay in the travel magazine *Holiday*—entitled "One Man's Chicago" by the magazine's surprised but contractually obligated editors (October 1951)—*Chicago* was published in book format in 1951 by Doubleday and has seen five editions and several reprintings by various presses over the years. Algren added an introduction to the second edition (Contact Editions, 1961) and changed the dedication. The 1968 edition (published by Angel Island) included photographs by Stephen Deutch, a new dedication, and, as epilogue, the twenty-nine-page poem "Ode to Lower Finksville" (entitled "Ode to Kissassville or: Gone on the Arfy-Darfy" in one hundred copies printed for Algren's use). The fourth edition, published by McGraw-Hill and reprinted by the University of Chicago Press, added an introduction by Studs Terkel. The Fiftieth Anniversary edition retains the Terkel introduction, moves Algren's 1961 introduction to book's end as an afterword, and adds a preface, twenty-two pages of notes, and a bibliography.

5. Carlo Rotella, *October Cities: The Redevelopment of Urban Literature* (Berkeley: University of California Press, 1998); see especially 20–25 and 35–38.

6. The reason is not only to move the reader but to invest the author emotionally and personally in his subject matter. As Algren argues in *Nonconformity,* an "accurate ear" and a "retentive" memory may produce the "stenographic fidelity" of the journalistic report (*Nonconformity,* 26–27) but by themselves do not communicate the sorts of truths that matter.

7. On the prose poem as a means of saying the unsayable, see Brooke Horvath, "Why the Prose Poem?" *Denver Quarterly* 25, no. 4 (Spring 1991): 105–15.

8. Algren, "Matters of Manhood," review of *Summer Street*, by Hal Ellson, *Saturday Review*, July 25, 1953, 15.

9. Geismar quoted by Daniel Simon, afterword to *Nonconformity*, 101.

10. "'Truth Will Be Known in Time'—Rosenbergs," *Daily Worker*, March 3, 1952, 3.

11. *Nonconformity: Writing on Writing*, ed. Daniel Simon (New York: Seven Stories Press, 1996), 4. Parenthetical references are to this edition.

12. Algren acknowledges that one need not be socioeconomically disadvantaged to number among the lost, noting that there are people everywhere "so submerged emotionally that they are unable to belong to the world in which they live," and that consequently it is "possible to live underground even while skiing at Aspen" (42). This is the fate, he feels, of the young in great numbers and a fact that explained many social ills, including the rise of drug addiction.

13. David Riesman et al., *The Lonely Crowd: A Study of the Changing American Character* (New Haven: Yale University Press, 1950).

14. Simon, afterword to *Nonconformity*, 103.

15. Debs quoted in Algren, *Chicago: City on the Make*, 128.

Chapter Seven—*A Walk on the Wild Side*

1. Bettina Drew, *Nelson Algren: A Life on the Wild Side* (New York: G. P. Putnam's Sons, 1989), 237.

2. Drew, *Nelson Algren: A Life on the Wild Side*, 225.

3. Algren to Brand, quoted in Drew, *Nelson Algren: A Life on the Wild Side*, 253; $8,200 in debt: Drew, *Nelson Algren: A Life on the Wild Side*, 271. Algren's money problems were the result of a combination of factors. He was gambling heavily, and he was engaged in legal battles related to the filming of *The Man with the Golden Arm*, challenging what he had been paid for the rights to his book and his percentage of the movie's profits as well as producer-director Otto

Preminger's advertising of the movie as "a film by Otto Preminger." Additionally, Amanda Kontowicz, whom Algren had divorced in 1946, remarried in 1953, and sued for divorce in 1955, had countersued and been awarded $7,000 (Drew, *Nelson Algren: A Life on the Wild Side*, 273).

4. Algren and de Beauvoir first met through a mutual acquaintance when she visited America in 1947. Although the relationship lasted for years, their love affair, hampered by the fact that the two were apart more than they were together, was over by the mid-1950s. Distance, differing expectations (and attitudes toward the possibility of taking other lovers when apart), de Beauvoir's refusal to leave Paris, and Algren's reluctance to relocate to France caused the affair to flounder.

5. Thomas Hill Schaub, *American Fiction in the Cold War* (Madison: University of Wisconsin Press, 1991). What happened to American literature and its criticism during the cold war is a complicated story. In brief, as Schaub tells it, Marx gave way to Freud, and radical/liberal ideology to a conservatism (the New Critics being the most obvious example) that privileged psychological and formal complexity (achieved via the employment of ambiguity, paradox, irony). See, too, Richard Ohmann, "The Shaping of a Canon: U.S. Fiction, 1960–1975," *Critical Inquiry* 10 (September 1983): 199–223. For a partisan defense of *A Walk on the Wild Side* against the book's critics, see Lawrence Lipton, "A Voyeur's View of the Wild Side: Nelson Algren and His Critics," *Chicago Review* 10, no. 4 (Winter 1957): 4–14.

6. H. E. F. Donohue, *Conversations with Nelson Algren* (New York: Hill and Wang, 1964), 294–95.

7. Letter to Maxwell Geismar quoted in Drew, *Nelson Algren: A Life on the Wild Side*, 253.

8. William Brevda, "The Rainbow Sign of Nelson Algren," *Texas Studies in Literature and Language* 4, no. 4 (Winter 2002): 408.

9. Alston Anderson and Terry Southern, "Nelson Algren," *Writers at Work: The "Paris Review" Interviews,* ed. Malcolm Cowley (New York: Viking Press, 1960), 247.

10. *A Walk on the Wild Side* (New York: Farrar, Straus and Giroux, 1998), 270. Parenthetical references are to this edition. Published by Farrar, Straus and Cudahy in 1956, the novel has passed through eight previous editions. The edition being used here was first published by Thunder's Mouth Press (New York, 1990). The lyrics to two of the songs Algren and Fran Landesman wrote for the musical stage version of the novel can be found in Martha Healsey Cox and Wayne Chatterton, *Nelson Algren,* Twayne's United States Author Series 249 (Boston: Twayne Publishers, 1975), 88–90.

11. Russell Banks has also compared Dove to Tom Jones and Candide. See his foreword to *A Walk on the Wide Side* (New York: Farrar, Straus and Giroux, 1998), viii.

12. *A Walk on the Wild Side* occasionally gives new meaning to the term *prose poetry.* Consider, for instance, this paragraph from the novel's midpoint, into which I have inserted slashes to indicate where, had this been verse, lines would end in what is essentially a rhymed trimeter quatrain: "Out in the lake-palmed suburbs, / far from the dong and the glare, / in a house that had once been human, / Dove climbed a soundless stair" (174).

13. Algren quoted in Kenneth Allsop, "A Talk on the Wild Side," *Spectator,* October 16, 1959, 511.

14. Algren, "The Chateau at Sunset or It's a Mad World, Master Copperfield," (*Wayne State University*) *Graduate Comment* 3 (December 1959): 7.

15. Ibid., 7.

16. A recurrent Algren strategy is to preface serious remarks with a slapstick opening. See, for instance, the opening pages of *Who Lost an American?* as well as the essay "The Mafia of the Heart" (*Contact* 2 [October 1960]) and the texts of speeches such as "The Chateau at Sunset" and "The Role of the Writer in America"

(*Michigan's Voices: A Literary Quarterly* 2 [Spring 1962]): in all four texts, as elsewhere, Algren enters playing the clown.

17. Whether Harding was part African American may never be known. See, for instance, Francis Russell, *The Shadow of Blooming Grove: The One Hundred Years of Warren Gamaliel Harding* (New York: McGraw-Hill, 1968).

18. Consider, as a few, randomly chosen examples, Lou Reed's 1972 hit "Walk on the Wild Side"; Murray Kempton's 1988 *New York Newsday* column "A Walk on the Wild Side," which tells of a man with a "taste for outré enjoyments" who is kidnapped, sodomized, and "threatened with murder" (Murray Kempton, *Rebellions, Perversities, and Main Events* [New York: Times Books, 1994], 319–21); and sociologist Jim Thomas's use of the phrase "a walk on the wild side" to describe the need to cultivate the "undomesticated side of [one's] scholarly nature" (*Doing Critical Ethnography* [Newbury Park: Sage Publications, 1993], 7). Algren himself seems to have taken his title from a song he claims to have heard in New Orleans in 1931, "Walking the Wild Side of Life" (Drew, *Nelson Algren: A Life on the Wild Side*, 35); there was also a Hank Thompson hit of 1952 (written by William Warren and Arlie Carter) called "Wild Side of Life."

19. Leslie A. Fiedler, "The Noble Savages of Skid Row," review of *A Walk on the Wild Side*, by Algren, *Reporter*, July 12, 1956, 43–44; Norman Podhoretz, "The Man with the Golden Beef," review of *A Walk on the Wild Side*, by Algren, *New Yorker*, June 2, 1956, 139, 132.

20. James T. Farrell, "On the Wrong Side of Town," review of *A Walk on the Wild Side*, by Algren, *New Republic*, May 21, 1956, 19; James Kelly, "Sin-Soaked in Storyville," review of *A Walk on the Wild Side*, by Algren, *Saturday Review*, May 26, 1956, 16; Maxwell Geismar, "Against the Tide of Euphoria," review of *A Walk on the Wild Side*, by Algren, *Nation*, June 2, 1956, 473.

21. David Ray, "A Talk on the Wild Side: A Bowl of Coffee with Nelson Algren," *Reporter*, June 11, 1959, 32.

Chapter Eight—*Who Lost an American?* and *Notes from a Sea Diary*

1. On Algren's removal from reading lists and textbooks, see James A. Lewin, "Nelson Algren," *American Writers: A Collection of Literary Biographies: Supplement IX,* ed. Jay Parini (New York: Charles Scribner's Sons-Gale, 2002), 4. On Algren's response to the National Book Award committee, see Irv Kupcinet, "Kup's Column," *Chicago Sun-Times,* March 15, 1959, sec. 1. As for the Beats, Algren dismissed them (Jack Kerouac in particular) on numerous occasions; for a concise example, see "'Chicago is a Wose [*sic*],'" *Nation,* February 28, 1959, 191.

2. John Clellon Holmes, "Arm: A Memoir," *Representative Men: The Biographical Essays,* vol. 2 (Fayetteville: University of Arkansas Press, 1988); reprinted in *The Man with the Golden Arm,* Fiftieth Anniversary Critical Edition, ed. William J. Savage Jr. and Daniel Simon (New York: Seven Stories Press, 1999), 357, 356.

3. Bettina Drew, *Nelson Algren: A Life on the Wild Side* (New York: G. P. Putnam's Sons, 1989), 281, 286–87.

4. Algren, "The Strange Sleep," *Cavalier,* September 1962; "The Daddy of Them All," *Taboo: Seven Short Stories Which No Publisher Would Touch from Seven Leading Writers* (Chicago: New Classics House, 1964), 42, 44. The story's material is clearly important to Algren: it was reworked again as "Decline & Fall of Dingdong-Daddyland" for *Commentary* (September 1969) before appearing as "The Mad Laundress of Dingdong-Daddyland" in *The Last Carousel.*

5. Algren, "How the Man with the Record One Eighth of an Inch Long Was Saved by a Bessarabian Rye," *Esquire,* June 1960; "Say a Prayer for the Guy," *Manhunt,* June 1958. The former story, revised, appeared again under the title "Ipso Facto" in *Audience* (November–December 1971) before being collected as "I Guess You Fellas Just Don't Want Me" in *The Last Carousel;* "Say a Prayer for the Guy," revised, appeared as "A Ticket on Skoronski" in *Saturday*

Evening Post (November 5, 1966), only to be revised again for inclusion in *The Last Carousel*. Another lighthearted story from these years is "Shlepker, or White Goddess Say You Not Go That Part of Forest," *Cavalier,* February 1963: a slapstick account of Algren's misadventures in Hollywood.

6. Algren, "Down with Cops," *Saturday Evening Post,* October 23, 1965, 10, 14; "Moon of the Backstretch: Still and White," *Rogue,* August 1961, 12–16, 24; "G-String Gomorrah," *Esquire,* August 1957, 8.

7. "A Talk on the Wild Side: A Bowl of Coffee with Nelson Algren," by David Ray, *Reporter,* June 11, 1959, 32; Algren, "The Role of the Writer in America" (symposium transcript), *Michigan's Voices: A Literary Quarterly* 2, no. 3 (Spring 1962): 23–24.

8. Algren, "The Mafia of the Heart," *Contact,* October 1960, 15; "Remembering Richard Wright," *Nation,* January 28, 1961, 85.

9. Algren, "Ain't Nobody on My Side?" *The Race for Space!* ed. Paul G. Neimark (Chicago: Camerarts, 1957), 13; H. E. F. Donohue, *Conversations with Nelson Algren* (New York: Hill and Wang, 1964), 212; Algren, introduction to *Nelson Algren's Own Book of Lonesome Monsters* (New York: Bernard Geis Associates, 1963), 5.

10. The book's reviewers noticed such features although for the most part they saw them as shortcomings. Thus, Hilton Kramer, objecting to *Who Lost an American?* as unserious, fragmentary, self-exhibiting, and self-parodying, concluded that it was "written out of fatigue or disgust" ("He Never Left Home," *Reporter,* June 30, 1963, 46–47). The more sympathetic Herbert Gold found the book an eclectic "collection of memories, notes, burlesques and prejudices . . . that is part fact, part fiction" ("After All, Who Is the Enemy," *New York Times Book Review,* June 2, 1963, 23). Similarly, Sol Yurick described *Notes from a Sea Diary* as "clownish," a "petulant amalgam" that exploits "the fiction of the *real* self" ("Correspondent to the Underworld," *Nation,* 25 October 1965, 283). Kramer's impression that *Who Lost an American?* was perhaps "written out of fatigue" recalls one of the classic early descriptions of postmodern

fiction, the novelist John Barth's essay "The Literature of Exhaustion" (1967); see John Barth, *The Friday Book: Essays and Other Nonfiction* (New York: G. P. Putnam's Sons, 1984), 62–76.

11. See, for instance, Algren, "The Catch," review of *Catch-22*, by Joseph Heller, *Nation*, November 4, 1961, 357–58; "The Donkeyman by Twilight" (essay on Terry Southern), *Nation*, May 18, 1964, 509–12; and "The Radical Innocent" (essay on Bruce Jay Friedman), *Nation*, September 21, 1964, 142–43.

12. Kurt Vonnegut, introduction to *Never Come Morning*, by Algren (New York: Seven Stories Press, 1996), xix.

13. *Who Lost an American?* (New York: Macmillan Company, 1963), 274. Parenthetical references are to this edition, the only American edition (there were two British editions). The book is currently out of print.

14. Algren claimed that, among other offenses, Preminger had improperly acquired the rights to and then destroyed the spirit of *The Man with the Golden Arm*, cheated Algren out of his fair share of the film's profits, and implied via advertising that he, Preminger, was the story's author. See Drew, *Nelson Algren: A Life on the Wild Side*, 274.

15. In his *Paris Review* interview, Algren defined a "reader's book" as one in which the writer must play the clown and keep the reader laughing. See Alston Anderson and Terry Southern, "Nelson Algren," *Writers at Work: The "Paris Review" Interviews*, ed. Malcolm Cowley (New York: Viking Press, 1960), 247.

16. Asked by H. E. F. Donohue if the ship was in fact a "tramp steamer," Algren replied, "I was on it, wasn't I?" (*Conversations with Nelson Algren*, 172).

17. Donohue, *Conversations with Nelson Algren*, 176–77.

18. *Notes from a Sea Diary: Hemingway All the Way* (New York: G. P. Putnam's Sons, 1965), 21. Parenthetical references are to this edition. *Notes* has been out of print since 1967.

19. It is perhaps no accident that *Notes from a Sea Diary* has had little if any impact on Hemingway scholarship.

20. Algren, "The Emblems and the Proofs of Power," *Critic* 25 (February–March 1967): 24, 22.

21. "Interview with Dave Peltz," *The Works: Arts Documentaries for BBC2*, series four, *BBC Online*, November 22, 1997, http:www.bbc.co.uk/works (click on "Walk on the Wild Side," then "Info," then "Dave Peltz"), February 16, 2000.

Chapter Nine—*The Last Carousel* and *The Devil's Stocking*

1. Conrad Knickerbocker, "Scraping the Barnacles off Papa," review of *Notes from a Sea Diary*, by Algren, *Book Week*, August 15, 1965, 3.

2. Algren quoted in Henry Kisor, "Nelson Algren, Hale and Salty at Sixty-four," *Chicago Daily News Panorama*, October 27–28, 1973, 2.

3. The most charming account of Algren as teacher is Burns Ellison's "The First Annual Nelson Algren Memorial Poker Game," *Iowa Review* 18, no. 1 (1988): 61–97.

4. Algren quoted in Kisor, "Nelson Algren, Hale and Salty at Sixty-four," 2. During the final sixteen years of his life, Algren wrote almost eighty reviews, including for the first time a couple film reviews (of *The Exorcist*, *The Great Gatsby*, and *Last Tango in Paris*).

5. Algren, "The Emblems and Proofs of Power," *Critic* 25 (February–March 1967): 25. As a second example, see "The Rest of the Way Is by the Stars," *Chicago Free Press*, October 5, 1970. John William Corrington, "Nelson Algren Talks with NOR's Editor-at-Large," *New Orleans Review* 1 (Winter 1969): 131. See also "Pottawattomie Ghosts," *Chicago Free Press*, October 26, 1970.

6. James David Harkness, "Nelson Algren: Sixty Years from Mack Avenue, He Still Likes 'The People Underneath,'" *Detroit Free Press*, May 26, 1974, 9.

7. Algren, "Let's See Your Hands" (essay on Richard Wright), *Chicago Free Press*, November 2, 1970, 27; "'We Never Made It

to the White Sox Game'" (essay on James T. Farrell), *Chicago Tribune Book World*, September 2, 1979, 1. Algren's poems on Asian topics are "Nobody Knows," *Nation*, September 3, 1966, 15, and "The Country of Kai-Li" and "The Cockeyed Hooker of Bugis Street," *Chicago Tribune Magazine*, October 8, 1972, 29, 30. His poems about America include "Gentlemen: The Law Is Present" and "It Don't Matter How You Spell It," *Chicago Tribune Magazine*, October 8, 1972, 29, 30, and the twenty-nine-page "Ode to Lower Finksville." Added to the 1968 edition of *Chicago: City on the Make* (Oakland: Angel Island), "Ode to Lower Finksville" is a collage of free verse and prose that reiterates the themes and concerns of *Chicago: City on the Make*.

8. Algren, "Requiem," *Chicago*, September 1975.

9. Algren, "Where Did Everybody Go?" (essay on Edward Hopper), *Chicago Tribune Magazine*, February 13, 1972, 20; "Nelson Algren," interview by John F. Baker, *Publishers Weekly*, December 31, 1973, 12; "The Best Novels of World War II," *Critic* 31 (January–February 1973): 77.

10. Algren, "On Kreativ Righting," *New York Times*, March 29, 1975, 23; "Literary 'Exile' Is Pleasant for Algren," interview by Jim Gallagher, *Chicago Tribune*, March 29, 1977, 4.

11. Another selection that derives from *A Walk on the Wild Side*, "The House of the Hundred Grassfires," also has a more complicated publication history than the acknowledgments indicate. Although a note explains that the story first appeared in *Nelson Algren's Own Book of Lonesome Monsters*, which is true, the note adds that the story consists of "material deleted before publication from *A Walk on the Wild Side*," which is not the case: the story is virtually identical to the scene in the novel in which a naval officer hires a prostitute to impersonate his black mammy.

12. *The Last Carousel* (New York: Seven Stories Press, 1997), 62. Parenthetical references are to this edition (pagination of which replicates that of the first edition).

13. Despite Algren's sundry disembowelments of Preminger, none is as scathing as the letter actually written to the filmmaker

and reproduced in Stuart Brent, *The Seven Stairs* (Boston: Houghton Mifflin, 1962), 47–48.

14. Algren, *Nonconformity: Writing on Writing,* ed. Daniel Simon (New York: Seven Stories Press, 1996), 77.

15. See, for example, the dreams with which "A Ticket for Skoronski" and "Bullring of the Summer Night" begin and the defeats that follow in the wake of those dreams.

16. Because Algren could not secure from American publishers the advance on royalties he thought he deserved, the American edition of *The Devil's Stocking* (New York: Arbor House, 1983) was preceded by a German translation by Carl Weissner published under the title *Calhoun: Roman eines Verbrechens* (Frankfurt: Zweitausendeins, 1981). Parenthetical references are to the American edition. Pagination of the cloth edition is identical to that of the paperback.

17. Algren, afterword to *Chicago: City on the Make,* Fiftieth Anniversary Edition, ed. David Schmittgens and Bill Savage (Chicago: University of Chicago Press, 2001), 81.

18. Algren had, of course, relied heavily on material (slang, dialogue) drawn directly from life throughout his career. *Never Come Morning,* for instance, he had described as based upon "the lives of half a dozen men with whom the writer had grown up, as well as upon the newspaper reports of the trial of Bernard 'Knifey' Sawicki" (author's preface to *Never Come Morning* [New York: Seven Stories Press, 1996], xv). And in a 1956 interview he had remarked that his best lines were drawn from things overheard: "the lines people threw back at me years after they were written, were lines I never wrote. They were lines I heard, and repeated, usually [spoken by] someone who never read and couldn't write"; Luther Nichols, "An Author Explains His Views," *San Francisco Examiner Modern Living,* May 20, 1956, 14. On Sawicki, see chapter 3, note 15; on Algren's habit of working from life, see chapter 3.

19. Carter was still in prison appealing to the New Jersey Supreme Court for a new trial when Algren died. Following that court's 4–3 decision against a new trial, Judge H. Lee Sarokin of the

United States District Court in Newark (New Jersey) overturned the retrial verdict and released Carter without bail in November 1985. The original indictments against him were dropped in 1988.

20. The reader interested in comparing *The Devil's Stocking* with the facts upon which it is based might begin with Rubin Carter's autobiography, *The Sixteenth Round: From Number 1 Contender to #45472* (New York: Viking Press, 1974). For accounts of the entire story through Carter's exoneration, see Sam Chaiton and Terry Swinton, *Lazarus and the Hurricane: The Freeing of Rubin "Hurricane" Carter* (New York: St. Martin's Griffin, 2000) and James S. Hirsch, *Hurricane: The Miraculous Journey of Rubin Carter* (Boston: Houghton Mifflin, 2000). See also the movie *The Hurricane* (Universal 2000), directed by Norman Jewison and starring Denzel Washington.

21. See Selwyn Raab, "Despite Setbacks, Carter Hopes for Freedom," *New York Times,* September 29, 1975, 33, 61.

22. Algren, "The Last Interview," interview by W. J. Weatherby, *The Devil's Stocking,* 12.

23. The quotation comes from U.S. District Judge H. Lee Solokin (quoted in Chaiton and Swinton, *Lazarus and the Hurricane,* 286) on what he saw as the miscarriage of New Jersey justice in the Rubin Carter conviction.

24. Algren, "Let's See Your Hands," 27.

Chapter Ten—Conclusion

1. Joe Pintauro, "Algren in Exile," *Chicago,* February 1988, 157.

2. Algren, "Walk Pretty All the Way," *Chicago,* June 1981; "So Long, Swede Risberg," *Chicago,* July 1981. Algren's final work for the magazines remains true to form: "Topless in Gaza" (*New York,* October 30, 1978) finds the author refusing to pay for an overpriced drink in a topless bar (material worked into *The Devil's Stocking* with Algren transformed into the character Flash); "There Will Be

No More Christmases" (*Chicago,* July 1980), a comic story about Chicago's most inept cop, who loses his mind when his stupidity is exposed in the *Daily News;* "Last Rounds in Small Cafés: Remembrances of Jean-Paul Sartre and Simone de Beauvoir" (*Chicago,* December 1980).

3. Algren's books are all listed in the opening section of the bibliography.

4. John Seelye, "The Night Watchman," *Chicago,* February 1988, 69. All of Algren's books are currently available except *Somebody in Boots, Who Lost an American? Notes from a Sea Diary,* and *The Devil's Stocking.*

5. Algren, *He Swung and He Missed* (Mankato, Minn.: Creative Education, 1993); John Miller and Randall Koral, eds., *White Rabbit: A Psychedelic Reader* (San Francisco: Chronicle Books, 1995); Paul Levy, ed., *The Penguin Book of Food and Drink* (New York: Penguin, 1997); Nicholas Dawidoff, ed., *Baseball: A Literary Anthology* (New York: The Library of America, 2002). Algren's inclusion in *White Rabbit* was not his first appearance in such an anthology; see, for instance, Dan Wakefield, ed., *The Addict* (Greenwich: Fawcett Premier, 1963).

6. Matthew J. Bruccoli and Judith Baughman, *Nelson Algren: A Descriptive Bibliography* (Pittsburgh: University of Pittsburgh Press, 1985); James R. Giles, *Confronting the Horror: The Novels of Nelson Algren* (Kent: Kent State University Press, 1989). The only other book-length study is Martha Heasley Cox and Wayne Chatterton's *Nelson Algren* (Boston: Twayne-Hall, 1975).

7. Bettina Drew, *Nelson Algren: A Life on the Wild Side* (New York: G. P. Putnam's Sons, 1989).

8. Carlo Rotella, *October Cities: The Redevelopment of Urban Literature* (Berkeley: University of California Press, 1998); Thomas S. Gladsky, *Princes, Peasants, and Other Polish Selves: Ethnicity in American Literature* (Amherst: University of Massachusetts Press, 1992); Carla Cappetti, *Writing Chicago: Modernism, Ethnography, and the Novel* (New York: Columbia University Press, 1993).

9. An account of this symposium can be found in Robert Patrick Ward, "Nelson Algren: An International Symposium," *Dictionary of Literary Biography 2000,* ed. Matthew J. Bruccoli (Detroit: Gale Group, 2001), 377–78.

10. Wayne Kramer, *Adult World* (MuscleTone, 2002); Frankie Machine Blues Band, "Algren Street," available via the Web site of the Nelson Algren Committee http://www.nelsonalgren.org.

11. Russell Banks, foreword to *A Walk on the Wild Side,* by Algren (New York: Farrar, Straus and Giroux, 1998), vii–xi. Regarding the Brautigan novel, see, for instance, the chapter "The Shipping of Trout Fishing in America Shorty to Nelson Algren."

12. Edward Sanders, E-mail to the author, September 5, 2003; Richard Ford, letter to the author, April 7, 2003.

13. Don DeLillo, letter to the author, April 7, 2003; John Sayles, "Chicago Guy: Nelson Algren," *Conjunctions* 29 (1997): 20; Stuart Dybek, letter to the author, November 26, 2003.

14. Rick Hornung, "The Hustler: Nelson Algren's Neon Wilderness," *Village Voice Literary Supplement,* December 1990, 34.

15. Algren, afterword to *Chicago: City on the Make,* Fiftieth Anniversary edition, ed. David Schmittgens and Bill Savage (Chicago: University of Chicago Press, 2001), 81. For an example of how reprehensibly Algren could treat a woman, see David Ray, "Housesitting the Wild Side," *Chicago Review* 41, nos. 2/3 (1995): 107–16.

16. Algren quoted in Van Allen Bradley, "Author Nelson Algren —He Sits and Broods," *Chicago Daily News,* September 6, 1952, 24; Algren, "Algren Depicts Dire Straits, Hopeless Resignation of Italy," *Roosevelt (University) Torch,* November 14, 1949, 5.

17. "Searching for the Real Chicago" (transcript of 1957 symposium featuring Algren, Rudolph Ganz, Archibald MacLeish, and Frank Lloyd Wright), *Chicago,* January 1983, 125–26.

18. Simone de Beauvoir, *The Mandarins,* trans. Leonard M. Friedman (New York: W. W. Norton, 1991), 327. Algren, *Who Lost an American?* (New York: Macmillan Company, 1963), 285.

Bibliography

Works by Nelson Algren

Books

The first edition and, when one exists, the currently available edition of each of Nelson Algren's books are listed below in order of publication. Also noted are any editions containing additional supplementary material. See Matthew J. Bruccoli and Judith Baughman, *Nelson Algren: A Descriptive Bibliography* (under "Bibliography") for the publication histories of Algren's books through 1984.

Somebody in Boots. New York: Vanguard Press, 1935. The 1965 Berkeley-Medallion paperback edition (New York, 1965) included a new preface and afterword by Algren that were also included in the 1987 edition (New York: Thunder's Mouth Press). An abridged paperback edition appeared in 1957 (New York: Avon) under the title *The Jungle*.

Never Come Morning. New York: Harper and Brothers, 1942. New York: Seven Stories Press, 1996. The 1942 edition included an introduction by Richard Wright. The 1963 edition (New York: Harper Colophon) contained a new author's preface that is included in the Seven Stories edition along with an introduction by Kurt Vonnegut Jr., a memoir by H. E. F. Donohue, and excerpts from Donohue's *Conversations with Nelson Algren* (see below under "Interviews").

The Neon Wilderness. Garden City, N.Y.: Doubleday, 1947. New York: Seven Stories Press, 1986. The 1960 edition (New York: Hill and Wang) included a new introduction by Algren. The Seven Stories edition includes an introduction by Tom Carson, an afterword by Studs Terkel, and an excerpt from the 1955 *Paris Review* interview with Terry Southern and Alston Anderson (see below under "Selected Criticism and Commentary"). Includes twenty-four stories: "The Captain Has Bad Dreams," "How the Devil Came Down Division Street," "Is Your Name Joe?"

"Depend on Aunt Elly," "Stickman's Laughter," "A Bottle of Milk for Mother," "He Couldn't Boogie-Woogie Worth a Damn," "A Lot You Got to Holler," "Poor Man's Pennies," "The Face on the Barroom Floor," "The Brothers' House," "Please Don't Talk about Me When I'm Gone," "He Swung and He Missed," "El Presidente de Méjico," "Kingdom City to Cairo," "That's the Way It's Always Been," "The Children," "Million-Dollar Brainstorm," "Pero Venceremos," "No Man's Laughter," "Katz," "Design for Departure," "The Heroes," "So Help Me."

The Man with the Golden Arm. Garden City, N.Y.: Doubleday, 1949. New York: Seven Stories Press, 1990. The 1990 edition includes an introduction by James R. Giles. Fiftieth Anniversary Critical Edition, ed. William J. Savage Jr. and Daniel Simon. New York: Seven Stories Press, 1999. The critical edition contains one hundred pages of "Remembrances" (by John Clellon Holmes, Kurt Vonnegut, Studs Terkel, and others), early criticism (by Maxwell Geismer, George Bluestone, and Lawrence Lipton), and "New Views" (by the editors, Bettina Drew, James R. Giles, and others); the "Selected Criticism and Commentary" section of this bibliography annotates the most important of this material.

Chicago: City on the Make. Garden City, N.Y.: Doubleday, 1951. Fiftieth Anniversary Edition, ed. David Schmittgens and Bill Savage. Chicago: University of Chicago Press, 2001. The anniversary edition contains Algren's afterword to the 1961 edition, an introduction by Studs Terkel, twenty-two pages of notes, and a bibliography. The 1968 edition (Oakland: Angel Island) includes as epilogue a twenty-nine-page poem entitled "Ode to Lower Finksville" (entitled "Ode to Lower Kissassville" in one hundred copies printed especially for Algren).

A Walk on the Wild Side. New York: Farrar, Straus and Cudahy, 1956. New York: Farrar, Straus and Giroux, 1998. The 1998 edition includes a foreword by Russell Banks.

Nelson Algren's Own Book of Lonesome Monsters. New York: Lancer Books, 1962. Includes an introduction by Algren, an excerpt from *A Walk on the Wild Side,* and fourteen stories by

Saul Bellow, James Blake, Chandler Brossard, Brock Brower, H. E. F. Donohue, George P. Elliott, Bernard Farbar, Bruce Jay Friedman, Joseph Heller, Joan Kerckhoff, Thomas Pynchon, and Hughes Rudd. The 1963 edition (New York: Bernard Geis Associates) adds stories by James Leo Herlihy and Terry Southern.

Who Lost an American? New York: Macmillan, 1963.

Notes from a Sea Diary: Hemingway All the Way. New York: G. P. Putnam's Sons, 1965.

The Last Carousel. New York: G. P. Putnam's Sons, 1973. New York: Seven Stories Press, 1997. Includes thirty-seven selections (stories, essays, poems): "Dark Came Early in That Country," "Could World War I Have Been a Mistake?" "Otto Preminger's Strange Suspenjers," "I Never Hollered Cheezit the Cops," "The Mad Laundress of Dingdong-Daddyland," "The Leak That Defied the Books," "Tinkle Hinkle and the Footnote King," "Hand in Hand through the Greenery *with the grabstand clowns of arts and letters,*" "Come In If You Love Money," "Brave Bulls of Sidi Yahya," "I Know They'll Like Me in Saigon," "Airy Persiflage on the Heaving Deep," "No Cumshaw No Rickshaw," "Letter from Saigon," "What Country Do You Think You're In?" "Police and Mama-sans Get It All," "Poor Girls of Kowloon," "After the Buffalo," "The Cortez Gang," "The House of the Hundred Grassfires," "Previous Days," "Epitaph: *The Man with the Golden Arm,*" "The Passion of Upside-Down-Emil: *A Story from Life's Other Side,*" "Merry Christmas, Mr. Mark," "I Guess You Fellows Just Don't Want Me," "Everything Inside Is a Penny," "The Ryebread Trees of Spring," "Different Clowns for Different Towns," "Go! Go! Go! Forty Years Ago," "Ballet for Opening Day: *The Swede Was a Hard Guy,*" "A Ticket on Skoronski," "Ode to an Absconding Bookie," "Bullring of the Summer Night," "Moon of the Arfy Darfy," "Watch Out for Daddy," "The Last Carousel," "Tricks Out of Times Long Gone."

The Devil's Stocking. New York: Arbor House, 1983. This novel was first published in German as *Calhoun*, translated by Carl

Weissner (Frankfurt: Zweitausendeins, 1981). The Arbor House edition includes a foreword by Herbert Mitgang and an interview by W. J. Weatherby.

America Eats. Edited by David E. Schoonover. The Iowa Szathmáry Culinary Arts Series. Iowa City: University of Iowa Press, 1992. Includes a preface by Louis I. Szathmáry, foreword by David E. Schoonover, and forty-two pages of recipes tested and revised by Szathmáry.

The Texas Stories of Nelson Algren. Edited by Bettina Drew. Austin: University of Texas Press, 1995. Includes two previously uncollected stories ("Lest the Traplock Click" and "A Holiday in Texas"); four excerpts from *Somebody in Boots;* three stories from *Neon Wilderness* ("So Help Me," "El Presidente de Méjico," and "Depend on Aunt Elly"); and two stories from *The Last Carousel* ("After the Buffalo: Bonnie and Clyde" and "The Last Carousel").

Nonconformity: Writing on Writing. Edited by Daniel Simon. New York: Seven Stories Press, 1996. Includes an afterword, historical note, and annotations by Simon, and, as an appendix, a version of "Hollywood Djinn with a Dash of Bitters" (see below under "Essays").

Selected Periodical Appearances

The lists below contain only those stories, essays, and poems mentioned in this study that were not incorporated into one of Algren's books. Items are grouped by genre and listed in chronological order. For a complete listing of Algren's contributions to books and periodical publications (including book reviews), see Bruccoli and Baughman (under "Bibliography"). It should also be noted that material appearing in magazines often differs substantially from the book version of that material.

Stories
"Forgive Them, Lord." *A Year Magazine* 2 (December 1933–April 1934): 144–49.

"A Lumpen." *New Masses,* July 2, 1935, 25–26.

"Hank, the Free Wheeler." *A Treasury of American Folklore: Stories, Ballads, and Traditions of the People,* edited by B. A. Botkin, 540–42. New York: Crown Publishers, 1944.

"Single Exit." In *Cross Section 1947: A Collection of New American Writing,* edited by Edwin Seaver, 217–24. New York: Simon and Schuster, 1947.

"Say a Prayer for the Guy." *Manhunt,* June 1958, 31–35.

"How the Man with the Record One Eighth of an Inch Long Was Saved by a Bessarabian Rye." *Esquire,* June 1960, 105.

"The Strange Sleep." *Cavalier,* September 1962, 24–25, 27.

"Shlepker, or White Goddess Say You Not Go That Part of Forest." *Cavalier,* February 1963, 12–14, 84–89.

"The Daddy of Them All." In *Taboo: Seven Short Stories Which No Publisher Would Touch from Seven Leading Writers,* 31–59. Chicago: New Classics House, 1964.

"There Will Be No More Christmases." *Chicago,* July 1980, 132–34.

"Walk Pretty All the Way." *Chicago,* June 1981, 160–64.

Essays

"For the Homeless Youth of America." *Masses* 12 (March–April 1934): 4. Unused material from *Somebody in Boots.*

"'Politics' in Southern Illinois." *New Republic,* August 1, 1934, 307. Unsigned article.

"American Obituary." *Partisan Review* 2 (October–November 1935): 26–27.

"Within the City." *Anvil* 3 (October–November 1935): 9.

"A Middle-Aged Clerk in a Faded Army Coat." *Galena Guide.* American Guide Series. Federal Writers' Project, Works Progress Administration. Galena, Ill.: City of Galena, 1937.

"Do It the Hard Way." *Writer* 56, no. 3 (March 1943): 67–70.

"Laughter in Jars—Not as Sandburg Wrote of It: Two Poems Show How Chicago Has Changed." *Chicago Sun Book Week,* July 20, 1947, 2.

"Algren Depicts Dire Straits, Hopeless Resignation of Italy." *Roosevelt Torch,* November 14, 1949, 5.

"One Man's Chicago." *Holiday,* October 1951, 72–73, 75, 77–78, 80–83, 86–87, 89, 117, 119–20. Original version of *Chicago: City on the Make.*

"Things of the Earth: A Groundhog View." *California Quarterly* 2 (Autumn 1952): 3–11.

"American Christmas, 1952." *Nation,* December 27, 1952, inside front cover. Reprint of a piece first published in the *Chicago Daily News* (December 3, 1952).

"G-String Gomorrah." *Esquire,* August 1957, 47–48.

"Ain't Nobody on My Side?" In *The Race for Space!* edited by Paul G. Neimark, 13. Chicago: Camerarts, 1957.

"'Chicago Is a Wose.'" *Nation,* February 28, 1959, 191.

"The Chateau at Sunset; or, It's a Mad World, Master Copperfield." *Graduate Comment* 3 (December 1959): 5–7, 12. Text of a speech delivered at Wayne State University.

"The Mafia of the Heart." *Contact,* October 1960, 9, 11–15.

"Remembering Richard Wright." *Nation,* January 28, 1961, 85.

"Moon of the Backstretch: Still and White." *Rogue,* August 1961, 12–16, 24.

"The Donkeyman by Twilight." *Nation,* May 18, 1964, 509–12.

"The Radical Innocent." *Nation,* September 21, 1964, 142–43.

"Down with Cops." *Saturday Evening Post,* October 23, 1965, 10, 14.

"The Emblems and the Proofs of Power." *Critic* 25 (February–March 1967): front cover and 20–25.

"The Rest of the Way Is by the Stars." *Chicago Free Press,* October 5, 1970, 22–27.

"Pottawattonie Ghosts." *Chicago Free Press,* October 26, 1970, 26–29.

"Let's See Your Hands." *Chicago Free Press,* November 2, 1970, 25–27.

"Where Did Everybody Go?" *Chicago Tribune Magazine,* February 13, 1972, 20, 22–25.

"The Best Novels of World War II." *Critic* 31 (January–February 1973): 74–77.

"On Kreativ Righting." *New York Times*, March 29, 1975, 23.

"Requiem." *Chicago*, September 1975, 120–24.

"Topless in Gaza." *New York*, October 30, 1978, 88–90.

"We Never Made It to the White Sox Game." *Chicago Tribune Book World*, September 2, 1979, 1.

"Last Rounds in Small Cafés: Remembrances of Jean-Paul Sartre and Simone de Beauvoir." *Chicago*, December 1980, 210–13, 237–38, 240.

"So Long, Swede Risberg." *Chicago*, July 1981, 138–41, 158.

Poems

"Makers of Music." *New Anvil* 1 (March 1939): 23.

"Utility Magnate." *New Anvil* 1 (April–May 1939): 16–17. Published under the pseudonym "Lawrence O'Fallon."

"Program for Appeasement." *New Anvil* 1 (June–July 1939): 12.

"Home and Goodnight." *Poetry*, November 1939, 74–76.

"Travelog." *Poetry*, November 1939, 76–77.

"This Table on Time Only." *Esquire*, March 1940, 78–79.

"How Long Blues." *Poetry*, September 1941, 309.

"Local South." *Poetry*, September 1941, 308–9.

"The Swede Was a Hard Guy." *Southern Review* 7 (1942): 873–79.

"Tricks Out of Times Long Gone." *Nation*, September 22, 1962, 162.

"Nobody Knows." *Nation*, September 3, 1966, 15.

"The Cockeyed Hooker of Burgis Street." *Chicago Tribune Magazine*, October 8, 1972, 30.

"The Country of Kai-Li." *Chicago Tribune Magazine*, October 8, 1972, 29.

"Gentlemen: The Law Is Present." *Chicago Tribune Magazine*, October 8, 1972, 29.

"It Don't Matter How You Spell It." *Chicago Tribune Magazine*, October 8, 1972, 30.

Interviews

This section arranges selected interviews chronologically. For a complete list of interviews, consult section C of Bruccoli and Baughman (under "Bibliography").

"Nelson Algren" (1955). By Alston Anderson and Terry Southern. In *Writers at Work: The "Paris Review" Interviews,* edited by Malcolm Cowley. New York: Viking Press, 1960. Algren discusses writing *The Man with the Golden Arm* and *A Walk on the Wild Side,* influences on his work, his reasons for writing, and the profession of writing in America.

"Interview with Nelson Algren." By Robert A. Perlongo. *Chicago Review* 11 (Autumn 1957): 92–98. Reprinted in *Arizona Quarterly* 45 (1989): 101–6. Algren discusses what is wrong with America in the 1950s and what the writer's job is.

"A Talk on the Wild Side: A Bowl of Coffee with Nelson Algren." By David Ray. *Reporter,* June 11, 1959, 31–33. Algren comments on Ernest Hemingway, religion, the Beats, the state of America and of American literature, *The Man with the Golden Arm* and *A Walk on the Wild Side.*

"A Talk on the Wild Side." By Kenneth Allsop. *Spectator,* October 16, 1959, 509, 511. Algren offers not-always-accurate biography and thoughts on "the writing racket."

"3 Tapes." *Writer's Yearbook* 31 (1960): 45–49, 148, 150. Craft interview in which Algren discusses his composing process, formal concerns, influences, and aesthetic preferences.

"Nelson Algren Off the Cuff." By Hendrik L. Leffelaar. *Cavalier,* November 1963, 80–82. Profile/interview. Algren comments on politics and other writers, especially James Baldwin.

Conversations with Nelson Algren. By H. E. F. Donohue. New York: Hill and Wang, 1964. Eleven interviews conducted between February 1962 and June 1963 cover Algren's personal history and thoughts on Hollywood, the writer's vocation, politics, literature, and the state of American life and culture. Donohue correctly suggests the book might have been subtitled "Notes toward a Biography."

"Nelson Algren Talks with NOR's Editor-at-Large." By John William Corrington. *New Orleans Review* 1 (Winter 1969): 130–32. Algren discusses other writers, the Old versus the New Left, a writer's obligations, favorite books, and the connection of *Somebody in Boots* to *A Walk on the Wild Side*.

"Nelson Algren on the Make." By Irwin Saltz. *Chicagoland*, May 1970, 24–27. Profile/interview in which Algren talks about his life, drugs and his drug bust, his second wife, and current writing projects.

"Some Blunt But Not Unkind Words from Nelson Algren." By Tom Fitzpatrick. *Chicago Sun-Times*, March 26, 1973, 14, 16. Algren jokes about other writers and an award from *Playboy* magazine.

"Nelson Algren: Hale and Salty at Sixty-four." By Henry Kisor. *Chicago Daily News Panorama*, October, 27–28 1973, 2–3. Algren comments on the writer's need for struggle and risk, writing workshops, critics, and writing for money versus writing for posterity.

"Nelson Algren." By John F. Baker. *Publishers Weekly*, December 31, 1973, 12–13. Algren talks about his writing routine, first agent, other writers, and responses to his work.

"Nelson Algren: Sixty Years from Mack Avenue, He Still Likes 'The People Underneath.'" By James David Harkness. *Detroit Free Press*, May 26, 1974, 6–9. Profile/interview. Algren discusses politics, boxing, and the future of America.

"Literary 'Exile' Is Pleasant for Algren." By Jim Gallagher. *Chicago Tribune*, March 29, 1977, sec. 2. Profile/interview. Offering thoughts on his reputation and his work's worth, Algren also talks about growing old, working on the Rubin Carter book, and being married.

"The Last Interview." By W. J. Weatherby. In *The Devil's Stocking*, 7–12. (New York: Arbor House, 1983). On the day before he died, Algren discusses *The Devil's Stocking*, Simone de Beauvoir, and his election to the American Academy.

Motion Pictures

The Man with the Golden Arm. Directed by Otto Preminger. Written by Walter Newman, Lewis Meltzer, and Ben Hecht (uncredited). Starring Frank Sinatra, Eleanor Parker, Kim Novak, and Arnold Stang. 1955. Warner Home Video.

A Walk on the Wild Side. Directed by Edward Dmytryk. Written by Edmund Morris, John Fante, and Ben Hecht (uncredited). Starring Laurence Harvey, Capucine, Jane Fonda, Anne Baxter. 1962. Columbia/Tristar Studios.

Selected Criticism and Commentary

No up-to-date listing of secondary materials exists. This list is limited in several ways. First, it includes only work available in English. It omits unpublished dissertations and master's theses, book reviews, and criticism making only slight or passing reference to Algren. Omitted as well are a clutch of essays aimed at book collectors and bibliographies and checklists superceded by Matthew J. Bruccoli and Judith Baughman's *Nelson Algren: A Descriptive Bibliography* (see "Bibliography"). Finally, critical materials available only on the Internet are not listed simply because of uncertain future accessibility.

"Algren, Nelson 1909–1981." *Contemporary Authors,* New Revision Series, vol. 61. Edited by Daniel Jones and John D. Jorgenson. Detroit: Gale Research, 1998. 2–10. A review of Algren criticism; essay updates Anne Janette Johnson's original 1987 review of the literature in *Contemporary Authors,* New Revision Series, vol. 20.

Bassoff, Bruce. "Algren's Poetics in *The Man with the Golden Arm.*" *Études Anglaises* 40, no. 4 (1987): 413–20. Bassoff examines how imagery patterns in the novel turn on Algren's characteristic technique of making figurative use of literal details as a means of exploring the city as manufactured environment and the problem of identity in a fallen world.

Bluestone, George. "Nelson Algren." *Western Review* 22 (Autumn 1957): 27–44. Excerpted in Savage and Simon, eds., *The Man with the Golden Arm,* 393–97. Classic critique of Algren's strengths and weaknesses as a writer (through *A Walk on the Wild Side*); argues that Algren's characters possess an "impulse to destroy love," which leads inevitably through a "series of frozen images" of arrested consciousness to destruction and death.

Brent, Stuart. *The Seven Stairs.* Boston: Houghton Mifflin, 1962. Chapter 4 of bookseller Brent's memoir recalls Algren in the late 1940s.

Breslin, Jimmy. "The Man in a Twenty-Dollar Hotel Room" (1978). In *The World According to Breslin,* 270–73. New York: Ticknor and Fields, 1984. The newspaper columnist recalls Algren as tough guy.

Brevda, William. "The Rainbow Sign of Nelson Algren." *Texas Studies in Literature and Language* 4, no. 4 (Winter 2002): 392–413. This essay considers the use of religious symbolism in *Never Come Morning, The Man with the Golden Arm,* and *A Walk on the Wild Side.*

Cappetti, Carla. *Writing Chicago: Modernism, Ethnography, and the Novel.* New York: Columbia University Press, 1993. Chapter 6 discusses Algren's reputation and the critical reception of *Never Come Morning;* chapter 7 offers a reading of *Never Come Morning* as a book informed by the work of the Chicago school of urban sociology and the ethnographic training Algren received while working for the Federal Writers' Project.

Cox, Martha Heasley, and Wayne Chatterton. *Nelson Algren.* Twayne's United States Author Series 249. Boston: Twayne-Hall, 1975. This first critical study of Algren offers a biographical chapter followed by close examination of Algren's first four novels and the stories collected in *Neon Wilderness.* Themes (especially those of love and guilt), characterization, style and structure, symbolism, and critical reception are covered in each discussion. A useful chronology and a substantial bibliography are included. Algren cooperated in the book's preparation.

de Beauvoir, Simone. *The Force of Circumstance*. Translated by Richard Howard. New York: G. P. Putnam's Sons, 1965. This third installment of de Beauvoir's autobiography contains a passim account of her relationship with Algren.

———. *The Mandarins*. Translated by Leonard M. Friedman. Cleveland: World, 1956. This novel offers a fictionalized account of de Beauvoir's affair with Algren.

———. *A Transatlantic Love Affair: Letters to Nelson Algren*. Edited and translated by Sylvie Le Bon de Beauvoir and others. New York: The New Press, 1998. Collects 350 letters from de Beauvoir to Algren, February 1947 to November 1964. As Algren requested, his letters to de Beauvoir remain unavailable.

Drew, Bettina. *Nelson Algren: A Life on the Wild Side*. New York: G. P. Putnam's Sons, 1989. Readable and informative biography, tracing Algren from his family's old-world roots to his death. Drew conducted copious interviews with those who knew Algren and makes excellent use of the Algren archives at Ohio State University.

Eisinger, Chester E. *Fiction of the Forties*. Chicago: University of Chicago Press, 1963. Finding Algren simultaneously a poetic naturalist and a "romantic man of feeling" who has small use for ideas, Eisinger examines Algren's first four books to enumerate his novelistic flaws, to argue that the author was never more than a superficial leftist, and to track the recurring themes of love, guilt, and the search for identity.

Ellison, Burns. "The First Annual Nelson Algren Memorial Poker Game." *Iowa Review* 18, no. 1 (Winter 1988): 61–97. Memoir of Ellison's friendship with the writer.

Geismar, Maxwell. "Nelson Algren: The Iron Sanctuary." *College English* 14 (March 1953): 311–15. Revised version in Geismar, *American Moderns: From Rebellion to Conformity* (New York:

Hill and Wang, 1958), 187–94. Original version reprinted in Savage and Simon, eds., *The Man with the Golden Arm*, 387–92. Often-cited early critique defends Algren as heir to "the American heritage of dissent," an isolated late realist of social protest.

Giles, James R. *Confronting the Horror: The Novels of Nelson Algren.* Kent: Kent State University Press, 1989. Giles argues that Algren, concerned always with "the horror" of life for society's underclass, extended naturalism's emphasis on environmental determinism and social injustice by incorporating modernist complexity, existentialism, and Celine's absurdist "harsh compassion." The novels and *Who Lost an American?* receive in-depth examination.

Gladsky, Thomas S. *Princes, Peasants, and Other Polish Selves: Ethnicity in American Literature.* Amherst: University of Massachusetts Press, 1992. Chapter 6 recounts Polish-American reaction to *Never Come Morning* and Algren's rejection of his work's ethnic dimension (including *The Neon Wilderness* and *The Man with the Golden Arm*) despite its "probing examinations of ethnicity."

Grebstein, Sheldon Norman. "Nelson Algren and the Whole Truth." In *The Forties: Fiction, Poetry, Drama,* edited by Warren French, 299–309. Deland: Everett/Edwards, 1969. Overview of the first three novels that sees Algren as unwilling to tell any but "hard" truths about America's "mutilated" underclass.

Herman, Jan. "Nelson Algren: The Angry Author." *Chicago Sun-Times,* January 21, 1979, sec. C., 8–11. Algren comments on being poor at sixty and on being busted for possession of marijuana.

Holmes, John Clellon. "Arm: A Memoir." In *Representative Men: The Biographical Essays,* 243–62. Vol. 2. Fayetteville: University of Arkansas Press, 1988. Reprinted in Savage and Simon, eds., *The Man with the Golden Arm*, 349–61. Novelist and Beat fellow-traveler Holmes recalls his close friendship with Algren.

Klaw, Barbara. "Simone de Beauvoir and Nelson Algren: Self-Creation, Self-Contradiction, and the Exotic, Erotic Feminist Other." In *Contingent Loves: Simone de Beauvoir and Sexuality,* edited by Melanie C. Hawthorne, 117–52. Charlottesville: University Press of Virginia, 2000. Simone de Beauvoir's affair with Algren is analyzed to reveal the conflicts between de Beauvoir's "feminine and feminist tendencies."

Lewin, James A. "Algren's Outcasts: Shakespearean Fools and the Prophet in a Neon Wilderness." *MidAmerica* 18 (1991): 97–115. Offering a Judeo-Christian reading of *A Walk on the Wild Side* and *The Man with the Golden Arm,* Lewin argues that Algren exploits the stances of Shakespearean fool and "Biblical prophet-in-exile" to expose the ills of a sick culture.

———. "A Jew from East Jesus: The Yiddishkeit of Nelson Algren." *MidAmerica* 21 (1994): 122–31. Examining Jewish characters in "So Help Me," *Never Come Morning,* and *The Man with the Golden Arm,* Lewin argues that Algren "concealed his Jewishness" but was influenced by it.

———. "Nelson Algren." In *American Writers: A Collection of Literary Biographies: Supplement IX: Nelson Algren to David Wagoner,* edited by Jay Parini, 1–18. New York: Charles Scribner's Sons, 2002. Overview of Algren's life and work.

———. "The Radical Tradition of Algren's Chicago: City on the Make," *MidAmerica* 19 (1992): 106–15. A description of Chicago's radicalism.

Lid, R. W. "A World Imagined: The Art of Nelson Algren." In *American Literary Naturalism: A Reassessment,* edited by Yoshinobu Hakutani and Lewis Fried, 176–96. Heidelberg: Carl Winter, 1975. Offering an overview of Algren's accomplishment, Lid challenges the usefulness of classifying Algren as a literary naturalist, finding the author instead possessed of an "infernal vision" conveyed via Christian imagery. The discussion of "A Bottle of Milk for Mother" reworks Lid's earlier "A Commentary on Algren's 'A Bottle of Milk for Mother,'" in *The Short Story: Classic and Contemporary,* edited by R. W. Lid (Philadelphia: J. B. Lippincott, 1966), 504–12.

Lipton, Lawrence. "A Voyeur's View of the Wild Side: Nelson Algren and His Reviewers." *Chicago Review* 10, no. 4 (1957): 4–14. Reprinted in Savage and Simon, eds., *The Man with the Golden Arm*, 399–408. Lipton, a friend of Algren's, offers a spirited defense of Algren's work and a scathing dismissal of the negative reviews *A Walk on the Wild Side* received.

Maxwell, William J. *New Negro, Old Left: African-American Writing and Communism between the Wars.* New York: Columbia University Press, 1999. Comparing *Somebody in Boots* and Richard Wright's *Native Son,* chapter 6 charts the debt Wright's novel owed to Algren, offers a reading of Algren's antiracism, and presents both novels as challenges to the Communist Party's hopes for interracial solidarity.

McCarrell, Stuart. "Nelson Algren's Politics." In *The Man with the Golden Arm,* edited by Savage and Simon, 377–79. Sees Algren as a "gut radical."

McCollum, Kenneth G. "Nelson Algren." *Concise Dictionary of American Literary Biography.* Vol. 5, *The New Consciousness, 1941–1968.* Detroit: Gale Research, 1987. Overview of Algren's life and work; updates McCollum's original Algren entry in *Dictionary of Literary Biography,* vol. 9, *American Novelists: 1910–1945,* ed. James J. Martine (Detroit: Gale Research, 1981).

Murray, George. "Author of 'The Man with the Golden Arm' Takes a Walk amid His Old West Side Haunts." *Chicago American Pictorial Living,* October 7, 1956, 6–7. Profile.

Peddie, Ian. "Poles Apart? Ethnicity, Race, Class, and Nelson Algren." *Modern Fiction Studies* 47 (Spring 2001): 118–44. Examining "So Help Me," *Chicago: City on the Make,* and the first three novels, Peddie argues that, for Algren, race and ethnicity impacted class solidarity negatively, and that Algren's emphasis on these concerns as regards urban America earned him the negative reviews he began receiving in the 1950s.

Pintauro, Joe. "Algren in Exile." *Chicago,* February 1988, 92–101, 156, 163. Memoir recalling Algren's final years, death, and burial.

Pitts, Mary Ellen. "Algren's El: Internalized Machine and Displaced Nature." *South Atlantic Review* 52, no. 4 (1987): 61–74. Pitts interprets the elevated railroad as a symbol of an intrusive technology "that has displaced nature" and entrapped Algren's characters.

Ray, David. "Housesitting the Wild Side." *Chicago Review* 41, nos. 2/3 (1995): 107–16. The former editor of the *Chicago Review* recalls palling around with Algren in the late 1950s, offering anecdotes about Algren's fondness for crashing parties, his love of pranks and petty larceny, and his attitudes toward women.

Raymer, John D. "A Changing Sense of Chicago in the Works of Saul Bellow and Nelson Algren." *Old Northwest: A Journal of Regional Life and Letters* 4, no.4 (1978): 371–83. Raymer discusses how, from *Somebody in Boots* through *Who Lost an American?*, Algren's affection for Chicago "curdles" as the city becomes increasingly the "victim of a sterile corporate culture."

Robinson, James A. "Nelson Algren's Spiritual Victims." *The Gypsy Scholar* 3 (1975): 3–12. Robinson examines attitudes toward institutionalized religion and the use of religious imagery in Algren's first five books.

Rosen, Robert C. "Anatomy of a Junkie Movie." In *The Modern American Novel and the Movies,* edited by Gerald Peary and Roger Shatzkin, 189–98. New York: Frederick Ungar, 1978. Rosen argues that *The Man with Golden Arm* is an implicitly radical novel about the disinherited—a fact lost in the film adaptation.

Rotella, Carlo. *October Cities: The Redevelopment of Urban Literature.* Berkeley: University of California Press, 1998. *The Man with the Golden Arm* and *Chicago: City on the Make* are used to examine how American literature has imagined urban transformation since the 1940s. A comparison of *The Man with the*

Golden Arm to Theodore Dreiser's *Sister Carrie* reveals Algren as the endpoint of the tradition of Chicago literary realism; *Chicago* is read as providing the big historical picture that contextualizes *Arm*'s sense of unspecified but imminent urban decline.

Royko, Mike. "Algren's Golden Pen." *Chicago Sun-Times / Daily News,* May 13, 1981. Reprinted in Royko, *Sez Who? Sez Me* (New York: E. P. Dutton, 1982), 233–36. Reprinted in Savage and Simon, eds., *The Man with the Golden Arm,* 363–65. Affectionate character sketch by the syndicated newspaper columnist on the occasion of Algren's death.

Savage, William J. "The Quality of Laughter: Algren's Challenge to the Reader." In *The Man with the Golden Arm,* edited by Savage and Simon, 417–22. Savage argues that "humor is the key to understanding" Algren, who forces readers to attend to when, how, and at what they laugh.

Savage, William J., and Daniel Simon, eds. *The Man with the Golden Arm.* Fiftieth Anniversary Edition. New York: Seven Stories Press, 1999. Includes seventeen remembrances, early views, and new commentaries on the novel (see "Works by Nelson Algren: Books" above).

Seelye, John. "The Night Watchman." *Chicago,* February 1988, 69–72. Reflections on why Algren's books will never be widely popular.

Shay, Art. *Nelson Algren's Chicago: Photographs.* Urbana: University of Illinois Press, 1988. Algren's friend and a professional photographer, Shay offers a 115–image photobiography supplemented by reminiscences and detailed notes.

Silkowski, Daniel R. "Alienation and Isolation in Nelson Algren's 'A Bottle of Milk for Mother.'" *English Journal* 60 (September 1971): 724–27. The author focuses on Bruno's efforts to assert his identity.

Simon, Daniel. "Algren's Question." In *The Man with the Golden Arm,* edited by Savage and Simon, 411–15; also in *Nation,* December 20, 1999, 28, 30–32. Simon reads Algren as a lyrically complex revolutionary writer with a preference for asking questions rather than lodging accusations.

Stringer, Lee. "*Golden Arm*'s Song of Sweet Surrender." In *The Man with the Golden Arm*, edited by Savage and Simon, 439–43. Another writer about life on the streets admires Algren's skill and offers provocative ideas about *The Man with the Golden Arm* as social commentary.

Terkel, Studs. "Glasses." In *Talking to Myself: A Memoir of My Times*, 225–29. New York: New Press, 1973. Reprinted in Savage and Simon, eds., *The Man with the Golden Arm*, 371–75. A Chicago icon recalls Algren in 1973 as a prophet whose work still speaks to working men and women. This memoir has enjoyed various permutations: as the introduction to the 1983 edition of *Chicago: City on the Make;* as "Nelson Algren: An Appreciation" in *Nelson Algren: A Checklist,* compiled by Kenneth G. McCollum (Detroit: Gale Research, 1973), 1–4; and as the afterword to *The Neon Wilderness* (New York: Seven Stories Press, 1986), 287–93.

Writing in the First Person: Nelson Algren 1909–1981. Exhibit catalog. Chicago: Grand Army of the Republic Museum and the Chicago Public Library Cultural Center, 1988. In addition to photographs of Algren artifacts and an introduction to the author's life and work by curator Catherine Ingraham, the catalog contains Roger Groening's "Amateur Night Way Out West" (memoir of Algren in Vietnam and in New Jersey pursuing the "Hurricane" Carter story) and Michael Anania's "Nelson Algren and the City" (on Algren's use of light imagery and the Chicago tradition of realism to which Algren was heir).

Web Site

Leming, Warren. "The Nelson Algren Committee." http://www.nelsonalgren.org.

Bibliography

Bruccoli, Matthew J., with Judith Baughman. *Nelson Algren: A Descriptive Bibliography.* Pittsburgh Series in Bibliography. Pittsburgh: University of Pittsburgh Press, 1985. The indispensable volume for understanding the publication record of Algren's books, for locating his work's first appearances in anthologies and the like, and for researching the many essays, stories, poems, interviews, and reviews Algren contributed to newspapers and magazines. Two addenda to the bibliography have also been published: Matthew J. Bruccoli, "Addenda to Bruccoli, *Nelson Algren.*" *Papers of the Bibliographical Society of America* 82, no. 3 (1988): 367–69; and Robert A. Tibbetts, "Further Addenda to Bruccoli, *Nelson Algren*," *Papers of the Bibliographical Society of America* 83, no. 2 (1989): 214–17.

Archives

The bulk of Algren's papers are archived at the Ohio State University library, Columbus, Ohio. The Newberry Library of Chicago owns, in the words of one librarian, "a very small miscellaneous collection" of Algren manuscripts and letters.

Index

Fictional characters, followed by the title of the work in which they appear, are listed by first name. Titles appearing without author attribution are by Algren; Algren titles not mentioned in the text are indexed to the notes.

Abraham, Bernice, 4
Abraham, Gerson, 4, 123, 124
Abraham, Goldie, 4, 123
Abraham, Irene, 4
Abraham, Nelson Ahlgren. *See* Algren, Nelson
Achilles Schmidt (*A Walk on the Wild Side*), 103, 104, 105
Adamovitch, Sergeant (*Never Come Morning*), 48
Adams, John Quincy, 93
Addams, Jane, 86
Adventures of Huckleberry Finn, The (Twain), 113
Africa, 137, 141
"After the Buffalo" (*The Last Carousel*), 138
"Airy Persiflage on the Heaving Deep" (*The Last Carousel*), 137
Alabama, 19
Alexander, Grover Cleveland, 86
Alger, Horatio, 31
"Algren Depicts Dire Straits, Hopeless Resignation of Italy" (essay), 186n16

Algren, Nelson: book reviews, 36, 51–52, 63, 64, 115, 133, 174n8, 180n11, 181n4; composing process, 9, 33, 36–38, 52, 64, 67–68, 90–91, 93–94, l97, 99–101, 117–18, 132, 133–34, 135, 142–43, 144, 164–65n8, 168n12, 168–69n13, 173n6, 183n18; essays, 16, 52, 116, 117, 133, 134–42 passim, 163–64n2, 168n12, 168n13, 173n4, 176–77n16, 184–85n2; as fictional character, 77; life, 4–14 passim, 15, 33, 51, 66–67, 84, 88, 98, 99–100, 114–15, 123, 124, 128–31 passim, 132–33, 135–39 passim, 141, 149, 150, 153–54, 158n12, 159n18, 161–62n10, 174–75n3, 175n4, 181n3, 184–85n2; literary reputation, 2, 5–7, 9,10–11, 12, 20–21, 29, 37–38, 49–50, 63–64, 67, 68, 80, 82–83, 85, 88, 98–100, 112–14, 124, 150–54, 170n3, 178n1; poetry, 34–36, 66–67, 80, 85, 87, 90–91, 111, 112, 113, 133, 134, 135, 140, 150, 173n4, 176n12, 181–82n7; politics, 4, 8, 15–17, 20, 28–32, 34, 35, 51, 70, 71, 85, 89, 90, 92, 98–99, 111, 112, 118, 121, 172n2; prose style, 12, 31, 36–38, 52, 77–78, 80, 90–91, 112,

Algren, Nelson: prose style (*continued*)
117–18, 119–20, 124, 129–30, 134,142–43, 149, 164–65n8, 173n6, 176–77n16, 179–80n10, 183n18; short stories, 5, 6–7, 16–20, 51, 53–65, 66, 67, 99, 101, 106, 115, 134–42 passim, 150, 158n13, 163–64n2, 167n5, 168nn7, 8, 178n4, 178–79n5, 182n11, 183n15, 184–85n2; views on literature, 2–3, 5, 6, 8–13, 15–16, 20, 21, 29, 31–32, 34, 36, 38, 39, 51–52, 53, 55, 63, 64, 79–80, 81, 90, 91, 93–94, 97, 99, 109–10, 116, 123–24, 127–34, 142, 154

Algren's Folly (horse), 133

"Algren Street" (Leming), 152

Almería, Spain, 123

Alpert, Hollis, 82

Altgeld, John Peter, 160n27

America, 2, 4, 8, 16, 17, 26, 33–34, 70, 74, 75, 76, 84, 85, 88–96 passim, 98, 107, 116, 117, 121–27 passim, 130–31, 133, 147–49, 154

America Day by Day (de Beauvoir), 118

America Eats, 6, 33–34, 150, 151

American Academy and Institute for Arts and Letters, 11, 150, 160n25

"American Christmas, 1952" (essay), 172n1

American Communist Party, 5

American Dream, 5, 9, 11, 46, 70, 74, 101, 107–8, 111

American literature, 3, 11–12, 93–95, 114, 123–24, 127–31, 175n5

American Mercury (magazine), 167n5

"American Obituary" (sketch), 16

Anderson, Sherwood, 12, 168–69n13

Angry Dust (Stockbridge), 51

Ann Arbor, Mich., 153

Antek "Owner" Witwicki (*The Man with the Golden Arm*), 68, 73, 76

anti-Semitism, 18–19, 25, 28, 43, 57, 161–62n10

Anvil, The (magazine), 15

Appel, Benjamin, 38

Applejack Katz (*The Man with the Golden Arm*), 69, 77

Arroyo, Tex., 102, 111

Artis, John, 144

Asia, 124–31 passim, 132, 133, 137

Atlantic Monthly (magazine), 115

atom bomb, 68, 76, 84

Augie ("A Lot You Got to Holler," *The Neon Wilderness*), 59, 60

Baldwin, James, 39, 119, 122

"Ballet for Opening Day" (*The Last Carousel*), 135, 138

Banks, Russell, 152, 176n11

Banty Longobardi ("Stickman's Laughter," *The Neon Wilderness*), 60–61

"Barber, The." *See* Bonifacy "The Barber" Konstantine
Barcelona, Spain, 123
Barney Kerrigan (*The Devil's Stocking*), 145, 147
Barrett, Monte, 51
Barrow, Clyde, 138, 141
Barth, John, 179–80n10
baseball, 4, 35, 86, 88, 135, 137–38, 141, 150, 151
Baseball: A Literary Anthology (Dawidoff), 151
Baughman, Judith, 151
Beats, 114, 152–53, 178n1
Behan, Brendan, 119
Beiderbecke, Bix, 86
Bello, Alfred P., 143
Bellow, Saul, 134
Best American Short Stories, 158n13
"Best Novels of World War II, The" (essay), 182n9
Beth ("Dark Came Early in That Country," *The Last Carousel*), 139–40
Beth-Mary ("Watch Out for Daddy," *The Last Carousel*), 140–41
Bible, 3, 32, 81, 157n5, 163n20
Bibleback Watrobinski (*Never Come Morning*), 42, 47
"Biceps" (story), 158n13, 167n5
Bill of Rights, 93
Billy the Kid (folk hero), 66, 169–70n2
black humor, 11, 110, 115. *See also* humor

Black Sox, 35, 88, 137–38, 150, 151
Blind Pig (*The Man with the Golden Arm*), 69
Blue Boy (Giono), 51
Blue City (Millar), 64
Bluestone, George, 167–68n6, 170n9
Bombay, India, 124, 125
Bonifacy "The Barber" Konstantine (*Never Come Morning*), 40, 41, 42, 43, 47
book reviews by Algren, 36, 51–52, 63, 64, 115, 133, 180n11, 174n8, 181n4
Boone Terry ("A Holiday in Texas"), 17
boots: as symbol, 28
Borstal Boy (Behan), 119
Botkin, B. A., 36
"Bottle of Milk for Mother, A" (*The Neon Wilderness*), 56, 57, 158n13, 167n5, 168nn7, 10
boxing, 6, 10, 32, 35, 40, 43–44, 49, 55, 56, 59, 61, 132, 139, 142, 143
Bradley, Arthur Dexter, 143
Bradley, Van Allen, 159–60n24
Brand, Millen, 98
Brautigan, Richard, 152, 153, 186n11
"Brave Bulls of Sidi Yahya" (*The Last Carousel*), 137
Brent, Stuart, 14
Brevda, William, 99
Bromfield, Louis, 94

"Brothers' House, The" (story), 20, 53, 59, 158n13
Brown, Catherine Meredith, 63–64, 167n6
Bruccoli, Matthew J., 151, 163n2
Brueggemann, Walter, 157n5
Bruno "Lefty" Bicek: "A Bottle of Milk for Mother" (*The Neon Wilderness*), 56, 59; *Never Come Morning*, 6, 32, 39–50, 142, 166n15
Bryan McKay (*Somebody in Boots*), 21, 22, 23, 101
Buckley, Richard (Lord Buckley), 137
Bukowski, Charles, 153
"Bullring of the Summer Night" (*The Last Carousel*), 140, 183n15
Burroughs, William, 83
Busch, Niven, 51–52
business, 4, 29–30, 35, 72–73, 87, 89, 90, 95, 117, 120, 121, 123, 148
Butte, Mont., 138
Byron Linkhorn (*A Walk on the Wild Side*), 101

Cahan, Abraham, 31
Calcutta, India, 124, 126
Calhoun: Roman eines Verbrechens, 183n16
Calumet City, Ill., 116
Candide (Voltaire, *Candide*), 101, 105, 176n11
Cannery Row (Steinbeck), 104
capitalism, 15, 16, 21, 28–31, 108

Cappetti, Carla, 36, 152
"Captain Has Bad Dreams, The" (*The Neon Wilderness*), 53–54, 57
"Captain Is a Card, The" (story), 168n8
"Captain Is Impaled, The" (story), 168n8, 169–70n2
Carl Jusitska (*Somebody in Boots*), 26
Carson, Tom, 7
Carter, Arlie, 177n18
Carter, Rubin "Hurricane," 11, 132, 142, 143, 144, 149, 183–84n19, 184nn20, 23
Casey Benkowski (*Never Come Morning*), 44, 47
Cass McKay (*Somebody in Boots*), 21–31, 87, 101
Catch-22 (Heller), 134
Catfoot Nowogrodski (*Never Come Morning*), 42
Cavalier (magazine), 115
Céline, Louis-Ferdinand, 160n27
"Century of Progress, The." *See* Chicago World's Fair
Chaiton, Sam, 184n20
"Chateau at Sunset, The" (speech), 176–77n16
Chatterton, Wayne, 176n10
Chekhov, Anton, 160n27
"Chevalier of Vain Regrets, The" (essay), 168–69n13
Chicago (magazine), 152
Chicago Board of Health, 6
Chicago: City on the Make, 3, 8, 70, 81, 84, 85–91, 92, 97, 99,

122, 123, 135, 151, 159n18, 173n4, 181–82n7
Chicago Committee to Secure Justice for the Rosenberg Case, 85
Chicago Cubs, 86
Chicago Daily News (newspaper), 51, 172n1, 184–85n2
Chicago Free Press, 133
Chicago, Ill.: 4, 5, 6, 7, 14, 15, 16, 18, 26–31, 35–50 passim, 51, 55, 67, 70, 76, 85–91, 92, 98, 99, 107, 118, 122–24, 132, 133, 141, 152, 153, 154
"Chicago Is a Wose" (essay), 178n1
Chicago Press, University of, 151
Chicago Sun (newspaper), 51
Chicago Sun Book Week, 70
Chicago White Sox, 4, 35, 86, 88, 137–38, 141. *See also* Black Sox
Chicago World's Fair, 29–30, 32
Chickadee (*Never Come Morning*), 42
"Children, The" (*The Neon Wilderness*), 58, 167n5
Christ figure, 81
Christopher Morgan ("Forgive Them, Lord"), 19–20
Christy (Christiano) ("Design for Departure," *The Neon Wilderness*), 61
"City, The" (Wolff), 53, 170–71n10
Clemens, Samuel Langhorne. *See* Twain, Mark
"Cockeyed Hooker of Bugis Street, The" (poem), 181–82n7
Cohen, Leonard, 2
cold war, 2, 8, 84, 85, 88, 89, 92, 98–99, 112, 121, 175n5
comedy. *See* humor
"Come in If You Love Money" (*The Last Carousel*), 138
"Comintern, The" (song), 17, 161n7
Comiskey, Charles, 35, 137
Commentary (magazine), 135
Communism, 17, 26, 28, 31, 84–85, 95, 117
Communist Manifesto, The, 26, 28
composing process, 9, 33, 36–38, 52, 64, 67–68, 90–91, 93–94, 97, 99–101, 117–18, 132, 133–34, 135, 142–43, 144, 164–65n8, 168n12, 173n6, 168–69n13, 183n18
conformity, 88–98 passim, 111
Confronting the Horror: The Novels of Nelson Algren (Giles), 151
Conrad, Joseph, 94, 160n27
Conroy, Jack, 12, 63, 67
Conversations with Nelson Algren (Donohue), 10, 115, 151
"Cortez Gang, The" (*The Last Carousel*), 136, 138
Cortez, Gregorio, 138
"Could World War I Have Been a Mistake?" (*The Last Carousel*), 138
"Country of Kai-Li, The" (poem), 181–82n7
Cowley, Malcolm, 6, 38
Cox, Martha Healsey, 176n10
Crane, Stephen, 12, 93

"Creepy" Edelbaum (*Somebody in Boots*), 25, 161–62n10
Crete, 119, 120
crime and punishment, 1, 3, 5, 6, 7, 11, 12, 13, 22, 24, 26–28, 35, 39–43 passim, 46, 53–60 passim, 71, 72, 96, 97, 115, 116, 125, 137–38, 142–49 passim
Cross-Country Kline (*A Walk on the Wild Side*), 103, 110

Daddy ("The Mad Laundress of Dingdong-Daddyland," *The Last Carousel*), 136, 139
"Daddy of Them All, The" (story), 115, 135
Daily Worker (newspaper), 92
Daly, Richard, 133
Danielsen (*Notes from a Sea Diary*), 128
D'Arcy, Hugh Antoine, 168n11
"Dark Came Early in That Country" (*The Last Carousel*), 139, 142
Darrow, Clarence, 160n27
David ("The Brothers' House"), 20
David ("So Help Me"), 19, 59
"Dead, the Drunk, and the Dying, The" (working title), 67
Dealer. *See* Frankie Machine
de Beauvoir, Simone, 7, 8, 12, 98, 100, 114, 118, 119, 137, 153–54, 159n18, 175n4
Debs, Eugene V., 31, 86, 97, 160n27
"Decline & Fall of Dingdong Daddyland" (story), 178n4

DeLillo, Don, 13, 153
Democratic Convention (1968), 133
"Depend on Aunt Elly" (*The Neon Wilderness*), 54, 57–58
Depression, The (the Great Depression), 2, 4–5, 15, 16, 17–32 passim, 102, 139
"Design for Departure" (*The Neon Wilderness*), 55, 61, 168n12
DeSimone, Vincent, 143
determinism, 22
Detroit, Mich., 4, 26, 126, 152
Deutch, Stephen, 173n4
Devil's stocking: as symbol, 144
Devil's Stocking, The, 2, 11, 142–49, 183n16, 184n20, 184–85n2, 185n4
DeWitt (*The Man with the Golden Arm*), 69
Dexter Baxter (*The Devil's Stocking*), 143
Dickens, Charles, 160n27
"Different Clowns for Different Towns" (*The Last Carousel*), 137
Dill Doak (*Somebody in Boots*), 28, 29
Dillinger, John, 86
Diners' Club, 122
Dingdong Daddy ("The Daddy of Them All"), 115, 178n4
Doc ("Please Don't Talk about Me When I'm Gone," *The Neon Wilderness*), 60
Doc Dominoes (Dominowski) (*The Man with the Golden Arm*), 72
documentary realism, 11, 37, 42, 142–44, 166n15. *See also* realism

"Do It the Hard Way" (essay), 52, 168n12
"Donkeyman by Twilight" (essay), 180n11
Donohue, H. E. F., 2, 10, 80, 115, 117, 125, 151
Dostoyevsky, Fyodor, 130, 160n27
Doubleday & Company (publisher), 51, 84, 92, 98
Dove Linkhorn (*A Walk on the Wild Side*), 9, 87, 101, 102, 103–13, 135, 176n11
Dovie-Jean Dawkins (*The Devil's Stocking*), 144, 145
"Down with Cops" (essay), 116
"Dreary Black Hills" (song), 161n7
Dreiser, Theodore, 12, 86
Drew, Bettina, 114, 151, 157nn6, 8, 163n2, 170n3, 172n1
drugs, 3, 7, 46, 57, 60, 61, 66–72 passim, 74–75, 82, 95, 101, 102, 115, 116, 132, 139, 140, 151, 174n12, 185n5
Drunkie John (*The Man with the Golden Arm*), 69
Dublin, Ireland, 119, 121
Dude (magazine), 115, 140
Dybek, Stuart, 153
Dylan, Bob, 9, 149

Ed "Red" Haloways (*The Devil's Stocking*), 144, 145, 146
"Eggheads Are Rolling: The Rush to Conform" (essay), 172n1
Eisenhower, Dwight David, 93, 122
Eisinger, Chester, 37
Ellison, Burns, 181n3

Elly Harper ("Depend on Aunt Elly," *The Neon Wilderness*), 57–58
El Paso, Tex., 12, 24, 25
"Emblems and the Proofs of Power, The" (essay), 181nn5, 20
Emil ("The Passion of Upside-Down Emil," *The Last Carousel*), 139, 141
England, 121
"Entrapment" (unfinished Algren novel), 8–9, 98, 100, 115
"Epitaph: The Man with the Golden Arm" (poem), 66–67
Esquire (magazine), 11, 116
essays by Algren, 16, 52, 116, 117, 133, 134–42 passim, 163–64n2, 168nn12, 13, 173n4, 176–77n16, 184–85n2
Europe, 118–20
"Everything Inside Is a Penny" (*The Last Carousel*), 137, 138
Existentialism, 7, 11, 12, 152, 159n18, 165n11
Exorcist, The (movie), 181n4

"Face on the Barroom Floor, The": *The Neon Wilderness*, 56, 101, 167n5; poem by Hugh Antoine d'Arcy, 168n11
Fadiman, Clifton, 6
Fancy (bartender, "The Face on the Barroom Floor," *The Neon Wilderness*), 56, 59
fantasy, 113
Farrell, James T., 12, 38, 112, 133, 153

"Father & Son Cigar" (*The Last Carousel*), 141
Fat Josie (*Never Come Morning*), 42
Faulkner, William, 92, 154
Federal Bureau of Investigation (FBI), 8, 84–85, 86, 88, 98, 118, 157–58n8
Federal Writers' Project, 5, 33, 36, 38, 165n9, 166n15
feminism. *See* women
Fiedler, Leslie, 9, 99, 112
Fielding, Henry, 101
Finger Idzikowski (*Never Come Morning*), 42, 44
Finn, Mickey, 86
Fireball Kodadek (*Never Come Morning*), 42, 44
Fitzgerald, F. Scott, 94
Fitz Linkhorn (*A Walk on the Wild Side*), 101, 104
Flash (*The Devil's Stocking*), 145, 184–85n2
Floralee (*A Walk on the Wild Side*), 110–11
folk literature, 37, 66
Fonda, Jane, 112
Force of Circumstance, The (de Beauvoir), 159n18
Ford, Richard, 153
foreign policy (U.S.), 92–93, 117, 121–22, 125–26, 127, 133
"Forgive Them, Lord" (story), 18, 19–20
"For the Homeless Youth of America" (article), 16
Fortune (*The Devil's Stocking*), 146

Four Walls Eight Windows (publisher), 151
Frakes, James R., 159–60n20
France, 121
Franco, Francisco, 119, 120
Frankie Machine (*The Man with the Golden Arm*), 7, 64, 66, 68–81, 83
Frankie Machine Blues Band, 152
Frankie Majcinek. *See* Frankie Machine
Freud, Sigmund, 175n5
Friedman, Bruce Jay, 118
Fuller, Edmund, 64, 169n19

Galena Guide, 6, 33, 163n2
Galena, Ill., 6, 163n2
Gallagher, Jim, 158n9, 182n10
gambling, 10, 56, 60, 71, 115, 138, 140, 174–75n3
García Márquez, Gabriel, 13
Gary "Crooked-Neck" Smith (*Notes from a Sea Diary*), 125, 140
Geismar, Maxwell, 7, 21, 92, 112
General Motors, 121
Gent (magazine), 115
"Gentlemen: The Law Is Present" (poem), 181–82n7
Giang ("What Country Do You Think You're In?" *The Last Carousel*), 141
Gideon Planish (Lewis), 51
Giles, James R., 151–52, 165n11
Gino Bomagino ("No Man's Laughter," *The Neon Wilderness*), 55, 61

Giono, Jean, 51
Giovanni Johnson (*Who Lost an American?*), 119
Gladsky, Thomas S., 152
Gladys Sobotnik ("Poor Man's Pennies," *The Neon Wilderness*), 60–61
Gleason, Ralph, 9
"Go! Go! Go! Forty Years Ago" (*The Last Carousel*), 138
Gold, Herbert, 179–80n10
Gold, Michael, 31
Goldman, Emma, 31
Goodman, Benny, 166n16
Gortynia, Crete, 120
government (U.S.), 15, 28, 29–32, 57–58, 75, 84–85, 106, 117, 121, 124, 147–48
Grant, Ulysses S., 163n2
Great Gatsby, The (movie), 181n4
"Great Writing Bogged down in Fear, Says Novelist Algren" (essay), 172n1
Grebstein, Sheldon Norman, 10
Greece, 121
Greener (*Notes from a Sea Diary*), 129
"G-String Gomorrah" (essay), 116
Guggenheim Foundation, 164–65n8

Hackensack, N.J., 11, 132
"Hallelujah, I'm a Bum" (song), 161n7
Hallie Breedlove (*A Walk on the Wild Side*), 100, 103, 105
"Hand in Hand through the Greenery" (*The Last Carousel*), 138

Hand, Learned, 160n27
"Hank, the Free Wheeler" (story), 163–64n2
Hannah the Half-Girl Mystery ("The Last Carousel," *The Last Carousel*), 138
Hardheart, Corporal ("The Heroes," *The Neon Wilderness*), 63
Harding, Warren Gamaliel, 110, 177n17
Harper's Magazine, 159n18
Harvey, Laurence, 112
Havana, Cuba, 125
"He Couldn't Boogie-Woogie Worth a Damn" (*The Neon Wilderness*), 54, 61
Hefner, Hugh, 123, 136
Heller, Joseph, 9, 13, 118, 134
Hemingway, Ernest, 2, 6, 7, 38, 82, 124, 125, 127–31, 154, 160n27, 180n19
Henna, Hinky Dink, 86
Henriques, Robert, 52
Herlihy, James Leo, 63
"Heroes, The" (*The Neon Wilderness*), 58–59, 63
"He Swung and He Missed" (*The Neon Wilderness*), 55, 151, 167n5
Hiroshima, Japan, 68
Hirsch, James S., 184n20
Ho Chi Minh City, Vietnam, 137
Holiday (magazine), 173n4
"Holiday in Texas, A" (story), 16–18

Hollis Floweree ("Bullring of the Summer Night" and "Moon of the Arfy-Darfy," *The Last Carousel*), 140, 141
Hollywood, Calif., 8, 82, 84, 99, 137, 139, 178–79n5
"Hollywood Djinn with a Dash of Bitters" (essay), 172n1
Holmes, John Clellon, 49–50, 114
Holocaust, 153
"Home and Goodnight" (poem), 35
Homer ("So Help Me"), 18–19
Honeyboy Tucker (*Never Come Morning*), 44, 49
Hopper, Edward, 133
Hornung, Rick, 153
horse racing, 10, 116, 133, 138, 140
Horvath, Brooke, 173n7
Hostage, The (Behan), 119
"House of the Hundred Grassfires, The" (story), 182n11
House Un-American Activities Committee (HUAC), 84
Houston, Tex., 103
"How Long Blues" (poem), 35
"How the Devil Came Down Division Street" (*The Neon Wilderness*), 62, 158n13, 167n5, 168n7
"How the Man with the Record One Eighth of an Inch Long Was Saved by a Bassarabian Rye" (story), 115
Huck Finn (Twain, *The Adventures of Huckleberry Finn*), 101
humor, 11, 62–63, 77–78, 100–104, 110–12, 115, 119, 120, 122, 125, 126–27, 154, 168n13, 176–77n16
"Hurricane" (Dylan), 149
Hurricane, The (Jewison), 184n20
"Hustler's Heart" (working title), 67

Ibsen, Henrik, 160n27
"I Guess You Fellas Just Don't Want Me" (*The Last Carousel*), 140, 178–79n5
"I Know They'll Like Me in Saigon" (*The Last Carousel*), 137
Illinois, University of, 4
Illinois Writers' Project, 33, 36, 38, 150
"I'm a Ding Dong Daddy from Dumas" (Goodman), 166n16
"I Never Hollered Cheezit the Cops" (*The Last Carousel*), 140
"Internationale, The" (song), 17–18
Iowa Press, University of, 150
Iowa, University of, 132
Iowa Writers' Workshop, 132
"Ipso Facto" (story), 178–79n5
Irish Republican Army (IRA), 119
Isaac Bailey, PFC ("He Couldn't Boogie-Woogie Worth a Damn," *The Neon Wilderness*), 61
Istanbul, Turkey, 119, 121
"Is Your Name Joe?" (*The Neon Wilderness*), 56–57, 60
"It Don't Matter How You Spell It" (poem), 181–82n7

Jackson, Andrew, 21
Jackson, Shoeless Joe, 86

jail. *See* justice system
Jailer Schwabatski (*The Man with the Golden Arm*), 73, 76
Japan, 137
Jesse ("The Brothers' House"), 20
Jesse Gleason ("El Presidente de Méjico," *The Neon Wilderness*), 57
Jesus Christ, 79, 81
Jewison, Norman, 184n20
Jews without Money (Gold), 31
Joe Felso (*Chicago: City on the Make*), 90
John Henry (folk hero), 66, 169–70n2
Johnny (*Somebody in Boots*), 21
John Reed Club, 5, 15
Jonathan Harris ("Lest the Traplock Click"), 17–18
Judaism, 4, 153, 161–62n10. *See also* anti-Semitism
Judge Turner (*The Devil's Stocking*), 143
Jungle, The (Sinclair), 31, 82
Junkie (Burroughs), 83
justice system, 3, 11, 20, 25–26, 40, 41, 43, 47, 53–54, 56, 57–58, 70, 75, 83, 96, 123, 133, 142–49, 184n23

Kafka, Franz, 94, 160n27
Kalamazoo, Mich., 153
Katz ("Katz," *The Neon Wilderness*), 56, 60
"Katz" (*The Neon Wilderness*), 56
Kayo: World's Foremost Boxing Magazine, 44

Kazin, Alfred, 99, 138
Keller, Dean H., 163n2
Kelly, James, 112
Kempton, Murray, 177n18
Kennedy, John F., 13
Kent State University (library), 163n2
Kenyon Review (quarterly), 115
Kerouac, Jack, 178n1
Kesey, Ken, 9
"Kingdom City to Cairo" (*The Neon Wilderness*), 54, 56
King, Martin Luther, Jr., 146
Kitty Twist (*A Walk on the Wild Side*), 103, 104
Knickerbocker, Conrad, 10, 132
Kontowicz, Amanda, 5, 174–75n3
Korean War, 84, 88, 98
Kowloon, Hong Kong, 124, 126
Kramer, Hilton, 10, 179–80n10
Kramer, Wayne, 152
Kupcinet, Irv, 178n1
Kuprin, Alexander, 160n27
Kvorka, Sergeant (*The Man with the Golden Arm*), 69

labor unions, 15, 84, 104, 138, 141
Landesman, Fran, 112, 176n10
Lardner, Ring, 168–69n13
Larner, Samuel, 143
Lasch, Christopher, 157n2
Last Carousel, The, 10, 11, 99, 115, 129, 133, 134–42, 159–60n24, 178n4, 178–79n5, 183n15
"Last Carousel, The" (*The Last Carousel*), 136, 137, 139

"Last Rounds in Small Cafés: Remembrances of Jean-Paul Sartre and Simone de Beauvoir" (essay), 184–85n2
Last Tango in Paris (movie), 181n4
"Laughter in Jars—Not as Sandburg Wrote of It" (essay), 170–71n10
"Leak That Defied the Books, The" (*The Last Carousel*), 140
Lease, Mary Ellen, 31–32
Leeds, University of, 152
Leming, Warren, 152
"Lest the Traplock Click" (story), 17–18
"Let's See Your Hands" (essay), 181–82n7
"Letter from Saigon" (*The Last Carousel*), 137
"Letter to Joe Haas," 170n5
Lewin, James, 171n16, 178n1
Lewis, Sinclair, 51
Library of America (publisher), 151
Lid, R. W., 171n16
Life (magazine), 98
Lily Splits (*The Man with the Golden Arm*), 72
Lincoln, Abraham, 21
Lindsay, Vachel, 12, 93–94
Lipton, Lawrence, 175n5
literary naturalism. *See* naturalism
literary reputation, 2, 5–7, 9, 10–11, 12, 20–21, 29, 37–38, 49–50, 63–64, 67, 68, 80, 82–83, 85, 88, 98–100, 112–14, 124, 150–54, 170n3, 178n1
literary scene, 119, 138
literary tradition, 11–12, 22, 31, 33, 37, 42, 62, 90, 91, 101, 104, 120, 124, 127–29, 131, 143
Little, Frank, 138
Little Lester (*The Man with the Golden Arm*), 69
Live Bait Theatre (Chicago), 152
Lloyd Jenks ("Forgive Them, Lord"), 19–20
"Local South" (poem), 35
London, England, 119, 120, 123
London, Jack, 93
Lookingglass Theatre Company (Chicago), 152
Los Angeles, Calif., 126
Lost Men, The (Thielen), 52
"Lot You Got to Holler, A" (*The Neon Wilderness*), 58, 59
Louie Formorowsky. *See* Nifty Louie Fomorowsky
Luke Gospel, 163n20
"Lumpen, A" (story), 18
Luther "Fort" Morgan ("So Help Me"), 18–19

Macao, 137
MacArthur, General Douglas, 98
Maddow, Ben. *See* Wolff, David
"Mad Laundress of Dingdong-Daddyland, The" (*The Last Carousel*), 135, 136, 139, 141, 178n4
"Mafia of the Heart, The" (essay), 117, 176–77n16
Mailer, Norman, 119
Majurcek the Grocer (*The Man with the Golden Arm*), 76

"Makers of Music" (poem), 35
Malaysia Mail (ship), 125–28 passim
Maloff, Sal, 159–60n24
Mama Bicek (*Never Come Morning*), 41, 46–47, 48
Mama Orlov ("How the Devil Came Down Division Street," *The Neon Wilderness*), 62
Mama Tomek (*Never Come Morning*), 40, 41, 43, 44, 47, 49, 50
Mandarins, The (de Beauvoir), 159n18
Man in Modern Fiction (Fuller), 64
Manning (*Notes from a Sea Diary*), 125, 129
Man with the Golden Arm, The: movie, 8, 9, 98, 99–100, 102, 104, 174–75n3, 180n14; novel, 2, 6, 7, 8, 44, 60, 64, 66–83, 84, 97, 98, 113, 150–51, 153, 168n8, 169–70n2, 174–75n3, 180n14
Mao Tse-tung, 98
Maria Chan ("Poor Girls of Kowloon," *The Last Carousel*), 137
Marrakech, Morocco, 137
Martha (*Notes from a Sea Diary*), 126
Marxism, 2, 20–21, 100, 159n18
Marx, Karl, 175n5
Mary ("Design for Departure," *The Neon Wilderness*), 55, 57, 60, 61
masculinity, 122–23, 136
Masses (magazine), 15
Masters, Edgar Lee, 12, 86
Matches (*Somebody in Boots*), 25

Maxwell, William J., 162n17
McCarran Act, 84
McCarrell, Stuart, 152
McCarthy, Joseph, 84
McCollum, Kenneth G., 163–64n2
McCormick, Cyrus, 86
MC5 (rock band), 152
McMahon, Jeff, 170–71n10
Médenine, Tunisia, 137, 141
Melville, Herman, 12
"Merry Christmas, Mr. Mark" (*The Last Carousel*), 137
Mexican War, 88
"Middle-Aged Clerk in a Faded Army Jacket, A" (book chapter), 163n2
middle-class society, 3, 15–16, 29–30, 46, 47–48, 49, 50, 53, 64, 68, 73, 74, 76–77, 78, 82, 83, 87, 95, 97, 106–9 passim, 117, 119, 122, 123–24, 126, 128, 142, 144, 147, 149, 154, 174n12
Miles, Barry, 83
Millar, Kenneth, 64
Millay, Edna St. Vincent, 12
"Million-Dollar Brainstorm" (*The Neon Wilderness*), 55, 161–62n10
Mitgang, Herbert, 157–58n8
"Modern Hymn for Grief" (Widdemer), 168n12
modernism, 117
Molly Novotny (*The Man with the Golden Arm*), 69, 73, 74, 79, 81
Montana, 141

"Moon of the Arfy-Darfy" (*The Last Carousel*), 140, 141
"Moon of the Backstretch: Still and White" (essay), 116
movie reviews, 181n4
Musial, John, 152
Myer Salk ("Million-Dollar Brainstorm," (*The Neon Wilderness*), 59

Nancy McKay (*Somebody in Boots*), 21, 22, 23
Nation (magazine), 13, 135, 172n1
National Association for the Advancement of Colored People (NAACP), 146
National Book Award, 82, 114
National Book Award Committee, 114
Native Son (Wright), 6
naturalism, 11, 12, 22, 31, 37, 38, 42, 45, 99, 151, 164–65n8, 165n11
Nelson Algren: A Descriptive Bibliography (Bruccoli and Baughman), 151
Nelson Algren: A Life on the Wild Side (Drew), 151
"Nelson Algren: An International Symposium," 152
Nelson Algren Award for Short Fiction, 152
Nelson Algren Committee, 152
Nelson Algren: For Keeps and a Day (play), 152
Nelson Algren's Own Book of Lonesome Monsters, 10, 115, 118, 182n11

"Nelson Algren Stopped By" (Kramer), 152
Nelson & Simone (Musial), 152
neon wilderness: as metaphor, 54
Neon Wilderness, The, 6–7, 51, 53–65, 66, 67, 99, 103, 167n5, 168n7
Never Come Morning, 2, 6, 32, 37, 38–50, 51, 52, 85, 99, 102, 106, 142, 152, 159n18, 164–65n8, 165n9, 166n16, 168nn8, 10, 183n18
New Anvil (magazine), 35
New Criticism, 175n5
New Jersey, 132, 142, 143, 144, 183–84n23
New Jersey Supreme Court, 183–84n19
New Masses (magazine), 15
New Orleans, La., 101–4 passim, 177n18
New Republic (magazine), 15
Newsweek (magazine), 159n18
New Yorker (magazine), 9, 82
New York Times (newspaper), 82, 112
Nick Iello (*The Devil's Stocking*), 143
Nifty Louie Fomorowsky, 68, 69, 71, 72
"Night without Mercy" (working title), 67
"Nobody Knows" (poem), 181–82n7
"No Cumshaw No Rickshaw" (*The Last Carousel*), 137
"No Man's Laughter" (*The Neon Wilderness*), 55, 61

nonconformity. *See* conformity
Nonconformity: Writing on Writing, 8, 70, 74, 81, 84, 91–97, 98, 150, 151, 172n1, 173n6
Norah Egan (*Somebody in Boots*), 26–29
Norman Manlifellow (*Who Lost an American?*), 119
Norris, Frank, 12
Notes from a Sea Diary: Hemingway All the Way, 10–11, 99, 115, 117, 124–31, 132, 133, 134, 140, 179–80n10, 185n4
Nubby O'Neill (*Somebody in Boots*), 25, 26–27, 29–30

O'Connor ("Pero Venceremos," *The Neon Wilderness*), 56, 60
"Ode to an Absconding Bookie" (poem, *The Last Carousel*), 140
"Ode to Kissassville" (poem), 173n4
"Ode to Lower Finksville" (poem), 87, 135, 173n4, 181–82n7
O'Fallon, Lawrence, 164n5
O. Henry Award, 158n13
Ohio State University, 84, 158n12, 159n2
Ohio State University Press, 150
Ohmann, Richard, 175n5
"Old Chisholm Trail" (song), 161n7
Old Husband. *See* Old Stash
Old Stash (*The Man with the Golden Arm*), 73, 77
Oliver Finnerty (*A Walk on the Wild Side*), 103, 106, 108–9, 110
Oliver, King, 86

"One-Eye" Tenczara, Captain (*Never Come Morning*), 45, 47, 48
O'Neill, Eugene, 12
"One Man's Chicago" (essay), 173n4
"On Kreativ Righting" (essay), 134
Oswald, Lee Harvey, 13
"Otto Preminger's Strange Suspenjers" (*The Last Carousel*), 136, 137

Papa Orlov ("How the Devil Came Down Division Street," *The Neon Wilderness*), 62
Paris, France, 119
Parker, Bonnie, 138, 141
Partisan Review (quarterly), 15
"Passion of Upside-Down Emil, The" (*The Last Carousel*), 139, 141
Paterson, N.J., 11, 132, 142
Peddie, Ian, 162n17
Peltz, Dave, 131
Penguin Book of Food and Drink, The (Levy), 151
People's History of the United States, A (Zinn), 83
Perkins, Maxwell, 7
"Pero Venceremos" (*The Neon Wilderness*), 56
Pintauro, Joe, 150
Playboy (magazine), 115, 122, 123, 128, 136
"Please Don't Talk about Me When I'm Gone" (*The Neon Wilderness*), 57, 59
Podhoretz, Norman, 99, 112

Poe, Edgar Allan, 93
poetry: by Algren, 34–36, 66–67, 80, 85, 87, 90–91, 111, 112, 113, 133, 134, 135, 140, 150, 173n4, 176n12, 181–82n7; by others, 52
Poetry (magazine), 51
police. *See* justice system
"Police and Mama-sans Get It All" (*The Last Carousel*), 137
Polish Americans, 6, 38–50, 51, 85, 99, 152
politics, 4, 8, 15–17, 20, 28–32, 34, 35, 51, 70, 71, 85, 89, 90, 92, 98–99, 111, 112, 118, 121, 172n2
"'Politics' in Southern Illinois" (essay), 161n2
"Poor Girls of Kowloon" (*The Last Carousel*), 136, 137
"Poor Man's Pennies" (*The Neon Wilderness*), 55, 60
Poor Peter Schwabatski (*The Man with the Golden Arm*), 69, 73
Poore, Charles, 63
populism, 31–32
Portillo ("El Presidente de Méjico," *The Neon Wilderness*), 57, 59
postmodernism, 11, 117–18, 179–80n10
"Pottawattomie Ghosts" (essay), 181n5
Pottawattomies, 87
poverty, 2, 3, 5, 7, 13–14, 15–16, 18, 22–23, 25, 26, 31, 51, 53–65 passim
Powers, Richard, 2

Preminger, Otto, 8, 99, 119, 137, 139, 174–75n3, 180n14, 182–83n13
"Presidente de Méjico, El" (*The Neon Wilderness*), 54, 57, 101
"Previous Days" (*The Last Carousel*), 136–37
"Program for Appeasement" (poem), 36
Progressive Party, 31
proletarian literature, 30–31, 37
proletarian revolution, 3, 15–19 passim, 24, 28–31
prose poem, 85, 90–91, 176n12
prose style, 12, 31, 36–38, 52, 77–78, 80, 90–91, 112, 117–20, 124, 129–30, 134, 142–43, 149, 164–65n8, 173n6, 176–77n16, 179–80n10, 183n18
prostitutes/prostitution, 6, 22, 24, 26, 28, 35, 39, 40, 41, 43, 44, 45, 49, 102–10 passim, 116, 119, 120, 121, 123, 125, 126, 134, 137, 138, 144, 146
Psalms, 32
Publishers Weekly (magazine), 134
Pulitzer Prize, 82
Pullman, George Mortimer, 86
Pusan, South Korea, 124, 126
Pynchon, Thomas, 2, 13, 118

Raab, Selwyn, 184n21
Race for Space!, The (Neimark), 117
racism, 3, 18, 19, 20, 22, 24–26, 28–29, 43, 103, 104, 105, 110, 123, 138–39, 142, 143–45, 148

"Radical Innocent, The" (essay), 180n11
Ragged Dick (Alger), 31
Rahv, Philip, 6, 38
Rahway Prison, 143
Railroad Shorty ("The Face on the Barroom Floor," *The Neon Wilderness*), 56, 59
Rampants (magazine), 159n18
Ray, David, 186n15
readers, 1–2, 13–14, 23, 31, 46, 50, 52, 65, 71, 79–80, 81, 111, 123–24, 134, 173n6, 180n15
realism, 2, 31, 82, 117
Reba (*A Walk on the Wild Side*), 104, 106, 107, 110
Record-Head Bednar, Captain (*The Man with the Golden Arm*), 77, 78–79, 97
"Red" Haloways. *See* Ed "Red" Haloways
Reed, Lou, 177n18
religion, 3, 4, 11, 19, 20, 23, 27–29, 47, 54, 60, 61, 64, 76, 79–81, 89, 90, 95, 96, 101, 104, 119, 123, 146, 148, 171n15
"Remembering Richard Wright" (essay), 179n8
"Requiem" (essay), 133
"Rest of the Way Is by the Stars, The" (essay), 181n5
Rhino Gross (*A Walk on the Wild Side*), 103, 104, 135
Rideout, Walter B., 5, 21
Riesman, David, 95
Risberg, Swede, 88, 141

Rise of David Levinsky, The (Cahan), 31
Rizk, Salom, 51
Rocco (Young Rocco) ("He Swung and He Missed," *The Neon Wilderness*), 55–56, 61
Roger Holly ("Dark Came Early in that Country," *The Last Carousel*), 139–40, 142
Rogue (magazine), 13, 115
"Role of the Writer in America, The" (speech), 176–77n16, 179n7
roman á clef, 143
Roman Orlov ("How the Devil Came Down Division Street," *The Neon Wilderness*), 62
Romans, Epistle to the, 171n13
Roosevelt, Franklin Delano, 5
Roosevelt University (Chicago), 154
Rosenberg, Ethel, 84, 92
Rosenberg, Julius, 84, 92
Rotella, Carlo, 83, 88, 152
Roxy (*Never Come Morning*), 42
Ruby Calhoun (*The Devil's Stocking*), 143–48 passim
Rumdum (*The Man with the Golden Arm*), 73
Rushdie, Salman, 13
Russell, Francis, 177n17
"Ryebread Trees of Spring, The" (*The Last Carousel*), 137, 138

Sag Harbor, N.Y., 11, 154
Saigon, Vietnam, 137, 138
Saint Paul, 78

"Salomon and Morris: Two Patriots of the Revolution" (essay), 163–64n2
San Antonio, Tex., 103
Sandburg, Carl, 2, 7, 12, 38, 86
Sanders, Edward, 152–53
Sandy (*Who Lost an American?*), 119
San Francisco, Calif., 137, 141
Sarokin, H. Lee, 183–84n19, 184n23
Sartre, Jean-Paul, 8, 12, 38, 88, 119, 159n18, 160n27, 165n9
Saturday Evening Post (magazine), 115
Savage, William J., 77–78
Sawicki, Bernard "Knifey," 166n15, 183n18
"Say a Prayer for the Guy" (story), 115, 140, 178–79n5
Sayles, John, 153
Schaub, Thomas Hill, 99, 175n5
Schulberg, Budd, 85
Scott Naylor ("A Holiday in Texas"), 17
"Searching for the Real Chicago" (symposium transcript), 186n17
Seelye, John, 185n4
sentimentalism, 16, 80, 94, 99, 112, 154
Seven Stories Press, 151
Seville, Spain, 123
Shay, Art, 1, 14, 98
Sheeny McCoy (*The Neon Wilderness*), 161–62n10
"Shlepker, or White Goddess Say You Not Go That Part of Forest" (story), 178–79n5

short stories by Algren, 5, 6–7, 16–20, 51, 53–65, 66, 67, 99, 101, 106, 115, 134–42 passim, 150, 158n13, 163–64n2, 167n5, 168nn7, 8, 178n4, 178–79n5, 182n11, 183n15, 184–85n2
Shudefski the Bartender (*The Man with the Golden Arm*), 72
Simon, Daniel, 85, 97, 151, 172n1
Sinatra, Frank, 99
Sinclair, Upton, 12, 31, 82
"Single Exit" (story), 167n5
Sleep of Baby Filbertson and Other Stories, The (Herlihy), 63
Slicky-Boy (*Notes from a Sea Diary*), 126
Smiley (*A Walk on the Wild Side*), 109
Snipes (*Never Come Morning*), 161–62n10
sociological novel, 32, 91, 152
"So Help Me" (story), 5, 18–19, 53, 59, 101
Solly "Sparrow" Saltskin (*The Man with the Golden Arm*), 60, 68, 69, 72, 73, 75, 77, 78, 79, 81, 161–62n10
"So Long, Swede Risberg" (poem), 150
Somebody in Boots, 3, 5, 15, 20–32, 33, 38, 100–101, 108, 185n4
Sophie (Zosh) Majcinek (*The Man with the Golden Arm*), 44, 68, 69, 71, 73, 74, 76, 79, 81
Southeast Asia. *See* Asia
Southern Christian Leadership Conference (SCLC), 146

Southern, Terry, 13, 118
Soviet Union, 84, 117, 121
Spain, 119, 120, 121
Sparrow Saltskin (*The Man with the Golden Arm*). *See* Solly "Sparrow" Saltskin
Spectorsky, A. C., 83
Stagolee (Stackerlee) (folk hero), 66, 169–70n2
State Department (U.S.), 84
"State of Literature, The" (working title), 84
Steffi Rostenkowski (*Never Come Morning*), 6, 39–42, 44–50
Steinbeck, John, 104
"Stickman's Laughter" (*The Neon Wilderness*), 60, 167n5
Stockbridge, Dorothy, 51
Stowe, Harriet Beecher, 82
"Strange Sleep, The" (story), 115
Stubby McKay (*Somebody in Boots*), 21, 22, 23, 101
Studs Lonigan trilogy (Farrell), 153
style. *See* prose style
Suggs, Jon Christian, 30–31
Sun in Their Eyes (Barrett), 51
Superman comics, 44, 166n16
"Swede Was a Hard Guy, The" (poem), 35, 150
Swinton, Terry, 184n20
Syrian Yankee (Rizk), 51

Tarkington, Booth, 94
Temps Modernes (magazine), 88
Terasina Vidavarri (*A Walk on the Wild Side*), 103, 111
Terkel, Studs, 13–14, 63, 173n4

Texas, 5, 16–17, 21, 22–23, 26, 54, 57, 141, 161n10
Texas Press, University of, 150
Texas Stories of Nelson Algren, The, 150
"That's the Way It's Always Been" (*The Neon Wilderness*), 58
"There Will Be No More Christmases" (story), 184–85n2
They Dream of Home (Busch), 51–52
Thielen, Benedict, 52
"Things of the Earth: A Groundhog View" (essay), 172n1
"This Table on Time Only" (poem), 35
Thomas, Jim, 177n18
Thompson, Hank, 177n18
Tibbetts, Robert A., 163n2
"Ticket on Skoronski, A" (*The Last Carousel*), 140, 178–79n5, 183n15
Time (magazine), 82, 122
"Tinkle Hinkle and the Footnote King" (*The Last Carousel*), 138
Tiny Zion ("Million Dollar Brainstorm," *The Neon Wilderness*), 55, 59, 60, 61, 161–62n10
Tom Jones (Fiedling, *The History of Tom Jones*), 101, 176n11
"Topless in Gaza" (essay), 184–85n2
Tortilla Flat (Steinbeck), 104
tragedy, 111–12
"Travelog" (poem), 35
"Tricks Out of Times Long Gone" (poem, *The Last Carousel*), 135, 139

Trout Fishing in America (Brautigan), 152, 186n11
Trout Fishing in America Shorty (Brautigan, *Trout Fishing in America*), 152
Turkey, 121
Twain, Mark, 93, 101

Umbrella Man (*The Man with the Golden Arm*), 69
Uncle Tom's Cabin (Stowe), 82
unions. *See* labor unions
United States District Court of Newark, N.J., 183–84n19
Updike, John 134
urban decline, 88, 152
"Utility Magnate" (poem), 35

Vanguard Press, 5, 158n9
Vietnam, 10, 131, 133, 137, 141
views on literature, 2–3, 5, 6, 8–13, 15–16, 20, 21, 29, 31–32, 34, 36, 38, 39, 51–52, 53, 55, 63, 64, 79–80, 81, 90, 91, 93–94, 97, 99, 109–10, 116, 123–24, 127–34, 142, 154
Vincent De Vivani (*The Devil's Stocking*), 143
Violet (Vi) (*The Man with the Golden Arm*), 73, 75, 77
Voice of the Trumpet, The (Henriques), 52
Voltaire, Francois M., 101, 105
Vonnegut, Kurt, Jr., 64, 118

Wakefield, Dan, 185n5
Walker, Margaret, 52
"Walking on the Wild Side of Life" (Thomas), 177n18
"Walk on the Wild Side" (Reed), 177n18
Walk on the Wild Side, A: movie, 9, 112; novel, 9, 98, 100–13, 114, 115, 117, 134, 135, 150, 176n10, 182n11; stageplay, 9, 112, 176n10
"Walk on the Wild Side, A" (Kempton), 177n18
"Walk on the Wild Side, A" (working title), 84
"Walk Pretty All the Way" (story), 150
Ward, Robert Patrick, 186n9
Warren, William, 177n18
Washington, Denzel, 184n20
"Watch Out for Daddy" (*The Last Carousel*), 135, 140–41
"Weaker Sheep, The" (working title), 67
Weissner, Carl, 183n16
"We Never Made It to the White Sox Game" (essay), 181–82n7
Western Union, 126
"What Country Do You Think You're In?" (*The Last Carousel*), 137
"When You Live Like I Done" (unpublished manuscript), 165n9
"Where Did Everybody Go?" (essay), 182n9
Whitman, Walt, 12, 39, 93
Who Lost an American?, 10, 115, 117, 118–24, 135, 136, 176–77n16, 179–80n10

Widdemer, Margaret, 168n12
Widow Rostenkowski (*Never Come Morning*), 43, 47
"Wild Side of Life" (Warren and Carter), 177n18
Willy the Weeper (folk hero), 66, 169–70n2
Wilma ("Depend on Aunt Elly," *The Neon Wilderness*), 58, 60
"Within the City" (sketch), 16
Wolfe ("El Presidente de Méjico," *The Neon Wilderness*), 57, 60, 161–62n10
Wolff, David, 53, 168n7, 170–71n10
women, 7, 12, 41, 42–43, 102, 104, 136, 148, 153, 186n15
Woodburn, John, 63, 167n6
Works Progress (later "Projects") Administration (WPA). *See* Federal Writers' Project

World War I, 19, 21, 52
World War II, 6, 7, 35, 36, 51–52, 55, 58–59, 61, 67, 68, 74, 152
Wright, Richard, 5, 6, 12, 86, 117, 133, 160n27, 165n9
WTTW (Chicago), 152

Yerby, Frank, 94
"You Felons on Trial in Courts" (Walt Whitman), 39
Young Finnegan (*Somebody in Boots*), 32
Yurick, Sol, 179–80n10

Zero Schwiefka (*The Man with the Golden Arm*), 69, 72
Zinn, Howard, 83
Zosh. *See* Sophie (Zosh) Majcinek.
Zygmunt the Prospector (*The Man with the Golden Arm*), 72